EMPOWERMENT

THROUGH

MULTICULTURAL

EDUCATION

SUNY Series
Teacher Empowerment and School Reform

Henry A. Giroux and Peter L. McLaren, editors

In an age when liberalism and radicalism have come under severe attack, American education faces an unprecedented challenge. The challenge has now moved beyond the search for more humanistic approaches to schooling and the quest for educational equality. Today's challenge is the struggle to rebuild a democratic tradition presently in retreat.

Laboring in a climate of anti-intellectualism and cultural ethnocentrism, educators are witnessing the systematic reduction of pedagogical skills and the disempowerment of the teaching profession; the continuation of privilege for select numbers of students on the basis of race, class, and gender; and the proliferation of corporate management pedagogies and state-mandated curricula that prescribe a narrow and sterile range of literacies and conceptions of what it means to be a citizen.

Under the editorship of Henry A. Giroux and Peter L. McLaren, this series will feature works within the critical educational tradition that define, analyze, and offer solutions to the growing dilemmas facing the nation's teachers and school systems. The series will also feature British and Canadian analyses of current educational conditions.

EMPOWERMENT

THROUGH

MULTICULTURAL

EDUCATION

edited by
Christine E. Sleeter

State University of New York Press

Published by
State University of New York Press, Albany

© 1991 State University of New York

For information, address the State University of New York Press,
State University Plaza, Albany, NY 12246

Library of Congress Cataloging-in-Publication Data

Empowerment through multicultural education / edited by Christine E.
  Sleeter.
      p.   cm. — (SUNY series teacher empowerment and school reform)
    Includes bibliographical references.
    ISBN 0-7914-0443-9. — ISBN 0-7914-0444-7 (pbk.)
    1. Intercultural education—United States. 2. Education—Social
  aspects—United States—Case studies. 3. Educational equalization—
  United States. 4. Political socialization—United States.
  5. Teachers—Training of—United States. I. Sleeter, Christine E.,
  1948-   . II. Series: Teacher empowerment and school reform.
  LC1099.3.E48   1991
  370.19′6′0973—dc20   89-77295
                                                                         CIP

10 9 8 7 6 5 4 3 2 1

CONTENTS

INTRODUCTION:
Multicultural Education and Empowerment

—————————— *Christine E. Sleeter*

Recently a principal of an urban elementary school expressed skepticism toward my interest in multicultural education, arguing that, with all the problems and difficulties low-income students and students of color face, shouldn't I instead be promoting the effective schools movement or programs for at-risk students? Isn't multicultural education a leftover from the 1960s that might be nice to add to a strong education program, but relatively unimportant given other reforms needed in schools for "disadvantaged" children? In the course of attempting to explain "why multicultural education," I concluded that she and I held very different visions of what it is, and probably also of society now and in the future.

A discussion with another colleague surfaced a different set of issues. Somewhat disdainful of my interest in multicultural education, he told me that it merely tries to co-opt Black people into the system rather than directly challenging White racism. Multicultural education, he argued, tries to make everyone like one another rather than to address issues of social inequality. Rather than being a strategy for empowerment and social change, he said, it is really an accommodationist strategy for defusing anger brought about by oppression. He pointed to "touchy-feely" lessons and lessons about group differences in food preferences as examples; he was unconvinced when I pointed out, first, that these were poor examples of multicultural education and, again, when I argued that empowerment for social change is an inextri-

Thanks are extended to Dick Ammann, Kathleen Bennett, Carlos Cortes, Henry Giroux, and Peter McLaren for helpful comments and suggestions on an earlier draft of this section.

cable component of multicultural education.

Yet, on reflection, I am aware that many people approach multicultural education without thinking about social inequality or empowerment at all. I have seen lessons containing a rich assortment of content drawn from different ethnic groups and both sexes that taught nothing about racism, sexism, or classism, and that made students passive recipients of someone else's version of the world. Such lessons have always struck me as inadequate because they so clearly ignore the issue of empowerment.

For me, as well as for many other advocates and theorists of multicultural education, *empowerment* and *multicultural education* are interwoven, and together suggest powerful and far-reaching school reform. But both terms mean different things to different people. Many people discuss empowerment without ever addressing social change, what a better society would look like, or society's racial, gender, and social-class groups. Many other people discuss multiculturalism, human relations, or "at-risk" populations as if oppression and collective power were irrelevant considerations or lenses for analysis. This book links power and empowerment with race, social class, and gender issues in education, and it amplifies attention to multicultural education's social change mission.

Empowerment has always been an important concern to oppressed groups, but it is especially crucial to focus on it now. The Civil Rights movement generated recognition on the part of the wider society that discrimination and oppression exist. During the 1980s, however, complacency and backlash replaced recognition. White America assumed that racial discrimination had been eliminated and felt threatened by so-called preferences given to Americans of color. Whites pointed to Asians as the "model minority," "proof" that racism no longer hinders a group's efforts to advance (Takaki, 1989). The presence of White women and a few Blacks in middle-management positions suggested that the doors of opportunity were now open to all. President Reagan addressed discrimination by simply removing sexist wording from laws, and the Supreme Court began dismantling civil rights rulings on the grounds that these are state issues. The "silent majority," with federal sanction, no longer sees the existence of a problem or the need to act. Within this context, action must be developed from within the ranks of oppressed Americans. Schooling, which usually serves to reinforce and legitimate the status quo, can also enlighten and emancipate, working with rather than against indigenous efforts for liberation. Chapters in this book illustrate how schooling can block efforts to advancement, as well as how it can create conditions for empowerment for liberation.

In this chapter, I will discuss what empowerment means in relation to social oppression, then how different conceptions of multicultural education address power and empowerment. I will then outline some issues and concerns that should be developed within the field of multicultural education; some of these issues are addressed by chapters in this book, some are not.

Empowerment

Empowerment has been defined in different ways. Ashcroft (1987) defines it as "bringing into a state of belief in one's ability/capability to act with effect" (p. 145). Her definition stresses the individual's power to achieve his or her own goals. McLaren (1989) stresses the social purpose of empowerment, defining it as "the process through which students learn to critically appropriate knowledge existing outside their immediate experience in order to broaden their understanding of themselves, the world, and the possibilities for transforming the taken-for-granted assumptions about the way we live" (p. 186). His definition highlights the need to transform "the way we live" so that the social world better serves the interests of all its members.

Empowering relationships differ markedly from the benevolent helping relationships that characterize much of education and social service work. Brickman and his colleagues (1982) have described four models of helping relationships, differentiating on the basis of who is believed responsible for causing a problem and who should take responsibility for its solution. The "moral model" blames the victim by viewing persons as responsible for both their own problems and their solutions; the rest of society is absolved of responsibility, and the "have-nots" are supposed to pull themselves up by their bootstraps out of problems presumed to be of their own making. The "medical model" and the "enlightenment model" are both benevolent helping relationships in which "experts" with power and knowledge help those who presumably lack these resources. These two models differ in that the first views society or the environment as having caused people's problems, and the second views persons as having created their own problems through ignorance. The fourth model directs us toward empowerment, viewing persons as victims of problems created by society but as potentially active solvers of their own problems.

The first three models are familiar features on the education landscape. Examples of the "moral model" include exhorting students with low grades or in lower groups to try harder, blaming low-income parents for lack of interest in their children's school success, and painting a picture of American society as an equal opportunity enterprise in which anyone who wishes can get ahead through hard work. Educators who subscribe to this model support treating all students "alike" and giving little or no special help to members of oppressed groups or making special considerations for discrimination they may have experienced. The "medical model" includes programs that place students in the hands of experts to diagnose special needs and recommend prescriptions for meeting those needs. Special education fits this model well; however, the model also includes any program that may not subscribe to biological causality but that still requires highly trained experts to understand a problem and decide what to do about it. Examples of the "enlightenment model" include discipline programs that instruct students on how they ought to behave, compensatory education programs that teach students skills their homes "failed" to teach them, and English as a second language or transitional bilingual education programs. The assumption is that students from "disadvantaged" groups need special instruction to "catch them up" with everyone else, and once they have the information or skills they had lacked, they will learn and behave "appropriately," and thus succeed.

These benevolent helping models, although they may be implemented with good intentions and produce some positive results, tend to reinforce the status quo and disable members of oppressed groups. Writing about family services, Dunst and Trivette (1987) argue that benevolent helping relationships produce learned helplessness, suggest that the "help seeker is inferior, incompetent, or inadequate" (p. 446), foster indebtedness, often produce poor solutions to family needs, and as a result disable people from working constructively on their own behalf. Hughes (1987), writing about services for rural communities and families, argues that benevolent helping relationships are often simply ineffective because they tend to ignore the strengths and competencies people have, as well as people's analysis of their own needs and problems, to promote homogeneity by standardizing solutions, and to weaken the small, intimate social institutions that impact most directly on people. These authors advocate empowerment strategies that capitalize on people's ability to understand their own needs and that build on the energy, networks, and strengths people have. Kramer (1989), for example, describes health care programs Indian tribal governments have established which build on the resources and networks within Indian communities.

Cummins (1986) has made similar arguments for empowering students of color through education. He distinguishes between empowering and disabling orientations in four areas: (1) whether students' culture and language are incorporated into or excluded from the education program; (2) whether community participation is collaborative or exclusionary; (3) whether pedagogy is oriented toward reciprocal interaction or transmission; and (4) whether assessment is oriented toward advocacy or legitimation of failure. Empowering education programs work with students and their home communities to build on what they bring; disabling programs ignore and attempt to eradicate knowledge and strengths students bring, and replace them with those of the dominant society.

Too often education for members of oppressed groups takes the form of benevolent helping, which in the process disables. A very dedicated teacher in a low-income school described her students to me like this: "They need lots of help with everything. They're Basic Level [lower track] kids, so they're not at grade level, so they need help with just about anything you could help them with." Although her genuine concern for the students' achievement is important, her description does not hint that students might bring with them to the classroom prior learning from outside school, motives, goals, insights, strategies for learning, or personal identities that give direction to their growth.

Chapters 1 through 4 in this book illustrate how schools disable many young people, especially members of oppressed groups, and how young people perceive their own power to control their lives. In Chapter 1, Bennett describes the formation of stratification in a first grade class in a low-income Appalachian community. She shows how the use of four reading groups placed a ceiling on the pace and type of instruction children received, and provided a context within which students constructed identities that matched their position in a hierarchical order. In Chapter 2, Sleeter and Grant examine how junior high students in a desegregated working-class school learn to view public institutions as being controlled by others, through their school experience. Even while students develop power over their personal and social worlds, they learn to comply passively with the demands of a public institution. In Chapter 3, Fordham examines how the organizational structure of a high school depressed the achievement of Black students by trying to separate high achievers from their peers. She develops the concept of "fictive kinship" among Black Americans, arguing that competitive individualism in schools forces Black students to choose between an identity as Black people versus an identity as high achievers. In Chapter 4, Weis examines female identity formation and White male dominance in a postindustrial community. Referring to a case study of a high school, she argues that female students' partial insights into patriarchy are blocked and fragmented as they experience a strong White male voice and patriarchal relationships among teachers.

Chapters 5 through 12 develop strategies for empowerment. It is important to explain what empowerment means in the context of education, as it is used in this book. Education for empowerment demands taking seriously the strengths, experiences, strategies, and goals members of oppressed groups have. It also demands helping them to analyze and understand the social structure that oppresses them and to act in ways that will enable them to reach their own goals successfully. In part, this means helping them succeed as individuals in the mainstream of schools and other social institutions. Academic achievement is a necessary part of empowerment for members of oppressed groups. The importance of achievement within existing realities cannot be overemphasized. As Simon (1987) points out, "If we do not give youth a sense of how to 'make it' within existing realities, all too often we doom them to social marginality: yet another high-minded way of perpetuating the structural inequalities in society" (p. 375).

Education for empowerment also means teaching students how to advocate effectively for themselves as individuals as well as collectively. Chan, Brophy, and Fisher (1981), for example, have developed a teaching model "to help people assert control over their own lives" (p. 195). It involves helping people learn to use the law and administrative procedures of due process to assert their interests when they feel they are being treated unfairly. Rather than feeling frustrated and powerless, or depending on someone else to advocate for them, individuals learn specific procedures for analyzing problems, investigating alternative courses of action, and carrying out actions that translate legal standards into fair treatment. This model is limited in that it does not change institutions, but at least it helps oppressed individuals mobilize power on their own behalf.

Education for empowerment also means developing the insights and skills to work collectively for social justice. McLaren (1988b) points out that educators who use the term *empowerment* to refer only to "acquiring the cognitive and social skills necessary to adapt to a rapidly-changing capitalist society" (p. 3) generally view society as fair and just, and believe that people can go forward successfully if their own capabilities are strengthened. Educators who view society as unfair and unjust use the term *empowerment* to mean "enabling students to do more than simply adapt to the social order but rather to be able to transform the social order in the interests of social justice" (p. 3).

Wilkerson (1983) emphasizes skill for social transformation. Writing about the agendas and historic social activism of women of color, she asks: "Are personal advancement and social mobility the only ends that we seek? Do we seek more money? Greater influence? To what end?" (p. 61). She goes on to answer these questions:

> Lift as We Climb was the answer given a century ago as newly freed blacks struggled to loose the bonds of slavery and ignorance. The commitment of the historically black colleges to admit students whom other institutions might reject and to open the world of learning to these students was embodied in that phrase. It is still pertinent to women of color in the 1980s, for it acknowledges their need and desire for personal advancement while connecting them with a collective effort to improve the quality of life for many. (p. 61)

Members of other oppressed groups also recognize the need to achieve and climb as individuals while simultaneously working collectively to further the interests of the group. Checkoway and Norsman (1986), for example, describe a project for empowering citizens with disabilities. They point out the need to organize for collective action, noting that people with disabilities often do not see themselves as part of a potentially powerful collective: "Disabled persons often use facilities as individuals, or do not consider disabilities as an organizing vehicle, or are unaware about their rights as citizens in society. Instead they may operate in isolation, or hesitate to intrude in matters which seem beyond reach, or accept the notion of institutional control over resources even when these are intended to meet their special needs" (p. 274).

This brings us to a crucial issue: If empowerment involves collective action based on common interests, which collectives and which social issues do we have in mind? Who is articulating a particular group's agenda, who is analyzing its current status, who is deciding the boundaries defining its membership? Who is framing what empowerment means in practice? Who is deciding what constitutes legitimate discourse and rules for debate? Sometimes those who define the discourse on empowerment in the process shut out and exclude members of oppressed groups. Magda Lewis and Roger Simon (1986) recently published an intriguing (and brave) example of how Simon and male class members silenced female graduate students in a seminar on language and power relations. By deciding himself on the language, conceptual lenses, and processes to be used, Simon enabled the male class members to take over and render the women silent, in spite of his limited attempts to involve them. They described the silencing process that occurred:

> The men monopolized not only the speaking time but the theoretical and social agenda as well . . . [W]omen's experience and discursive forms are defined by men as illegitimate *within the terms of men's experience and men's discursive forms* . . . Being muted is not just a matter of being unable to claim a space and time within which to enter a conversation. Being muted also occurs when one cannot discover forms of speech within conversation to express meanings and to find validation from others. (pp. 207-211)

Members of traditionally dominant groups cannot be the main definers of what empowerment means, what its agendas are, and how it is to be implemented. If they are, they are using language of empowerment to silence and continue to oppress others. Many discussions of education for empowerment that one reads today are framed mainly by Whites and/or males, but often with reference to students of both sexes and of various racial and ethnic groups. Such discussions do not necessarily reflect the interests, concerns, experiences, and language of oppressed groups who are not White or male. This book questions who speaks for members of oppressed groups. It develops ideas that have been articulated within the field of multicultural education, not just *about* women and men of color and White women, but also *by* members of these groups.

Multicultural Education as a Strategy for Empowerment

In order to view multicultural education as an empowerment strategy, one must first take seriously the notion that education can serve as an effective vehicle for social change and emancipation. Considerable research over the past two decades portrays schools as agents of dominant groups that select and socialize the young into a highly stratified society. Yet at the same time, this socialization is somewhat contradictory and provides space for teaching the young to question. Banks (1981) notes that "the school itself is contradictory, since it often expounds democratic values while at the same time contradicting them. The school does socialize students into the existing social structure; it also enables some students to acquire the knowledge, attitudes, and skills needed to participate effectively in social action and social change" (p. 166). Advocates of multicultural education, feminist teaching, and critical pedagogy have sought to develop and amplify the school's power to validate students' experiences and identities, to promote democratic values and critical thought, and to empower young people.

Multicultural education is an imperative dimension to empowerment, and empowerment is a fundamental goal of multicultural education. This statement is not immediately obvious to many, however, because of the different perspectives regarding what multicultural education is. Suzuki (1984) points out that "many widely differing conceptualizations of multicultural education have been formulated. As a consequence, the various programs in the field often appear to have conflicting purposes and priorities. Many educators have come to view multicultural education as ill defined, lacking in substance, and just another educational fad" (p. 294). This is particularly a problem for people who know little about it, since many well-intentioned but superficial school practices parade as multicultural education, such as food fairs, costume shows, and window-dressing contributions by people of color.

How prominently empowerment for social action fits into any given educator's conception of multicultural education varies. How explicitly an educator announces this varies also. Multicultural education originated within a context of social activism and has always drawn its main energy and inspiration from struggles against oppression. It developed in the ferment of the 1960s and early 1970s, receiving its major impetus from struggles against racial oppression; it subsequently was joined to some extent by feminist groups struggling against sexual oppression. According to Gay (1983), in the mid-1960s, "the ideological and strategic focus of the [civil rights] movement shifted from passivity and perseverance in the face of adversity to aggression, self-determination, cultural consciousness, and political power" (p. 560). On college campuses this activism took the form of demands for ethnic studies courses and the elimination of stereotypic and derogatory treatment. Some of this energy was directed toward the public school curricula and to the "ethnic distortions, stereotypes, omissions, and misinformation" in textbooks (p. 561). At the same time, social science research undermined cultural deprivation theories which blamed racial minority people for their own problems by describing pathologies thought to characterize their cultures. This research suggested that "the academic failure of minority youths was due more to the conflicting expectations of school and home and to the schools' devaluation of minority group cultures" (p. 561). Although the field is still in the process of conceptualizing and developing its political strategy, it has always been grounded in a vision of equality and has served as a mobilizing site for struggle within education.

Multicultural education has been a highly political change strategy; many of its writings are attempts to bring about changes in schooling on the part of individuals who would resist those changes. Since schools, as well as the colleges and job markets they serve, are controlled mainly by White males, and substantive changes must have their support, advocates have had to address them in terms that will not be rejected outright. Having had considerable experience with White and male educators, advocates have known that they can easily be antagonized or alienated by words or ideas that seem "too radical." The politics of bringing about change has necessitated frequently couching arguments for school reform in relatively benign language. To radical educators who do not understand this, sometimes the words of multicultural education advocates seem soft and accommodationist. For example, using the term *human relations*, educators in Wisconsin, Minnesota, and Iowa institutionalized state requirements for teacher certification that have led many campuses to develop courses about oppression. Several campuses have hired faculty who specialize in "human relations" to develop and teach the courses. These "human relations" educators have networked quite effectively to exchange resources and ideas for their programs. In the process, oppression based on race, social class, gender, disability, and sexual orientation has become a shared framework for their work. Paradoxically, the benign term *human relations* was quite useful in institutionalizing radical activity.

Within the field, educators define and conceptualize multicultural education differently according to its goals and practices and the social groups it deals with. Some educators address only race and ethnicity (e.g., Bennett, 1986; Gay, 1983), some address race, ethnicity, and gender (e.g., Baptiste and Baptiste, 1979), some focus on race, ethnicity, and language (e.g. Hernandez, 1989), and some address multiple forms of oppression, including race, ethnicity, language, gender, social class, and disability (e.g., Banks and Banks, 1989; Gollnick and Chinn, 1986; Grant, 1977; Sleeter and Grant, 1988). Deciding with which groups one should be concerned presents some important issues that will be addressed later in this chapter.

One also can distinguish between five approaches to multicultural education which differ quite significantly and have different conceptions of empowerment (see Sleeter and Grant, 1987, 1988). These approaches include human relations, teaching the culturally different, single-group studies, multicultural education (or cultural democracy),[1] and education that is multicultural and social reconstructionist.

The *human relations* approach aims toward sensitivity training and teaching that "we are all the same because we are different." Human relations advocates talk of the power of love, unity, and harmony, and of the need for individuals to try to change the attitudes and behavior of other individuals who thwart loving, harmonious relationships. Inner and interpersonal well-being are much more a concern than social change. The human relations approach has less to say about empowerment as it is discussed in this book than does any other approach. Unfortunately, many people equate multicultural education with the human relations approach (e.g., McCarthy, 1988), and in so doing, miss entirely multicultural education's challenge to oppression.

The *teaching the culturally different* approach attempts to raise the achievement of students of color mainly through designing culturally compatible education programs. It conceptualizes empowerment as the development of the skills and capabilities needed to succeed in schools and society. For example, Trueba (1988) argues that "at the heart of academic success, and regardless of the child's ethnicity or historical background, an effective learning environment must be constructed in which the child, especially the minority child, is assisted through meaningful and culturally appropriate relationships in the internalization of the mainstream cultural values embedded in our school system" (p. 282). This approach assumes that society is sufficiently open that once mainstream values and skills have been acquired, individuals can "make it."

The other three approaches all conceptualize empowerment as collective social action in addition to achievement. The *multicultural education* approach, or *cultural democracy*, attempts to redesign classrooms and schools to model an unoppressive, equal society which is also culturally diverse. Explicitly this approach does not strongly teach social criticism and social change, but implicitly it does so in that a multicultural classroom or school implementing this approach is clearly different from the existing society. Students are empowered as individuals by achieving and receiving validation for who they are, and are empowered for social change by having lived a pluralistic model. The *single group studies* approach includes such programs as Black studies, Chicano studies, or women's studies, which explicitly teach students about the history of the target group's oppression and how oppression works today, as well as the culture the group has developed within oppressive circumstances. More than the other approaches, it promotes identification with and solidarity among members of the specific ethnic or gender target group, clearly defining boundaries between the in-group and out-groups. Finally, *education that is multicultural and social reconstructionist* forges a coalition among various oppressed groups as well as members of dominant groups, teaching directly about political and economic oppression and discrimination, and preparing young people directly in social action skills.

Advocates of these three approaches stress the need to help students acquire basic academic skills and develop an understanding of their own background as well as that of other groups in society. But equally important is helping them to develop a vision of a better society and to acquire the knowledge and skills necessary to bring about constructive social change. As Bennett (1986) has argued, "In view of the fact that certain ethnic groups are unable to gain, maintain, and effectively use political power, to ignore this goal is to make a sham out of the [other] goals" of multicultural education (p. 212). According to Suzuki (1984), multicultural education must

> foster [students'] ability to analyze critically and make intelligent decisions about real-life problems and issues through a process of democratic dialogical inquiry. Finally, it should help them conceptualize a vision of a better society and acquire the necessary knowledge, understanding, and skills to enable them to move the society toward greater equality and freedom, the eradication of degrading poverty and dehumanizing dependency, and the development of meaningful identity for all people. (p. 305)

Similarly, Banks (1989) has described the social action approach to multicultural curriculum development:

> To participate effectively in social change, students must be taught social criticism and must be helped to understand the inconsistency between our ideals and social realities, the work that must be done to close this gap, and how students can, as individuals and groups, influence the social and political systems in U.S. society. In this approach, teachers are agents of social change who promote democratic values and the empowerment of ethnic students. (p. 198)

To the extent that school programs ignore the analysis of issues of oppression and collective social action, they are ignoring a fundamental part of these last three approaches to multicultural education.

Chapters 5 through 12 discuss strategies for empowerment through multicultural education. Collectively, they advance the last approach, education that is multicultural and social reconstructionist. Individually, some of them more closely resemble other approaches. Readers are urged to seek linkages among chapters and the "gestalt" they form. I have tried to facilitate this linkage by cross-referencing chapters, since some elaborate on ideas mentioned in others.

Banks discusses the development of a curriculum for liberation in which students analyze social issues and learn to take action. He illustrates with several examples, developing an excellent picture of a junior high teacher's social studies curriculum. Cortés examines media literacy for empowerment, arguing that media constitute a very powerful source of education. He suggests that schools can teach young people to analyze media as critical consumers and to influence as well as use media as modes of communication about diverse groups in society. Sapon-Shevin and Schniedewind argue that cooperative learning supports many goals of multicultural education and that it should be used to help students develop a sense of collective power and self-efficacy. They suggest strategies for using it to accomplish this goal, emphasizing its potency when used in conjunction with a curriculum that analyzes oppression. Pang argues that empowerment is not just for older students, but that it can begin when children are young. She presents examples of young children's perspectives and suggests strategies for developing critical awareness and action skills at their developmental level. Williams examines African American Language in schooling, suggesting strategies for its use that will develop students' self-concept, teach Standard American English, promote bilingual communication, and help students learn to assert themselves as positive social actors in school as well as in the community. Ruiz distinguishes between language and voice, arguing that language-minority students need opportunities to use their own voices and be heard, not just to use a language other people consider "theirs." He urges language minority communities to marshall power within the "private" sphere of home and community, and to use voice for taking control of their own lives.

Chapters 11 and 12 examine the implementation of some strategies suggested in this book and discuss how students respond. Bell describes a project involving consciousness raising around gender issues with a multiracial group of elementary school girls. Takata describes a project that involved "nontraditional" undergraduate students in constructing a community-based research project.

Chapters 13 and 14 discuss issues in teacher education for multicultural education and urban schools. Haberman points out that teachers are self-selected and that those entering teacher education are most often late adolescents. He argues that, because of their level of development, it is not reasonable to expect them to empower urban children effectively; adults generally are developmentally more able to focus on those outside their own families and to comprehend the complexities of urban schools. Martin discusses how universities should work with student teachers, and preferably those who desire multicultural teaching. Using an analogy of the theater, she argues that schools are political "stages"; universities can work with several factors related to power in the classroom to empower student teachers to implement multicultural teaching.

As we develop further our thinking about empowerment through multicultural education, we encounter some important issues that must be addressed. I will discuss three: the extent to which 'powerlessness' is a useful idea, the extent to which different forms of oppression should be treated separately, and the dilemma of inviting students to think their own thoughts when those thoughts reaffirm rather than question the social order. Multicultural education theorists do not necessarily agree with one another on their resolutions to these issues; authors of chapters in this book do not necessarily agree. Nevertheless, they are important conceptual as well as practical issues that should be discussed.

Problems with the Concept of Powerlessness

Power is often conceived as a commodity one either has or lacks. This conception is reflected in the language we use and presents a serious conceptual as well as psychological problem. Consider the book titles *Educating the Powerless* (Charnofsky, 1971) and *The Powerholders* (Kipnis, 1976). One would think these refer to two different groups. However, they do not necessarily. Rather, they refer to two very different ways of viewing power.

The concept of powerlessness implies that "the powerless" have no power and no recourse but to wait for those who have power to share some of it. Charnofsky (1971), for example, in writing about "the powerless," advised that "those in positions of power must willingly relinquish some of it if the emerging poor [the powerless] are to have a chance to try it for themselves" (p. 191). If those in positions of power do not choose to relinquish some of it, presumably the powerless can do nothing.

I am reminded of a recent conversation with a teacher who was feeling powerless to change some conditions in his school that he saw as oppressive to students of color. As I asked him what actions he could take, I discovered how his analysis of change strategies reinforced his feeling of powerlessness. The main change strategy he voiced was the individual (himself) attempting to change attitudes of other individuals, a strategy he saw doomed to failure because so many other individuals had "hard core" attitudes he could not change. He also identified the school administration as the main locus of power, but doubted his ability as one lone teacher to influence it much. Power, viewed as a commodity, was something he felt he did not have and could not get.

This teacher illustrates well how many people conceive of power and its mobilization: the individual rather than the collective is the unit for accessing and using power; powerholders are an impenetrable collective the individual can rarely access effectively, which renders the individual powerless; and one's own strategies for attempting to make changes consist mainly of persuasion or coercion. This conception of power is reinforced in schools, which stress individual efforts and rarely teach students to analyze power structures and mobilize collective power. Those involved in empowerment must help people recognize and learn to use various power bases, as both individuals and collectives. This requires first rejecting the idea of powerlessness, which both conservative and radical educators have tended to hold, although for different reasons. Giroux (1983) puts it this way: "Too often, as I have pointed out, radical theorists have portrayed the use of power in schools in strictly negative and one-dimension terms. This not only distorts the reality of schools; it ends up being a more 'radical' version of management ideology which sees human beings as infinitely malleable. Power in the service of domination is NEVER as total as this image suggests" (p. 199). Ruiz, in Chapter 10, furthers this point, writing that "the radical pedagogue who treats empowerment as a gift is not yet radical. Teachers do not empower or disempower anyone, nor do schools. They merely create the conditions under which people can *empower themselves*" (p. 223, emphasis his).

Ashcroft (1987) provides a useful alternative metaphor for viewing power, from physics: "In the realm of physical science, energy is the ability/capability to do work. A distinction is made between potential energy, which is stored and latent, and kinetic energy, which is in use and active. This transformed kinetic energy science calls power" (p. 149). To the physicist, energy is never powerless: it is either latent or active. Similarly, oppressed people do not lack power, but are not mobilizing their power as effectively as possible. Power is inherent in a dialectical relationship between parties; both parties act in response to one another, although the acts of oppressed people often are not viewed as potentially powerful.

Giroux (1983) argues that power manifests itself in various forms and acts of resistance to domination that oppressed people make all the time. He points out that "much of the opposition in both schools and the workplace represents forms of symbolic resistance, i.e., the struggle is thereby limited to the world of cultural symbols of dress, taste, language, and the like. In order for such opposition to move to a more effective level of action, it will have to be extended into a form of resistance linked to political action and control" (p. 200). This requires developing "social awareness" (p. 200), or recognizing one's own oppositional behavior and viewing it as a creative, although not necessarily politically effective, act taken in response to certain conditions.

With training, oppositional behavior can become politically effective. The field of political science provides some guidance in political mobilization; multicultural educators should draw more on this guidance. Wrong (1979), for example, describes the characteristics of effective political groups. They have solidarity "based on an awareness by the members of their collective identity as a group and their common commitment to a goal, interest or set of values" (p. 148). Members are aware of their collective conflict with another group, and the group has developed a "social organization specifically designed to promulgate and promote" the group's interests (p. 149).

Developing group consciousness and solidarity can be difficult. One must first define who the group is and with whom it conflicts over what. For example, Weis, in Chapter 4, shows how the beginnings of female group consciousness and awareness of conflict of interest are thwarted by male dominance among faculty; Bell, in Chapter 11, describes a school-based project specifically designed to build female group consciousness and their awareness of conflicts of interest between the sexes. Another difficulty in developing group consciousness and solidarity is the ideology of individualism which pervades schooling. Fordham, in Chapter 3, illustrates clearly how school processes oriented around competitive individualism undermine the collective advancement of Black students.

Oppressed people can maximize their power by assessing and learning to use a variety of power bases. Kipnis (1976) discusses this in some detail, drawing on the five power bases described by French and Raven (1959): reward power, coercive power, legitimate power, expert power, and referent power. He argues that those who feel powerless tend to use coercive power only, and often violently; this is not necessarily the most effective power base. Power can be mobilized by expanding an individual's or group's power bases and by learning to judge more effectively when to use which base. Youkin (1989) illustrates, describing how people with disabilities are learning to use both litigation and public protest, making each form of power work with and strengthen the other. Williams, in Chapter 9, examines language as a power base, arguing that facility in multiple dialects and languages increases power by providing access to multiple language communities. Over the long run, according to Kipnis, those who use power effectively begin to view themselves as strong and effective, and are viewed by others in the same way, which furthers their ability to use power effectively.

Which Forms of Oppression?

The term *multicultural education* is usually associated with race and ethnicity, although, as mentioned above, many educators address additional forms of diversity. Terms themselves reflect differing conceptions of how to deal with different forms of oppression. For example, some authors distinguish between multicultural education and multiethnic education (Banks, 1981); some specify multicultural-nonsexist education (Colangelo, Foxley, and Dustin, 1979). Is White ethnicity part of multicultural education? What about women's studies? Bilingual education?

Arguments have been made for addressing each form of oppression separately, on the one hand, or oppression broadly conceived, on the other. At issue is the extent to which attending to multiple forms of oppression maximizes power or fragments it. As noted above, successfully organized groups have clearly defined membership, a sense of solidarity, and a clearly articulated agenda of concerns.

Gay (1983) argues that multicultural education's assault on racism will be weakened considerably if it is also attempting to deal simultaneously with additional forms of discrimination. She emphasizes the importance of Black Americans siding with each other against White racism; introducing other forms of oppression such as sexism can only fragment Blacks, as well as other groups of color, and weaken opposition to racism. Issues are often different for different groups and are sometimes contradictory. Hicks (1981) terms this problem "nonsynchrony." For example, while White women have been struggling to enter the workplace, Black women have been struggling for the economic security to leave the workplace and spend more time at home.

While many groups of color have struggled for access to mainstream social institutions, American Indians have struggled to retain control over Indian institutions.

On the other hand, all people are members simultaneously of at least one racial group, ethnic group, language community, gender group, social-class group, and other groups based on age, religion, and so forth. To address only one form of diversity forces many people artificially to separate out other loyalties and interests. Butler (1989) describes the particular difficulty in which she feels this places many women of color, for whom the "struggle against sexism and racism [and classism] is waged simultaneously" (p. 151). She suggests that women of color are natural "agents of transformation" (p. 151) because of their simultaneous membership in multiple oppressed groups.

Therefore, many people advocate building coalitions to address multiple forms of oppression simultaneously, focusing on oppression broadly rather than the oppression of one group (Grant and Sleeter, 1986; Schniedewind and Davidson, 1983). The issue then becomes determining which instances of oppression are most worth challenging collectively, how to build coalitions that will work together for common ends, and how to develop group consciousness on the part of members *without* asking groups constituting the coalition to give up their own identities or agendas. Sapon-Shevin and Schniedewind, in Chapter 7, discuss cooperative learning as a strategy for coalition building. They point out that cooperative learning helps students who are members of diverse groups to work together and appreciate each other. But they also emphasize that students who have learned to work together should then examine various issues involving oppression and learn to act on them collectively. Students' individual membership in various social groups become important resources for collective thinking and acting. Coalitions that bring together oppressed people can create powerful groups. For example, discriminatory housing practices can affect people of color, single parents with children, and people with disabilities. The exact form housing discrimination takes may vary across these groups. However, a coalition that addresses housing discrimination as it is experienced by multiple groups is not only larger and more powerful, but is also able to view the problem of housing discrimination more comprehensively. Scotch (1988) describes how the disability rights movement joined a coalition in Washington with other "liberal-left advocacy groups" in common struggle against conservative policies of the Reagan administration. The long-term stability of such coalitions is problematic, however, being constantly threatened by very real differences among groups. A related issue concerns the role of members of dominant groups. If one is mobilizing a challenge to sexism, for example, what role should men who support feminist concerns occupy? Women who are active in the women's movement vary on this issue, with some rejecting participation of men and others encouraging it. The same issue occurs with relationship to race, language, ethnicity, class, and disability. If one examines the models of helping relationships presented earlier (Brickman, et al., 1982), one can see that members of dominant groups who wish to "help" members of oppressed groups usually adopt either the "medical model" or the "enlightenment model." In both, the helper assumes he or she has the knowledge to determine the goals, agendas, strategies, and so forth, for others. In empowering relationships, members of dominant groups need to work with oppressed people, taking direction from them and contributing expertise only insofar as it is asked for and judged appropriate.

Empowerment as a Process or as Having Correct Information?

Radical educators face the dilemma of wanting students to develop the power to construct their own understanding of themselves and the world, on the one hand, and wanting them to know certain information and view the world in a certain way, on the other. Giroux (1988) illustrates with

> the middle-class teacher who is rightly horrified at the sexism exhibited by male students in her classroom. The teacher responds by presenting students with a variety of feminist articles, films, and other curriculum materials. Rather than responding with gratitude for being politically enlightened, the students respond with scorn and resistance. The teacher is baffled as the students' sexism appears to become even further entrenched. (pp. 70-71)

Should empowerment mean teaching these students to recognize and reject sexism, thereby accepting the teacher's definition of the world, or should it mean developing their power to examine the world and act upon it for themselves, which might not involve questioning sexism and could even strengthen it? Sometimes this is a dilemma, because although multicultural and radical educators advocate valuing and legitimating student experience and student perceptions, those perceptions always embody self-interest and personal experience. The teacher's definition of the world also reflects the teacher's self-interests and political affinities; nobody's definition is universal or neutral.

Simon and Dippo (1987) put this dilemma very well: "how to acknowledge student experience as a legitimate aspect of schooling while being able to challenge both its content and its form during the educational process" (p. 106). Describing a work education program, they show some common patterns in students' perceptions of experience. First, students commonly explain unfairness in terms of individual personalities: "'Harv was a cheap-o.' 'The boss is a jerk'" (p. 111). Second, students draw on what they have experienced to confirm the world rather than to question it. Third, their own life histories and assumptions help shape their interpretations of the world in ways they do not recognize.

As educators we want students to analyze events in terms of patterns and structures rather than just individual personalities, to question why things are as they are and how they might be different, and to hear and value the voices of those whose life histories have been very different from theirs. Probably most radical educators have experienced a process of learning to view the world differently from the mainstream and have invested considerable time and effort in questioning the social world as well as conventional explanations of it. We want exuberantly to convey to our students the "truth," being aware that students often accept and take for granted much of what they see and hear every day. So our teaching often takes the form of providing students with a different vision of the world, namely, ours.

Users of critical pedagogy and feminist pedagogy, on the other hand, attempt to help students develop the power to analyze and create meaning by working *with* rather than *on* students in the construction of knowledge. Maher (1987) explores similarities and differences between critical pedagogy and feminist pedagogy. In critical pedagogy, "oppressed groups name, describe, and then analyze salient features of their world as they experience it. As students come to recognize certain features of their reality as not 'natural' but as socially and historically constructed, they can act on these to change them" (p. 93). Feminist pedagogy emphasizes the private sphere and the personal; it holds that "all knowledge must be contextualized, and rooted in a particular framework and world view . . . [Knowledge] always has, and indeed should have, an emotional component, a feeling component, that cames from the knower's sense of purpose, sense of connection to the material, and particular context" (p. 96). Critical pedagogy emphasizes the collective analysis of oppression and feminist pedagogy focuses more on personal feelings and experiences, but both place the student at the center of teaching and learning. Neither imposes the teacher's view of reality on the students.

Freire insists that real learning can came about only by first "starting from THEIR description of THEIR daily life experiences" and moving "from concreteness, from common sense, to reach a rigorous understanding of reality" (Shor and Freire, 1987, p. 20). Tetreault (1989) explains as follows:

> Whereas previously my purpose in teaching was to set objectives that taught the students predetermined and objective generalizations, I now want to help students recognize, use and enlarge their own perspectives in relation to the themes of the courses, as well as to present views reflecting a fuller range of male and females lives . . . I seek to build a more complex conceptualization of a given issue, one that legitimizes students' voices and puts them in a larger explanatory context. (p. 137)

Takata, in Chapter 12, describes very clearly a project in which students controlled the learning process, directing and carrying out research on gangs in their community. In fact, Takata does not reveal to us her own perspective on gangs; she may be criticized for possibly not leading students toward a "politically correct" analysis, but her purpose was to help students collectively construct their own analysis, not adopt hers.

Helping students critique society in the interests of social justice, through their own experience, is not necessarily easy with students who are members of oppressed groups. As lower-class students explore their lives and experiences, for example, they can learn to analyze the social-class structures that institutionalize their poverty. They may resist doing so; oppressed people often maintain a belief in the openness of the social structure to individuals' attempts to achieve mobility since this view validates their own efforts to escape poverty. However, their life experiences at least are congruent with critiques of social oppression.

But it is much more difficult to help students who are members of dominant groups learn to view the world critically through their own experience (or through anyone else's, for that matter). Members of dominant groups usually believe they have a vested interest in maintaining the world as it is and in adopting mainstream understandings of that world. One of my colleagues struggles with her White male students more than with any other group. Her perspectives on the social order, particularly with respect to gender, are diametrically opposed to those of many of these students. They resist actively her attempts to reorient their view of society away from oppression to one of freedom and openness for all individuals regardless of gender or background.

Ellsworth (1989) explores further difficulties with critical pedagogy on the basis of her own attempts to use it in a university course. She has found that proclaiming a course to validate student voice tends to mask very real unequal power relationships in which all participants are enmeshed. The teacher not only occupies power in relation to students, which does not disappear by fiat, but is also embedded within his or her own network of interest groups, identities, and experiences. Students react to each other on the basis of the trust and understanding they perceive they can expect from peers who are of particular races, social-class backgrounds, sexes, sexual orientations, and so forth. Their attempts, as well as the teacher's, to interpret, understand, and act against oppression still embody partial insights, biases, and oppressive relations of some sort.

The process of instruction for multicultural education is very important to consider. It is inadequate just to tell students what to think, but equally inadequate to validate whatever students believe, in a relativistic and individualistic fashion. Helping students articulate, critically examine, and develop their own beliefs and action agendas for the emancipation of oppressed people is very difficult; it is not discussed sufficiently in concrete terms by multicultural education practitioners or theorists.

Furthermore, given that most teacher education students are middle-class White late adolescents and many will be teaching predominantly White student populations, how can we empower them to empower White children to struggle against oppression? This issue needs to be discussed and debated much more. Haberman, in Chapter 13, argues that much more attention needs to be given to who teaches, and that late adolescents are usually not good prospects for becoming teachers who will empower children of color from low-income families.

Conclusion

Multicultural education grew out of the social movements of the 1960s. It was grounded in social protest, emancipation, and social change. The climate of the 1990s is very different from that of the 1960s: the problems are still very much present, but protest movements in the United States are not nearly as visible. Therefore, it is imperative that multicultural educators give voice and substance to struggles against oppression and develop the vision and the power of our future citizens to forge a more just society. This book represents an effort to amplify the voices of oppressed groups and to articulate and further develop strategies for empowerment through an education that is multicultural.

PART I

*Schooling and the Disempowerment
of Children from Oppressed Groups*

Chapter 1

Doing School in an Urban Appalachian First Grade

Kathleen P. Bennett

Introduction

Appalachian people share a rich cultural heritage which includes a strong sense of kinship, a love of the land, a rich oral tradition, and a commitment to personal freedom and self-reliance. They also share a long history of poverty, economic exploitation, and inadequate schooling. Many rural and urban Appalachians today continue to struggle to provide for basic survival needs for their families; the poverty rate in central Appalachia is twice the national average. High rates of unemployment, illiteracy, and school dropouts continue to plague the region (Tickamyer and Tickamyer, 1987).

This chapter is about schooling for one small group of urban Appalachian children. I begin the chapter with a discussion of the Appalachian region to acquaint the reader with the geographical context. Next, I present a discussion of the study, its participants, and the reading program as it was implemented in this first-grade classroom. In this portion of the chapter I describe an ideology of stratification which served as the basis for the entire reading program. Then I present a summary of the constraining impact of district policies on the classroom reading program. I conclude the chapter with a discussion of the conflict between the reading program and the culture of the students as well as the implications this has for children whose home culture is not congruent with the culture of the school.

The Region

The Appalachian region has been defined differently through the years by social scientists, writers, and politicians. The most recent political definition of Appalachia grew out of efforts to establish the Appalachian Regional Commission (ARC) to address social, educational, and economic concerns of the area. In 1965, the federal government, at the urging of the region's state governors, created the ARC with representatives from thirteen states. By 1970, the total Appalachian region included 397 counties with a population of approximately eighteen million people. The Urban Appalachian Council of Cincinnati (1985) defines an Appalachian as one who was born, or whose parents or grandparents were born, in one of the counties making up the Appalachian region.

The Study

In this qualitative study, completed during the 1985-86 school year, I examined the means by which a first-grade teacher translated the district's mandated reading program into the reality of classroom instruction and interaction. I was particularly interested in the relationship between the students' Appalachian cultural background and the classroom reading program. I found that despite the district's written curriculum goals, which emphasized providing students with materials relevant to the students' experience and cultural backgrounds, the reading program in the classroom did not meet these goals. This district-mandated reading program, which was in conflict with the culture of the students, made learning to read especially difficult for these children. Rigid district policies and insufficient funding limited the teacher's classroom autonomy. In addition, her beliefs about the way children learn to read created a hierarchical system in which public assignments to reading groups established an instructional ceiling for each reading group as well as the beginnings of student identities based on a sense of failure for children in the lower groups .

Giroux's critical social theory (Giroux, 1983a, 1983b), which calls for schools to be examined as social sites that structure the experience of subordinate groups, informed this project. In this case, the subordinate group was a class of low-SES, urban Appalachian first-grade students. The theory calls for an examination of the ways in which schools reproduce the dominant culture through ideological interests embedded in the curricula, systems of instruction, and evaluation methods. It is concerned with the ideology underlying the curriculum, with its hierarchically organized bodies of knowledge, and how this curriculum marginalizes students. Giroux's theory calls for an examination of the linguistic and cultural knowledge of students and the extent to which this knowledge is congruent with the dominant culture of schooling.

Critical theory also emphasizes the transformative aspects of the schooling process in the power of human agency to ameliorate the oppressive aspects of schools for children who are not part of white, middle-class society. In other words, critical theorists argue that classroom teachers can resist merely reproducing the class structure of the dominant society and can structure the schooling process so that students from oppressed groups are able to successfully attain the education they need to empower themselves. In this particular study, I believed that despite inadequate school funding, an excellent teacher could make a difference in providing the necessary literacy base for students. In designing the study, I decided to examine what did work by studying the way an "excellent" teacher implements a reading program in the daily school experiences of a class of urban Appalachian children.

This theoretical framework directed the study in an examination of the experience of Appalachian first graders in a hierarchically arranged, ability-grouped reading program. Specifically, the project explored reading instruction in the mandated curriculum and how an "excellent" teacher implemented instruction for differing ability groups of students. Two major questions guided the study:

1. How is the mandated curriculum carried out as reading instruction for differing ability groupings when the learners are urban, low-SES, Appalachian first graders?
2. Is the curriculum differentiated for ability groups? If so, what is the relationship between ability groups and the outcomes of the learners?

Methods

The research project involved a variety of interactive and noninteractive ethnographic methods. The interactive approaches relied primarily on daily participant observation in the classroom and interviews. Field notes were used to record the who, what, where, why and when of the classroom events and interactions. More than sixty reading lessons were observed during the course of the study. In addition, daily observations included whole group instruction during the early morning period prior to the formal reading groups. There were also observations of Education Consolidation Improvement Act (ECIA) Chapter I reading classes, faculty meetings, and student placement meetings. During the course of the study, many informal interviews were conducted with the cooperating first-grade teacher, other classroom teachers in the school, ECIA teachers, and the principal. Following the data collection in the classroom, formal interviews were conducted with the first-grade teacher, her supervisor, and the school's principal.

Noninteractive methods included using stream-of-behavior chronicles (Goetz and LeCompte, 1984) during small-group reading lessons and audiotaping throughout the reading lessons and during the early morning period, in which board work directions were given. The artifact collection included student report cards, district curriculum guides, absentee records, California Achievement Test (CAT) scores, and criterion-referenced test scores. An instrument designed to measure a teacher's orientation to the reading process, a Theoretical Orientation to the Reading Process (DeFord, 1985), was completed by the participating teacher.

The Setting

Fairview, the community surrounding the school in which I conducted this study, is a small urban Appalachian neighborhood within a large midwestern metropolitan area. Fairview forms its own pocket just west of the downtown area and is surrounded on all sides by natural and constructed boundaries so that it is isolated from the city's center. Although it is only a matter of blocks from the busy downtown area, a river valley and a parallel interstate highway which run north and south separate the community from the east side of the city. Fairview is the first community to the west of this river and the major highway.

Despite this location, Fairview is rural in flavor. It seems to be more "small town" than part of a city. The neighborhood itself is only a few blocks wide and about a mile in length. The distinct isolation from the main portion of the city creates a feeling of community. Fairview Hill to the west helps to create an urban version of an Appalachian hollow. As one drives into the neighborhood from the north, east, or west, there is a feeling of going down into an isolated little pocket of Appalachia.

The community is one in which people frequently socialize, visiting with one another on the sidewalks or in other community gathering places. The school yard before and after school is one such meeting place. Parents walk their preschoolers and school-aged children to the playground and converse until it is time for the children to go into school. This type of community interaction is different from what we usually expect in an urban area, but neighborliness and a strong sense of family are typical of Appalachian families (Jones, 1975).

The community was described to me by one of the district supervisors as an area of "poverty, high crime, child abuse, and despair." Rather than the middle-class German neighborhood it once was, with attractive, narrow brick townhouses, it is now an aging, crowded, "port of entry" neighborhood for Appalachians who have moved from the rural areas looking for economic opportunities in the northern cities. This movement was part of a large migration from southern and central Appalachia (Kentucky, Tennessee, West Virginia) that was sparked by the promise of factory work in the northern cities of Detroit, Akron, Cleveland, Dayton, and Cincinnati during the war years of the 1940s. Fairview today is not a community in transition, but it is fairly stable in that the Appalachians who live here are generally second-, third-, and fourth-generation people who have settled permanently in this urban community.

The Participants

Four criteria were established to guide the search for a teacher to cooperate in this research project:

1. An experienced first-grade teacher was sought so that well-established instructional routines and familiarity with the first-grade reading curriculum would be evident.

2. The teacher was to be regarded as successful by other professionals. This person had to be considered an "excellent first-grade teacher" by her peers.

3. A self-contained classroom in which the teacher provided reading instruction to at least three ability groups was sought so that this organizational structure could be studied.

4. The teacher was to be located in a setting in which the participants were primarily low-SES, urban Appalachian, the population of interest to this study.

The Teacher

Doris Walker, an Anglo in her early forties, was a pleasant woman with a quiet, comfortable manner. She was appropriately described to me by one of the kindergarten teachers as someone who "always has everything under control. She has such a quiet manner. She's an excellent teacher." Two of the other teachers as well as her principal described Walker to me as an "excellent" teacher during my observations at the school.

Walker had been teaching at Thomas Elementary School for her entire career of eighteen years. She taught at the third-grade level prior to working with first graders. Because of her experience and longevity at the school, she was sought out by the other teachers for assistance and advice. Her mentoring role was especially evident during the last days of the school year, when necessary paperwork and placement decisions were to be turned in to the principal's office.

Although she was perceived by other teachers to have everything under control, Walker commented to me on several occasions that she was not a disciplinarian. She considered the disciplining of children to be of secondary importance to the work that she performed in the back of the classroom during small-group reading instruction: "It's what happens back there [in the reading group] that's important. If you focus on behavior rather than reading, you lose. The children know if they disrupt the room, they can get your attention . . . I think the work they do independently is important, but reading group is really the most important thing." However, she was somewhat concerned with her lack of ability in classroom discipline. On several occasions, Walker expressed to me a desire to return to college to take some refresher courses in classroom management.

The Students

The students in Walker's classroom, with the exception of four Black students, came from the neighborhood in which the school was located. The other four were from outside the community and were siblings of students attending a magnet program of Thomas Elementary designed to integrate neighborhood schools. Mr. Foster, the principal, described this group of first-grade students as "low income" with the exception of two students. This judgment was based on the fact that they qualified for free lunch and breakfast programs. The two exceptions were at opposite extremes in their classroom academic achievement levels. Ronald, a Black student considered to be of middle-class background and from outside the community, was in Walker's "top" reading group. He also obtained the highest scores in the class on the California Achievement Test (CAT). Charles, a White Appalachian, also considered to be middle class, was in the "slowest" group and was not included in the CAT scoring because he had qualified for placement in a learning disabilities class for the 1986-87 school year.

During most of the study, there were thirty-two students in the first-grade classroom. They included fifteen females and seventeen males with abilities ranging from kindergarten readiness level in reading to independent second-grade reading level. Walker described her group of students as follows: "Different years are different. Sometimes I can have just two groups, if they aren't spread out so much. This year they're too spread out in abilities. I like years [when] they're not, so there's more time to work individually with students to push them ahead."

At the beginning of the 1985-86 school year, Walker divided her students into four reading groups. These groups were in hierarchical order from the most to the least skilled readers. The Red Group was the "top," Yellow was next, then Orange, and finally Blue. She described the Orange Group as "slow" and the Blue Group as the "slowest." In order to provide a more vivid view of the students in these reading groups, a sampling of some of the statements Walker made about individual children is provided. These comments were made on different occasions and in different settings throughout the course of my research. The descriptions are arranged according to reading groups.

Red Group

Sharon was always in the top group. Her mom helps her a lot.

Ronald was in another school [at the beginning of the year]. I seem to see him reading, following, listening, understanding the stories and anytime I would ask a question, he knew the answers. Usually he was paying attention, watching, knowing what was going on.

Bobby sure moved up. Sometimes, though Bobby, wasn't always comprehending. I was kind of worried for him a little bit in here. Maybe I should have kept him in two groups a little bit longer. He had a good attitude toward reading. He enjoyed it.

Yellow Group

Terri is doing well. I think I'm going to push her. Mrs. Farrell [ECIA teacher] doesn't think Terri should be moved to the Yellow Group. She doesn't think her skills are good enough for that group, but I'm going to try her. I think she's capable of reading. I don't know about her skills either. But she tries. Her handwriting and coloring are good.

Alfred's plodding along, too. He's a slow reader. I have to watch him. I'll keep him in the Yellow Group as long as he doesn't keep the others behind too much.

Bobby [was in Yellow, moved to Red], Billy and Gene tend to be in a competition with each other. Billy and Gene are not quite as good as Bobby. They tend to copy from each other in order to compete. Gene's attendance and his behavior influence his reading.

Orange Group

Andrew fiddles around. He's not too good on sounds, though. If he has a blend sheet to do, he's out of his seat. He's my behavior problem. His mother spoils him. Buys him things. He and his brother fight constantly. I don't know how his mother can stand it. I think that's why he's like that. Some days he'll be good and others, he has trouble. He's so changeable. Andrew has the ability. He didn't test very high. If he applied himself, he'd do much better in his reading. He doesn't listen or pay attention. He wanders. He can't work in group. Andrew was referred to the Social Skills Program for his behavior, but his mother wouldn't agree to let him participate.

Jason couldn't do anything when he first came. He's a first-grade repeater and he could not read the word *the*. He was not willing to do anything. He was very embarrassed. Could not handle being in a group. Was very timid and shy. Of course, he's a little timid and shy yet. He couldn't handle being with the other kids. I think Mary kind of made friends with him and he felt more accepted. He was more willing to take risks. He's come a long way.

Blue Group

Charles knows his sounds and words. He acts immature, but is really picking up sounds. He's going into an LD class for next year. When he first came, he had runny ears, couldn't see and couldn't talk. He couldn't do anything. He did know his alphabet. I asked his mother how he knew his ABC's so well and she told me that his sister helped him with those. His sister is really smart. When you really talk to him, you'll see. He's a cute kid. Charles, I think, has more knowledge than he uses. I'm not sure if it's immaturity or some kind of learning problem with him. He knows more. He has a 93 I.Q. And when he tested, he tested higher. I didn't realize where he really was, but just could not function. Could not work. He has some kind of a learning disability. Because of his eyes and because of his ears, too. That was his real problem. He had a physical problem. Charles was referred to the Social Skills Program because he has difficulty staying on his work and getting his jobs done. He still doesn't stay on task.

Jim still needs to be tested. He doesn't have the ability. He tries, but he just doesn't have it. He's real quiet. Jim was referred to the Social Skills Program because he was isolated from the other children. He wouldn't play or talk to anyone.

Ned can't stay with his work. He doesn't try. He's a behavior problem. If they don't place him [in an LD class], I've told Mr. Foster it's his responsibility. Poor kid.

Ned and Charles and some of the other kids in that one group shouldn't be in first grade. They really shouldn't. They should be getting more kindergarten experience, playing and learning to do things before they go to first grade.

Timmy in the beginning was doing fine. Now he doesn't try. His behavior is bad. Timmy was referred to the Social Skills Program for his behavior. He hits and pinches other children and misbehaves in the classroom.

Implementation of the Reading Program

The following discussion illustrates how Doris Walker implemented the district's reading program for this group of urban, low-income, Appalachian first graders. The basis for this description is an ideology of stratification which served as the cornerstone for reading instruction in this classroom. Then, I analyze the way in which other district policies and practices reinforced Doris Walker's teaching behaviors.

Grouping for Reading Instruction

The practice of organizing children into homogeneous ability groups for reading instruction has become a standard practice in most elementary schools in the United States. This system of dividing a class into three or four reading groups enables a teacher to manage large groups of students for the purpose of teaching the basic reading skills required by the mandated curriculum. Grouping by ability at the beginning of each school year is generally an automatic process used by elementary teachers to sort their class into categories according to perceived ability levels

in reading. The groups fall into the general classifications of above average, average, or below average, indicating the rate at which they are
expected to be able to process and learn the reading skills presented.

District policy as well as the large number of children per classroom
in this school required the teacher to organize her classroom reading
program into smaller, manageable groups based on the perceived ability levels of the students. The children were viewed as members of these
specific reading groups rather than as individuals. The group identification helped to characterize the abilities and needs of the children within
that group. This hierarchical arrangement of reading groups was translated into public knowledge in the classroom through a variety of forms.
The scheduling of the reading groups was such that the "top" group
was scheduled to have its small-group reading instruction first. The
other groups followed in hierarchical order throughout the morning.
The teacher's perceptions of each reading group became public in the
early morning period prior to reading groups, during which she
explained the children's individual seatwork assignments. A typical
example from an audiotaped segment illustrates this process:

Doris—All right. Look over here. [She points to an assignment written
which deals with words that are opposites.] Blue Group, you will *not* do
this, but everybody else will. Maybe the Orange Group . . . Orange
Group, you don't do this either. It might be a little too hard for you, but
I *know* the Yellow Group and the Red Group can do this easily. Listen
up, Red Group and Yellow Group. Today I want you to do opposites.
Write the word in the first box and then look over here at the list of
opposites. Find the one that fits with *on*. What would be the opposite of
on? It's a word over here [points to the list at the left of the blackboard].

These public expectations of the reading groups helped to determine the students' expectations of themselves. "I can't do that. I'm not
in that group. I'm only in the Orange Group" was a typical statement in
children's conversations with each other.

The reading group identification was further used as an organizational means to structure nonreading activities such as getting in line
according to reading group to go to special programs, to lunch, or to the
restroom. The Red Group was first much of the time, and the Blue
Group brought up the rear. The children in the Blue and Orange reading groups tended to interact only marginally in the activities both in
and out of the classroom. In whole-group activities Blue group members were often the last to be chosen.

Ideology of Stratification

An ideology of stratification was embedded in the district's adopted basal reading program. By "stratification," I refer to a hierarchically organized curriculum in which different types of knowledge are considered more or less valuable than others. An ideology of stratification is the belief that curricular knowledge is best taught in these hierarchical levels according to the perceived abilities of students. This belief results in different learning experiences for students who are identified by school personnel as belonging to different levels in the hierarchy—top, average, and slow students.

In this reading program, although the teacher's edition described the program as designed for "average"-ability students, it recommended the grouping of students into above-average, average and below-average levels. It provided specific activities to be used by classroom teachers to meet the needs of the children perceived to belong to each of these group levels. The underlying philosophy of the program was that below average readers need structured instruction which reteaches and reinforces isolated sound and word skills. Above-average readers need independent, creative activities to develop critical thinking abilities.

Institutional Stratification

Ideological stratification was also evident in the structure of the Chapter I remedial reading program. Since placement in the program depended solely on Metropolitan or California Achievement Test scores, only those children who obtained scores below a certain level and who consequently were considered to be "below average" in their reading achievement were placed in the remedial reading program. Teachers in this school had no authority to recommend placement in the remedial program on the basis of any other criterion. This rule was strictly enforced by the district so as not to jeopardize the loss of federal funding for the program. Placement in the Chapter I remedial reading program helped to determine and maintain children's placement in classroom reading groups. Groups of children were scheduled to leave the classroom daily for remedial reading on the basis of their test scores. It was easier for Mrs. Walker's reading instruction schedule to keep those same groups of children together for reading in the classroom. Once the initial schedule was set up with the Chapter I reading teachers, flexibility in changing students in reading groups was limited.

An ideology of stratification was reflected in the scoring of the California Achievement Tests (CATs). The stanine scores were grouped by the publishers of this test according to the same three ability levels: above average, average, and below average. Stratification was realized in the means by which the CAT test scores were used in the school. For this particular group of first graders, reading achievement measured by CAT scores was closely related to the ability level of the reading group as perceived by the teacher. The use of these scores by the teachers to formulate reading groups for the following school year served to reinforce a hierarchically structured system of access to knowledge. CAT scores helped to ensure that the students remained in their assigned reading groups at one of the three levels of ability and received differential instruction, according to both content and mode of delivery.

The district's grading system was inherently stratified according to the reading performance of students. Formal guidelines specified that if the children were reading "below grade level," they must receive grades of D or F despite their classroom performance. Report card grades in the district were dictated by reading levels within particular grade-level expectations.

Classroom Stratification: Hidden Criteria for Reading

In addition to the institutional ideology of stratification, Walker's own beliefs about what constituted a "good reader" created a system of classroom stratification. The "hidden criteria" established by Walker identified "good readers" as follows: (l) The children must be able to use correct reading posture, in that they must sit still, quietly and with their feet in front of them. (2) They must watch and listen to the teacher and other students in the reading group. (3) They must use a "marker" (narrow strip of paper) to keep their place in the book. (4) They must demonstrate "comprehension" of the reading material in their answers to Walker's explicit questions on the text by restating in their answers exactly what was read in the text. These hidden criteria relating non-reading behaviors to reading ability were never explicitly explained to children in the classroom, but they were evidenced in statements throughout the observations. The following are a sampling of Walker's comments in the reading groups:

1. *The Reading Posture:*

Okay. I'm going to see who has their hands folded, who has their feet on the floor, who has their ears on tight.

Robert, come up here and sit by me. I don't know why you're so wiggly today. This is important.

2. *Watching, Listening, and Being Quiet:*

Be real quiet. If you're quiet you can hear me better. When you go ahead and don't listen, you get your work wrong.

I'll pick someone who's quiet and doesn't yell.

3. *Using a Marker:*

If you don't have your marker in the right place, you won't know where we are.

You don't have your marker at the right place. I don't know where you're reading.

Let's have Andrew read this page. Wait a minute till everybody has markers.

4. *Total Recall of Text Explicit Questions:*

Teacher: How did the horse run?
Ronald: Fast.
[No response from teacher]
Sharon: Very fast.
Teacher: Read line 5 [directed student to read exact sentence from text for correct answer].
Ronald: He ran as fast as he could.

The more students were able to incorporate her beliefs about good reading behavior into their own classroom performances, the more likely the teacher was to perceive them as better readers. The children who could meet her requirements for sitting properly, listening, watching, using their markers, and responding to teacher-directed questions in the appropriate text-explicit manner were rewarded with inclusion into the higher-ability groups. Those who, for whatever reason, did not understand this structure and could not present themselves in the appropriate manner were more likely to be perceived as poor readers.

Substantive Differences in Instruction

The complexity of the relationship between the structural requirements of the institution and the beliefs and methodologies of the teacher resulted in a hierarchical system of reading instruction. Once the grouping decisions were made, this organization served to determine the pace of the reading lessons. This finding supports the current research in ability-grouped reading (Allington, 1977, 1980a, 1980b, 1983, 1984; Barr,

1974, 1975, 1982; Borman and Mueninghoff, 1982, 1983; Dreeben, 1984; Featherstone, 1987; Gambrell, Wilson, and Gantt, 1981; McDermott, 1977; Shavelson and Stern, 1981). The higher-level groups read more actual text that the lower groups. The higher groups received more direct teacher instructional time. In Doris Walker's classroom, the higher groups were scheduled earlier in the morning when everyone was "fresher." The two lower-level groups participated in reading groups with the teacher at the end of the morning just prior to lunchtime, following a morning of independent "board work." The higher-level groups were provided with more opportunities for independent silent reading, in contrast to the public oral reading required of the Orange and Blue Groups (see Table 1.1). These factors tended to put a ceiling on the amount of actual reading practice the children received. The lower groups were given less opportunity actually to read text (see Table 1.2).

TABLE 1.1

Oral and Silent Reading During Text Phase of Lessons, Appalachian Students

Group	Oral Reading	Silent Reading
Red	64%*	36%
Yellow	34%	66%
Orange	92%	8%
Blue	100%	0%

* This group often read orally text which has been assigned and read silently and independently prior to coming to reading group.

TABLE 1.2

Phases of Reading Lessons According to Group Percentage of Time Spent in Each Phase, Appalachian Students

Group	G.R.*	Skills	Vocabulary	Text	Assignment
Red	1%	13%	16%	67%	3%
Yellow	0%	21%	17%	59%	3%
Orange	1%	16%	36%	45%	2%
Blue	9%	31%	15%	45%	0%

* Getting ready phase.

Therefore, students who entered first grade at a variety of skills levels completed this reading program in four relatively homogeneous groups. This not only reflected their teacher's perceptions of their individual abilities, but also the program's institutionalized hierarchy of above-average, average and below-average readers. At the end of the school year, the system of grouping children for the following year's reading groups on the basis of their current teachers' perceptions provided a legacy of past performance for students which reinforced the impact of the first placement. The first teacher's perception of a child's ability based on standardized tests and classroom performance, however accurate or inaccurate it might have been, was a crucial element in the students' acquisition of literacy skills.

The reading achievement of the group as a whole according to standardized test scores, as well as subsequent placement in reading groups for second grade, was startling. Of the thirty-one children in the class at the end of the school year, only ten of those children were considered to be "on grade level" and assigned to a second-grade reading book. Four of the children were retained in first grade for the following year, and one was assigned to a primary learning disabilities classroom. Of the other sixteen students, all of whom were assigned to a second-grade classroom, half were placed in groups which would continue to use first-grade reading books for instruction.

District Level Conflicts Between Ideology and Policy

During the course of the study, I found that there were conflicting ideologies about the reading program. Formally, the district recommended a reading program that was sensitive to the needs of low-income and culturally different students, and yet district policies prevented teachers from implementing such a program. The district's formal curriculum guide specifically emphasized the importance of utilizing the "pupil's particular language pattern" as a "powerful motivator for learning." The guide further described the importance of building self-worth and confidence in students through a system of flexible grouping, differentiated instruction, and providing for individual differences in children. It encouraged the use of a wide variety of instructional equipment and materials and encouraged teachers to select these materials on the basis of their relevance to their particular group of students. The guide stated that the materials selected "should be relevant to pupils, deal with problems of social evolution, and include content of lasting value." Informally, Walker's elementary supervisor espoused an ideology of reading which included a whole-language approach to reading instruction involving the use of language experience activities. He discouraged the use of the basal reading program as a total reading program. Both he and the principal, Ron Foster, emphasized the necessity of making the reading instruction meaningful to the children in order for effective learning to take place. They also placed primary importance on meeting the individual needs of their urban Appalachian student population.

Despite this formally stated ideology of reading described by the district's curriculum guide and school administrators, the Board of Education had adopted a basal reading program and then mandated it for use in the district's schools. Teachers did not have the authority to choose materials for use in their classroom reading program, as was suggested by the formal curriculum guide. They were required to use the materials provided to them by the district whether they met the needs of the children or not. As Principal Foster stated, "The Board says, 'That's your book.'" Despite the supervisor's belief that the basal reading program was not to be used as a total program, Walker reported that he checked with the teachers to see "how far" they had gotten in the series by the end of the year with each of their groups.

Structural Constraints

In addition to these conflicting curricular messages provided to teachers, there was also a system of structural constraints at the district level which further limited the teachers' ability to structure the mandated basal reading program to fit the needs of individual students as specified in the curriculum guide. The structural constraints included a formally recommended pacing schedule for moving the children along the curriculum according to grade levels. For example, in the first-grade classrooms, the teachers were provided with specific guidelines by their supervisors for the scheduling of the reading program. The schedule provided for the completion of the reading readiness book in four weeks. Three preprimers were to be completed in fourteen weeks. Nine weeks each were allotted for the primer and first-grade reader. This schedule was extremely important in that progress through it determined the placement of the students for the following school year. District policy required students to master skills at the primer level of the basal reading program before they could be promoted to second grade. Mastery of these skills was primarily determined by exposure to them in daily reading instruction. If students did not cover the material at a given level in their reading group, teachers assumed that the material had not been mastered. Teachers at the second- and third-grade levels put additional pressure on the first-grade teachers to have the students progress through the first-grade reading program as mandated by the district in order to have the students begin at the "appropriate" reading level in their classes. The frustration this caused for the teachers was expressed by one of the first-grade teachers at the primary faculty meeting: "This is impossible [the scheduled first grade reading program], but we have to cover this [pointing to the mandated schedule described above]. We get students who haven't mastered the letters of the alphabet and some of them can't even write their names. People don't realize what we have to cover."

In addition to these basal reader guidelines, there was a complex series of scheduling requirements which were to be accommodated by the classroom teacher, including a Chapter I remedial reading program and a social skills program for students with behavioral "problems." These rigid scheduling requirements limited the teachers' autonomy in implementing a reading program which would be flexible enough to meet the individual needs of their students.

Funding Limitations

Additional structural constraints included a limited amount of funds for the reading program, which determined the availability of reading materials and equipment. Although the district supervisor said the district gave "high priority to the reading program" and "does a pretty good job of supplying the staff with the necessary materials," at the school level this was not evidenced. The limited inventory of books and materials forced the first-grade teachers to share the basal readers each day. However, cost was not the only reason for the limited number of books. An unwritten administrative policy operated as well which was described by Foster:

> Well, there's a philosophy about that [having a limited number of texts available in the classroom]. That is forcibly to have the teachers have separate groups and not teaching the whole class. That was done forcibly. They don't buy thirty books. Their thirty kids would be in the same book, on the same page. Buy half-sets of books and the books don't go home. Reading books have been abused. A lot of schools do buy them. We unfortunately don't have that kind of money. Anytime you're in an economically deprived area, your funds are limited.

In other words, there were two separate issues here: (1) insufficient funding to supply each of the classrooms with enough books for all the children and (2) the underlying assumption that not all students were able to be on the same level, but should be in three reading groups. The informal philosophy of the district as presented by the principal was that by limiting the number of readers on each level of the curriculum available to teachers, teachers would be forced to group their children into approximately three instructional groups for reading. In the first-grade classrooms, the number of basal readers provided to the teachers at each level was about ten. This district-imposed practice of limiting resources removed the decision making from the level of the classroom teacher and resulted in a stratified pattern of reading instruction in the classroom. The reasoning of the administration was that, by limiting the availability of material resources, children would benefit by receiving more individual attention and time from the teacher in small groups. According to the principal, unlike schools in wealthier neighborhoods, his school was unable to raise funds to supplement those supplied by the district because of the low socioeconomic level of this community. But administrative control of the teacher's reading instruction was also maintained by controlling the number of books provided to each classroom.

The Reading Program in Conflict
with the Culture of the Students

The official policy statement of the school district as presented in the curriculum guide called for a text which would be relevant to the children's experience and cultural backgrounds and which would include "content of lasting value." It is the argument of this study that the "boring basal readers," as they were described by one of the first-grade teachers, did not meet the criteria of the reading program as set up by the Board of Education.

The content of the stories in the reading text had very little relationship to the lives of these low-SES, urban Appalachian students. Most of the stories were set in suburban or rural middle-class family situations. The two-parent families which were typically portrayed were happily involved with family projects and activities. Very few of the stories were placed in urban settings with which the children would be familiar. Those stories which were set in cities depicted an upper-middle-class lifestyle. The stories had little relevance to the lived daily experiences of poor, urban Appalachian children. An example of this lack of relevancy occurred during one of the reading lessons in which the children were reading a story entitled "Going Down to the Sea." In this story a grandfather and his granddaughter went to the harbor to look at a ship which was named "Lion." During the oral reading of the story it became evident that the setting was not part of one student's experiences and that he had no understanding of this text. He had no notion that ships are given names. He kept asking a fellow student next to him, "Where's the lion, anyway?" He knew what a lion was in animal form, but nothing in his own personal experiences could help him understand this application of the word.

The controlled language used by the basal readers was formalized and repetitive. The assumption of the reading series was that beginning readers need to read short sentences with reinforcement of a limited amount of vocabulary. However, this language pattern was not congruent with the natural, spoken language of the children. I argue that the use of more natural language in the reading text as well as content which is relevant to the lives of these children would increase students' ability to gain meaning from the text and to use contextual clues in order to comprehend the material.

Conclusions

This chapter paints a rather bleak picture of reading instruction in one urban Appalachian first-grade class. Despite formally stated district policies which celebrated the needs of culturally different and economically disadvantaged students, district practices limited the ability of the teacher to meet these needs. Inadequate funding for instructional materials, a standardized curriculum for all students, large class size, and constraining schedules contributed to limited academic achievement.

One of the major findings of this study is the dissonance between the formal philosophy of the district at the macrolevel and the actual reading program which was provided to students at the microlevel of classroom reality. The formal reading ideology as espoused by the district reflected a concern for the needs of culturally different and economically disadvantaged children as well as current research on how children learn to read. However, the basal readers and mandated curriculum guides which were provided for use by teachers in the form of a program of "scripted" lessons ignored the cultural backgrounds and experiences of Appalachian children. There was no place in the program for use of the children's natural language patterns and life experiences.

The administration gave lip service to the teachers as valuable professionals capable of providing quality instruction for students. However, in reality, teacher autonomy in decision making was denied through a complex series of curricular controls and structural limitations. Large class size, a strict timetable for the completion of a set curriculum, and prescribed materials dictate classroom activities and interactions. Mandated materials removed the control of the curriculum from the hands of practicing educators. As stated succinctly by Giroux and McLaren (p. 219, 1986):

> In place of developing critical understanding, engaging student experience, and fostering active and critical citizenship, schools are redefined through a language that emphasizes standardization, competency, and narrowly-defined performance skills.
>
> Within this paradigm, the development of curricula is increasingly left to administrative experts or simply adopted from publishers, with few, if any, contributions from teachers who are expected to implement the new programs. In its most ideologically offensive form, this type of prepackaged curricula is rationalized as teacher-proof and designed to be applied to any classroom context regardless of the historical, cultural, and socioeconomic differences that define different schools and students.

A second major finding of the study was that the ideology of stratification which permeated the reading program was the source of cumulative deficits in the reading abilities of students. Children were assigned to reading groups in kindergarten or first grade. There were limitations to the number of students placed in each of the groups. The instructional techniques and the pacing of the reading lessons served to put a ceiling on what was learned in each of the groups. Students in all groups were restricted to the material covered within the groups.

In this classroom, a mandated system of ability grouping in which at least one-third of each class was identified as "slow" learners determined the pace and type of instruction students experienced in the classroom and consequently limited their movement into higher-level groups. The school and social identities of these students were reinforced in classroom activities based on this ability-grouped reading program. The placement in reading groups had more to do with students' ability to exhibit correct or incorrect reading behaviors than it did with intellectual ability. Students identified as belonging to the lowest reading groups were provided with the most repetitive instructional practices. They were continually told through classroom practices and interactions that they were the less capable, "slower" students. I suggest that these are the students who we find in the lists of dropouts or "pushouts" when they reach junior and senior high schools.

We can see clearly that two-thirds of this group of Appalachian students failed to gain the first-grade reading skills prescribed by the school's curriculum. How can we explain this? The economic and cultural reproduction aspects of critical theory help us to understand this failure. For example, the school district, despite a stated goal of providing quality education to low-social-class children, provided inadequate funding to this poor, Appalachian neighborhood school. The school curriculum, despite its formal policy emphasis on cultural diversity, was in practice a standard White, middle-class way to "do school." This teacher, although competent, was not able to make a significant difference for these first graders. She did not provide a classroom in which the culture, natural language, and experiences of the children were used to engage them in the potentially exciting process of learning to read. The school structure as well as her own training limited her ability to do so.

Rather than dwell on the reasons for the failures of these children, this study points to the need for a reexamination of both the way we prepare teachers and the way we "do school." Colleges of education must be committed to preparing teachers to work effectively with students from a variety of economically, culturally, and ethnically different backgrounds. Educators and policymakers need to carefully address the issue of minority student failure. We have the research knowledge base to structure schools and to implement programs which provide quality educations for multicultural populations. It is essential to use this knowledge in schools to provide students like these urban Appalachian first graders with opportunities to succeed.

Chapter 2

Mapping Terrains of Power: Student Cultural Knowledge Versus Classroom Knowledge

——————————————— Christine E. Sleeter
——————————————— Carl A. Grant

Anna stared out the window, while the teacher droned on in the background. Anna's thoughts centered on an argument she had had with her best friend earlier in the week. The argument had been over interpersonal loyalty. On the surface, it was another case of one girl spreading secrets about another girl's feelings to a third party, who could be counted on to circulate everything she heard. But on a deeper level, the argument called into question what counts as private, what friendship and loyalty mean, and how kids legitimately gain status and acceptance in the social structure.

Anna's attention was wrenched back to the classroom when the teacher announced that "this information should be in your notes because it may appear on a test." Mechanically, Anna began to write as the teacher dictated some sentences about the differences between fiction and nonfiction, and how stories the class had read recently illustrated each. When the teacher had finished dictating notes, a student asked him a question and Anna's mind returned to her own concerns.

Most of us as students have been in Alma's shoes and can readily identify with the bifurcation Anna experienced between school knowledge and real-life knowledge, and with the potency of real life compared with the lifelessness of much school knowledge. For some of us, Anna's experience represents occasional moments of boredom and daydreaming in an otherwise interesting and engaging school experience. For others, Anna's experience is the main reality of classroom life; it is here these students learn in which terrains they have some power and in which they are powerless.

Knowledge and Power

Ashcroft (1987) defines power as "a capability to act" (p. 143). One exercises power when one desires a certain state of affairs and acts to bring it about. Power requires desire, interest, or passion; a vision of a state of affairs which is desirable or attractive and which differs from the current state of affairs; and the ability to act in a way that is sufficiently potent and informed to achieve what one desires. Greene (1986) describes teaching as "an undertaking oriented to empowering persons to became different, to think critically and creatively, to pursue meanings, to make increasing sense of their actually lived worlds" (p. 72).

Knowledge is central to power. Knowledge helps us envision the contours and limits of our own existence, what is desirable and possible, and what actions might bring about those possibilities. Knowledge helps us examine relationships between what is ethical and what is desirable; it widens our experience; it provides analytic tools for thinking through questions, situations, and problems. Knowledge that empowers centers around the interests and aims of the prospective knower. Apart from the knower, knowledge has no intrinsic power; in interaction with the knower's desires and purposes, knowledge has meaning and power. Dewey (1944) wrote the following:

> Such words as interest, affection, concern, motivation emphasize the bearing of what is foreseen upon the individual's fortunes, and his [her] active desire to act to secure a possible result . . . *What* is anticipated is objective and impersonal; tomorrow's rain, the possibility of being run over. But for an active being, a being who partakes of the consequences instead of standing aloof from them, there is at the same time a personal response. (p. 125)

It is the active being, then, who is the center of learning for the enhancement of personal power.

Ideally, education should help all students acquire knowledge that empowers. This implies that knowledge should include a perspective of history from the students' point of view and be selected and constructed in relationship to the students' desires, visions, descriptions of reality, and repertoires of action.

However, in schools the source of curriculum usually has very little to do with the students. The most common way educators select curriculum is to turn to traditionally accepted knowledge that has been encoded and passed down, in deference to the belief that schools exist for the "acculturation of the young to society's collective achievements"

(Reitman, 1981, p. 37). In order to base curriculum around those achievements teachers are often advised to determine "what major ideas (concepts) will be emphasized during the year" by examining "all available textbooks, curriculum guides, and course-of-study aids" (Hoover, 1982, p. 20). Presumably, if one transmits this knowledge to young people, it will inform their desires, interests, and thinking and help them gain power to achieve their own desires within society. Pickles (1985) describes this as the Cartesian model of teaching: "Knowledge as information is passed on from the teacher to the student as if it were a basket of eggs. Effective teaching and learning are achieved if the 'eggs' are conveyed safely, intact, and without damage" (p. 234). Failure to learn this predigested knowledge is often explained as a result of having low ability, being socially at risk, or having poor motivation for acquiring and retaining information and its organizing concepts. We will argue that for many students, the knowledge itself and the form it takes are disabling, both academically and socially.

Cummins (1986) argues that "students from 'dominated' societal groups are 'empowered' or 'disabled' as a direct result of their interactions with educators in the schools" (p. 21). Students who achieve and succeed in school experience a meshing or overlap between the knowledge taught in school and the knowledge that has personal meaning to them. According to Cummins, "they participate competently in instruction as a result of having developed a confident cultural identity as well as appropriate school-based knowledge and interactional structures" (p. 32). In the words of Shor and Freire (1987), knowledge that empowers is situated within and interacts with "the themes and language of the students" (p. 28). Students who are disabled by their school experience do not experience congruence between school knowledge and the knowledge they bring to school with them.

What they experience, illustrated by Anna, is a disjuncture between two different kinds of knowledge and the processes for engaging with it. Everhart (1983) has distinguished between reified knowledge and regenerative knowledge. Regenerative knowledge "is created, maintained, and re-created through the continuous interaction of people in a community setting"; it is "contextually based, meaning that understanding comes out of the specific historical context in which the actors are immersed" (pp. 124-125). It derives from the desires and experiences of the individuals who create it, and guides their thinking and behavior. Regenerative knowledge is also forged in the home and community. Walsh (1987) describes the meanings a community of Puerto Rican students attached to certain vocabulary words, showing how those meanings derive from the cultural context of their home and community.

Knowledge generated and learned within the context of everyday life structures how students think about themselves, their world, and experience.

Reified knowledge, on the other hand, "is knowledge that while abstract, tenuous, and problematic, is treated as it if is concrete and 'real'" (Everhart, 1983, p. 86). Reified knowledge, like regenerative knowledge, was created in a specific historical context by specific actors but has been encoded for transmission, and in the process decontextualized and converted to a static product. McLaren (1986) describes the "student state" in which students encounter reified knowledge: it usually places boundaries between emotion and knowledge; students do not control knowledge, but rather "must write their student roles and scenarios in conformity to the teacher's master script" (p. 88). Shor and Freire (1987) describe what usually occurs in classrooms: "Knowledge is already formed and must be verbally delivered to the students. Students in the traditional mode are expected to absorb preset formulations spoken by the teacher" (p. 15).

School knowledge empowers to the extent that it meshes with and augments students' regenerative knowledge. Pickles (1985) points out that teachers' knowledge and students' knowledge overlap in a range of "commonplaces." Seeking out these commonplaces and then engaging students from there provides a starting point for education."The task is democratic and empowering because it engages students in dialogue with their community, enhances their ability to unify reflection and action, and permits them to learn how to control change on the basis of principles and values that they have worked out in community with others" (p. 238). School knowledge disables to the extent that it silences students, usurps their minds or at least demands acquiescence, and alienates them from the major public institution in which they spend their growing-up years. Fine (1987) describes the epitome of a silenced student being disabled daily from developing the power to act on her own behalf in a public institution: "Patrice is a young black female, in eleventh grade. She says nothing all day in school. She sits perfectly mute. No need to coerce her into silence. She often wears her coat in class. Sometimes she lays her head on her desk. She never disrupts. Never disobeys. Never speaks. And is never identified as a problem" (p. 172).

Student Cultural Knowledge
and the Terrain of Students' Power

Regardless of the form or content of school knowledge, students exercise power over the creation and understanding of some parts of their world. This paper explores some of that world and juxtaposes it against the knowledge the students were encountering in the classroom. We will argue that students were learning to exercise power in the terrain of their own social lives and neighborhoods but that they were becoming disabled and silenced within a public institution, interpreting school knowledge as a series of tasks to complete for authority figures rather than as an instrument for advancing their own interests.

One can analyze students' cultural knowledge using principles of cognitive anthropology. Cultural knowledge refers to "the knowledge people use to generate and interpret social behavior" (Spradley and McCurdy, 1972, p. 8). It will be used here synonymously with Everhart's conception of regenerative knowledge. Drawing on the work of linguists, cognitive anthropologists have attempted to understand the "grammar" members of a cultural group use to generate and organize their cultural knowledge about the world. This is done by identifying domains of cultural knowledge, units of meaning and categories of units within those domains, relationships among units and categories of meaning, and criteria for distinguishing among categories. The anthropologist constructs representations of the cognitive maps that guide the sense that members of a cultural group make of their world. One then searches for underlying elements and principles that help account for the structure and content of those taxonomies. This procedure has been commonly used to understand kinship systems in traditional societies (e.g., Frake, 1980; Goodenough, 1956; Levi-Strauss, 1963), but, with exceptions such as Everhart (1983), it has been used very little to understand student culture in modern societies.

This study is based on a larger study of a desegregated junior high school in a working class neighborhood (Grant and Sleeter, 1986). Data were gathered by a team of three researchers between 1978 and 1981. As part of the larger study, we interviewed teachers and administrators, and spent a total of 143 hours observing in twenty-three of the school's forty-five classrooms. Twelve of these were in core academic subject areas (English, social studies, math, and science), six in electives (music, home economics, industrial arts, and multicultural education), and five in remedial and special education classes. During our first few days in the school we learned that student achievement scores were low. Although teachers were teaching and students were going through the motions of learning (discipline was not a problem in this school—most students obeyed teachers well), teachers lamented that not much learning was taking place. In interviews, teachers described their purposes as teaching basic skills and academic knowledge, largely at a remedial level, and preparing students for useful lives outside school. Most of them selected the knowledge to teach by determining the level of skills and knowledge students had mastered in relationship to what is traditionally taught within their subject areas. Most also made some attempt to include practical applications of academic knowledge. Thus, they saw their purpose as transmitting to students a body of knowledge and skills that would be practical but that could also provide a basis for further academic learning. They explained the students' low achievement primarily by citing deficiencies in the students' home backgrounds that were thought to limit their aptitude for learning.

The students spent the great majority of their classroom time, especially in core subject areas, sitting passively while teachers attempted to "fill" their heads with information. In ten academic and two home economics classrooms the prevailing instructional patterns consisted of a large-group lesson—usually lecture or recitation, followed by individual seatwork—usually reading from the text or doing worksheets. A few teachers occasionally varied this pattern using labs or projects in place of seatwork. Worksheets and tests in these classrooms emphasized recall and comprehension tasks to the virtual exclusion of higher-order thinking tasks. The two music classes consisted mainly of large-group rehearsal of songs (selected solely by the teacher in band and partially by students in chorus). Independent seatwork with a heavy drill-and-practice emphasis was used heavily in the remedial math and reading classes and often in special education classes, although two special education teachers made consistent attempts to build content lessons around student interests. Of the twenty-three teachers, only one social studies teacher and three teachers of electives consistently used varied teaching strategies that actively involved the students in discussing, applying, and creating some of the classroom content.

We came to wonder what was in the students' heads while they sat passively in most of their classrooms. To investigate the students' cultural knowledge, we interviewed 28 eighth- and ninth-grade students. We selected students to obtain a diverse cross-section of the student body. Thirteen were males; 15 were females. They represented the following racial or ethnic groups: Black American(3), Arab American (1), Mexican American (7), Native American (2), Filipino (1), White (11), and mixed Mexican White (3). Of the White students, three were physically impaired and were bused to the school. The students ranged academically from high achievers to low achievers placed in special education or remedial classes. We had been studying the teachers and administrators in the school for one and a half years by the time we interviewed students for this portion of the study. We were familiar to the students and had informally talked with or interviewed several of them already.

For this portion of the study, each student (with the exception of three who moved during the study) was interviewed on three different occasions, each interview lasting about an hour. Interviews were taped and transcribed for analysis. The first interview was used primarily to ascertain domains of knowledge students saw as important to their lives as students. Subsequent interviews were used primarily to gain more information about categories of meaning within these domains. Four kinds of interview questions were used (Spradley and McCurdy, 1972): grand tour questions (e.g., "Tell me what it's like to be a student here," "Tell me about the kids here."); structural questions (e.g., "You have listed four kinds of kids—are there any more?"); contrast questions (e.g., "What are the differences between a nice teacher and a mean teacher?"); and attribute questions (e.g.,"Tell me what a "hard guy" is.").

Transcribed interviews were analyzed to determine the structure and content of students' cultural knowledge about being students at this school. The three researchers first identified and agreed upon three major domains of cultural knowledge used by most of the students: things to do and whom to do them with (activities and friends were rarely discussed in isolation of one another), other kids, and school. These will be referred to as level 1 categories of cultural knowledge. These emerged primarily in response to grand tour questions. For example, when asked, "Tell me about your friends," and "Tell me about kids here at Five Bridges," students consistently and immediately differentiated between friends with whom they interacted or did things and other kids they saw but interacted with less or not at all. Further distinctions among kids were made after this. In determining categories of cultural knowledge at any level, we were careful to note whether a category was suggested by the student or the interviewer. Categories suggested and elaborated upon by the student, and particularly those used by the student in more than one interview, were designated as organizing categories for the students' cultural knowledge.

Subcategories under level 1 categories will be referred to as level 2 categories, and so forth. Level 2 categories emerged as students described each domain. For example, in describing the level 1 category of "going to school," students supplied their own categories and terms, such as teachers, classwork, and rules. Level 3 categories were further subdistinctions within that level 2 category. For example, several students distinguished between nice and mean teachers when asked to describe their teachers.

Each researcher separately examined each student's interviews and constructed a diagram of categories and subcategories of that student's cultural knowledge. After initial diagrams of students' cultural knowledge were made, they were compared, and any differences were discussed and checked again against the data or held in question until the student could be interviewed again. Each student (with the exception of three who moved and one who could not be located) was asked to examine his or her diagram and "walked through" it. All 24 students confirmed the diagrams as basically accurate, sometimes adding bits of information or making minor corrections.

The structure and content of students' cultural knowledge, and the location of the knowledge teachers were attempting to teach them, will be described below. First, however, it must be noted that most students did not confine all their remarks to these three categories. Most talked to some extent about their home life, and several talked about their neighborhood; for sake of space, since these domains were not directly concerned with their school experience and how they processed school knowledge, they will not be described here. However, these domains are important for understanding the student culture and for teaching students more productively. In addition to home and neighborhood, other level 1 categories discussed by one to three students included the following: preparing for the future, race (discussed by a new White student), other people's prejudice, music, getting around (discussed by a student in a wheelchair), my reputation, getting in trouble, my image to other people, and my personal philosophy. These seemed to represent concerns that were idiosyncratic to particular individuals.

Nevertheless, there was considerable similarity among the students in both the structure and general content of their cultural knowledge maps. We attempted to discover whether there were systematic differences among students on the basis of race, gender, handicap, or popularity. A few such differences, which will be noted, existed between the physically impaired and nonimpaired students; none were noted among other kinds of students. This issue is discussed more fully elsewhere (Grant and Sleeter, 1986).

Things to Do and Whom to Do Them With

This category occupied more attention than any other for most students. They frequently talked about things to do and whom to do them with when asked, "Tell me what it's like to be a student here." Students also tended to discuss their friends in terms of what they did with them when asked to talk about their friends, and activities in terms of whom they did them with when asked what they liked to do outside school.

Figure 2.1 shows an illustrative, simplified diagram of four levels of one student's cultural knowledge. This diagram is typical for the 28 students in several ways. Students differentiated among friends on the basis of where one saw them or what one did with them. Most students talked in detail about their friends, distinguishing among those they said "hi" to in school, those they "hung around" with in school, and those they "hung around" with outside (and often inside) school. What it meant to "hang around" differed somewhat from student to student, but this commonly included student-directed group activities such as going roller skating, shooting baskets, shopping, or listening to records. Opposite-sex friends constituted a distinct category from the larger and usually more differentiated category of "friends."

FIGURE 2.1

Four Levels of One Student's Cultural Knowledge

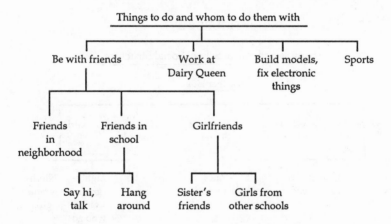

Sports was a level 2 category on half of the cultural knowledge diagrams (8 boys and 6 girls), and often students talked about friends with whom they played sports. Work of some sort was a category on several students' diagrams; usually this was not discussed in terms of friends and was mentioned rather than described. Finally, several students talked about a hobby, usually done alone, such as fixing things, taking pictures, or reading. A few additional level 2 categories some students discussed included parties, bike riding, and going shopping. These were usually discussed in terms of who participated in them.

There were a few variations to this pattern. Some students talked about only two or three level 2 categories (one boy confined his remarks to sports and girls), and a few others had seven or eight categories. One student discussed things to do, but not whom he did them with, and apparently did them alone (one of his teachers verified this). Two students—one in a wheelchair and one new to the school—discussed friends but made little mention of activities they did with their friends beyond talking at school. But on the whole, students shared a common way of organizing their understanding of things to do with friends.

Other Kids

This category represented a map of the student social structure in the school (usually), and sometimes included the student's own location in that structure. A few students included kinds of kids their age at other schools as well. Figure 2.2, although showing one of the more elaborated schemes, is typical of how most students described the student social structure.

FIGURE 2.2

Sample Scheme of School Social Structure

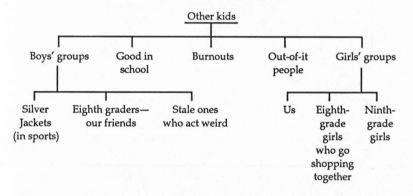

In the diagram represented in Figure 2.2, as in fourteen other students' diagrams, a level 2 distinction was made among kids on the basis of gender, although several categories of kids were not so divided. Students divided by gender those categories of other students with whom they had most contact, and referred to other categories (such as "burnouts" and those who are "good in school") without reference to gender. The categories of kids in Figure 2.2 were also named by many other students (i.e., kids in sports, good in school, burnouts, and out-of-its or bores), although students did not always name exactly the same people as belonging to these categories. The three additional categories that other students commonly named included "big mouths" and "hard guys" (girls and boys, respectively, who got in trouble by acting aggressively), "popular people," and (occasionally) handicapped kids (often referred to as "handicaps"). Most of these categories differentiated among kids on the basis of activities in which they chose to engage or personal identities over which they had some control. The two exceptions to this were gender and handicap.

One physically impaired student offered a variation which illustrates the main difference between how the physically impaired and nonimpaired students viewed the social system. This is shown in Figure 2.3.

FIGURE 2.3

One Physically Impaired Student's View of Social Structure

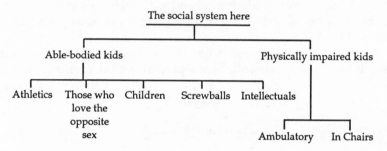

Notice this student's level 2 differentiation of physically impaired and able-bodied kids—a differentiation other physically impaired students also made. Although physical impairment was an ascribed difference among students, after physically impaired and nonimpaired students had become used to each other its main significance was that it restricted the activities in which one could engage.

Students offered more variation in the structure and content of this domain of cultural knowledge than the previous one. A few talked relatively little about other kids, for example, mentioning "kids we don't like" every once in a while, but little else. Others, on the other hand, talked at length and in great detail about other kids. Several students, while discussing different categories of kids, also discussed how kids judge each other (e.g., based on clothes, athletic skill, friends); these students appeared to dislike that aspect of their social system. A few students offered idiosyncratic systems for discussing their peers. Unique level 2 or level 3 distinctions included white versus minority (two students), those who like disco versus those who like rock (one student), those who smoke pot versus those who are straight (one student), talkative versus quiet kids (one student), and nice versus mean kids (one student). Still, even these students differentiated among students on the basis of student-directed activities. We found it particularly interesting that the great majority of the students did not classify each other on the basis of race (see Grant and Sleeter, 1986, for a discussion of this).

Going to School

This domain dealt directly with school. We had to probe students to talk about this domain more than we had to probe them to talk about the other two—several students said they simply did not think about school much. In the first interview, we asked students, "Tell me what it's like to be a student here." In subsequent interviews, we asked more direct questions about classwork, grades, and what they were learning. Two simplified cultural knowledge diagrams are depicted as examples in Figure 2.4.

Several features of these diagrams are typical. On most, teachers and classes and/or classwork were separate level 2 categories. Teachers

FIGURE 2.4

Two Views of School

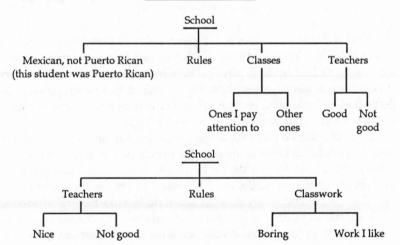

were usually discussed in terms of personal qualities and were usually divided into two categories, one positive and one negative, for example: good/bad, fair/not fair, nice/mean. Teachers were evaluated most positively if they expected students to work, communicated expectations clearly and enforced them evenly, and maintained pleasant relationships with students while doing so. As one student put it when asked how he would describe a good teacher: "One that would sit down with you and be there to help you all the time. One that wants to teach you. One that thinks you got something going." Classes and classwork were similarly divided into positive and negative categories ("boring" being the most common negative category). Positively evaluated classwork (e.g., discussing, doing projects) involved students actively and often with each other; the more passive their role (e.g., watching films, taking notes, doing worksheets), the less positively they evaluated the work. When students discussed their classes, they usually simply listed the name of a class and their evaluation of its worth. Only a few students spontaneously said very much about the content of a class, usually with reference to a class the student liked.

"Rules" appeared on several students' cultural knowledge diagrams. School rules became a category of concern when they encroached on what students saw as their own space. At the time of the study, the school had adopted a rule prohibiting students from leaving campus during lunch; this led several of them to describe the school as a "prison." Students did not mention rules in classrooms as a concern; schoolwide rules attempting to restrict their behavior between classes were what they grumbled about.

In addition to the level 2 categories on the diagrams in Figure 2.4, several students also talked about grades, school activities and school sports, and seeing friends in school.

What About Class Content?

After about two hours of interviews with each student, we realized they were saying very little about the content of most of their classes. We also noted that in the one and a half years of the larger study, we rarely heard students talk about classwork among themselves outside class (this has also been found in other ethnographic studies of students; see, for example, Cusick, 1973; Everhart, 1983). When we asked them to describe their classes, they tended to describe either the teacher or the classwork—for example, "In math we just sit there and listen to the teacher, and then at the end we get an assignment. And in English we do the work in class and then we go over it." Since they rarely mentioned what was being taught in class, we began asking students pointedly what they were learning, to what extent it was connected to their lives, and whether they thought about what they were taught when they were not in class.

Students usually described class content by listing topics; some students answered questions about content by describing instructional procedures more than content. About one-third said that none of the class content related to their lives outside class; almost half said that one or two classes related somewhat, but the rest of their classes did not. The other students named two or three classes they said related to their lives quite a bit. The most relevant classes included the following: government, because current events heard on the news were discussed there; oral history, because the content was about the students' own neighborhood; money and banking, because it would be useful later to know how to manage money and write checks; math, because it helps them deal with their money more skillfully; English, to some extent, because it teaches words one can use; and multicultural education, because some of the students or family members had experienced prejudice, which was a major focus of the class's content. But the great majority of the students we interviewed considered most or all of what the school was teaching them to be unrelated to their lives. Considering much of the content irrelevant, students often reported being bored in class, and some said they forgot what they had learned (been told) once they had been tested on it. This was true regardless of the grades they were getting or the academic ability teachers thought they had. As one student put it, "A lot of the reason why the kids screw up in class is because they can see no practical use for what they are learning."

Public Institutions as a Terrain
Outside One's Ownership

School is the first major public institution in which most of us spend a great deal of time, and it is where we first learn to act and interact in a public institution in a democratic society. For this reason, it is crucial that the school experience cultivates in students the habits and training for democratic participation. Dewey (1944) wrote the following:

> A society which makes provision for participation in its good of all its members on equal terms and which secures flexible readjustment of its institutions through interaction of the different forms of associated life is in so far democratic. Such a society must have a type of education which gives individuals a per-

sonal interest in social relationships and control, and the habits of mind which secure social changes without introducing disorder. (p. 99)

The students in this study were learning that they have little ownership in or control over public institutions and public learning. They had power to create, manipulate, and understand life, but that power was restricted to their own localized neighborhood and peer group. Their own cultural knowledge did not simply compete with school knowledge—school knowledge was subsumed within it, and understood as a set of tasks to do. School knowledge was not being absorbed by students as a conceptual system for helping them understand and act on the world—it was compartmentalized within their own conceptual system and thought of as sets of activities done for someone else in a social context.

We can understand why students paid little attention to school knowledge by considering it in relationship to the "grammar" of their own cultural knowledge. The students' cultural knowledge was made up of two basic elements that were usually related to one another: persons and events.

Students differentiated among persons mainly on the basis of age. They did not directly tell us that, but they talked most about age-mates and made reference to "older people," sometimes mentioning categories of older people such as parents and teachers. In addition, a sizable portion of the age-mates they talked about were personally known to the student, although categories such as "out-of-its" or "big mouths" were applied to people one had seen but not necessarily spoken with. Thus, although people constituted an important element of their cultural knowledge, the kinds of people to whom they directed most of their attention were age-mates with whom they had some personal contact. This category was then further subdivided on the basis of gender and other attributes. Older people, and especially older people with whom one had had no personal contact, were treated as an undifferentiated category that was not discussed much.

The other major element was events. Students talked most about events they could control, or at least choose whether or not to participate in (such as going roller-skating or talking). Most were social and may be considered frivolous by adults (e.g., parties, talking, sports, shopping); however, most were events in which students could make substantive choices regarding who would participate, when the event would occur, how it would be structured, and so forth. Student-controlled events constituted the main basis on which students distinguished among kinds of friends and kinds of kids. For example, in Figure 2.2 we find "Silver Jackets" who play sports together, "burnouts" who smoke and possibly take drugs together, and "eighth-grade girls who go shopping together." Even "out-of-it people" earned this designation by *not* participating in student activities of which this particular student was aware. Events students neither participated in nor controlled were not prominent categories in their cultural knowledge, unless these (e.g., pro football) were directly related to events in which they chose to participate. There was, for example, a direct relationship between professional football and students' own participation on football teams.

Students' cultural knowledge was rooted in their own concrete experience and reflected what was real to them. Collective separation from the adult world was a reality they experienced every day. Dividing their time between events under their own control and events controlled by others was also a reality they experienced. School knowledge usually concerned matters removed from the students' own existence, and came to the students by way of adults in verbal form without concrete analogues the students had experienced. People the school taught about (for example, in history or literature) were mostly adults and were not known personally by the students, or were described as important and significant others in the historical or contemporary lives of the students. Events the school taught about were mainly controlled by adults the students did not know personally and took place outside the students' realm of daily experience. Skills such as math were rarely contextualized within student experience. The concepts the school used to describe and explain phenomena were decided upon by adults and came out of their life experiences or the way they interpreted the students' life experiences. Our interviews with teachers and time spent in classrooms usually resonated to Greene's (1986) observation: "I think of how little many teachers know about their students' diverse lives and thinking processes, how little they can know because of the paucity of dialogue in the classroom space" (p. 80).

For example, in a geography unit we observed, students were taught about economic institutions and political events in states located one thousand miles away. Very little consideration or time was given to relating these concepts to economic institutions and political events pertinent to the lives of the students. Adult political figures were the only people included in the unit; historic and modern events shaped by adults in these states were the only events mentioned, and these were couched in abstract terms used by social scientists. Virtually none of this information was directly connected to the students' cultural knowledge about their own world. Classes students told us were relevant and interesting to them differed from other classes in that at least some of the content included people students knew (e.g., community members in oral history class) or events they would be choosing to participate in soon (e.g., writing checks).

Students encountered most school knowledge as a series of tasks to perform in a context of personal relationships. For example, math was encountered as a series of worksheets to complete with or without one's friends, for a teacher one either liked or disliked. English was encountered as a series of pages to read and questions to "do" in the company of peers for a teacher who was nice or mean, fair or unfair, strict or "lets us run all over" him or her. They thought about and learned school knowledge to the extent necessary for meeting demands placed on them in a manner that would maintain good relationships with teachers, peers, and parents they cared about. But just as the school had tacitly dismissed the importance of student's own cultural knowledge and the process through which it was constructed, so the students dismissed most school knowledge, seeing it as useless. Far from providing students with a way of understanding the world, school knowledge was lodged within the students' framework for understanding the world in a relatively unimportant niche, and thought of in terms of "work" to do for an older person.

The school, then, served as a public institution in which students learned to comply with the requirements of authority figures and experienced subject matter that was boring and not made relevant to their lives. The knowledge it dispensed was not so much a doorway to the broader society and its culture as it was a series of meaningless tasks to perform. In low-income communities and communities of Americans who are not White, this is often the reality of school.

Empowering Children from Disenfranchised Communities

Connecting the public knowledge that is found in books, works of art, and so forth with the knowledge and meanings students bring with them is always a challenge, no matter who the students are. Dewey (1944) reminded us that "the subject matter of the learner is not, therefore, it cannot be, identical with the formulated, the crystallized, and systematized subject matter of the adult . . . The latter represents the *pos-*

sibilities of the former; not its existing state" (p. 182). And no matter who the students are, their power to learn and act begins with knowledge generated within their own lived experience: "It is not true that the experience of the young is unorganized—that it consists of isolated scraps. But it is organized in connection with direct practical centers of interest . . . The problem of teaching is to keep the experience of the student moving in the direction of what the expert already knows. Hence the need that the teacher know both subject matter and the characteristic needs and capacities of the student" (Dewey, 1944, pp. 183-184).

School knowledge can be bridged very directly with students' life experiences and knowledge. For example, Saxe (1988) investigated mathematical concepts constructed by children who sell candy in Brazil, showing how mathematical systems generated in their everyday lives related to and helped them acquire schools' mathematics. Cummins (1986) described a school district in California that had a preschool program in which "Spanish is the exclusive language of instruction, there is a strong community involvement component, and the program is characterized by a coherent philosophy of promoting conceptual development through meaningful linguistic interaction" (p. 30). Spanish-speaking students participating in the program scored as well on school readiness tests as native English-speaking students; Spanish-speaking students participating in other programs scored much below either group. Cummins attributes students' achievement directly to the program's explicit attempt to eliminate walls separating the institution's knowledge from knowledge children develop in the home and community.

Let us emphasize that we are not advocating *not* teaching traditional school knowledge to children from disenfranchised communities. As Simon (1987) points out, "If we do not give youth a sense of how to 'make it' within existing realities, all too often we doom them to social marginality: yet another high-minded way of perpetuating the structural inequalities in society" (p. 375). What we are advocating is bridging school knowledge or public knowledge and students' own cultural knowledge, and thus encouraging students to analyze this interaction and then use the knowledge learned to take charge of their circumstances.

Freire emphasizes that his "insistence on starting from *their* description of *their* daily life experiences is based on the possibility of starting from concreteness, from common sense, to reach a rigorous understanding of reality" (Shor and Freire, 1987, p. 20, emphasis theirs). One can extend students' understanding and analysis of the world outward. For example, sports was a domain of interest to the students we studied. Within a study of sports one can learn to use a wide range of mathematical operations. One can study human physiology or the physics of motion and matter. One can also examine sociological questions, such as why coaches are disproportionately White but players on many high-revenue-producing sports are disproportionately Black, or why people of color mainly play "ghetto sports" such as football or basketball and rarely "country club sports" such as golf and tennis. One can study principles of economics starting with an investigation of the price of a season ticket to watch a professional football team or the money received by the NCAA and the colleges selected to play in the NCAA tournament (see, for example, Gup, 1989). Pickles (1985) argues that "the task of education then is to engage students in a dialogue with the commonplaces of their world in order that they can: (a) understand them and hold on to the commonplaces which are significant; (b) transcend those commonplaces which are parochial and constraining; and (c) change those commonplaces which they judge to be wrong" (p. 238).

The students we studied were very willing and able to tell us what concerned them, interested them, motivated them. They could tell us in rich detail about their world and their dreams. They could just as easily share their world with their teachers, if the teachers perceived the students' world as worth becoming engaged with. Were engagement and dialogue to occur, real learning and empowerment could begin for both teachers and students.

Chapter 3

Peer-Proofing Academic Competition Among Black Adolescents: "Acting White" Black American Style

———————————— *Signithia Fordham*

Introduction

Peer-proofing Black adolescents' school achievement practices is a widely sought, but rarely fully achieved, social goal of school and school officials. They maintain that this is a much desired goal because, among Black adolescents, peer influence is a critical deterrent to academic excellence (Hanna, 1982; MacLeod, 1987; Ogbu, 1974; Silverstein and Krate, 1975). Also, as I shall document in this analysis, among school officials a kind of reinvention ethos[1] exists in the American system of public schooling leading to the celebration of the dominant culture and,

An earlier version of this paper was presented at the eighty-seventh annual meeting of the American Anthropological Association in Phoenix, Arizona, November 20, 1988. I wish to thank all of my colleagues who commented on the paper at that meeting. Special thanks are extended to the National Institute of Education (NIE-G-82-0037), the Spencer Foundation for a grant in 1984-85, and a Spencer Foundation Fellowship during the academic year 1988-89. None of this would have been possible without the cooperation and helpfulness of the faculty, students, parents, and staff of Capital High School in Washington, D.C. Their willingness to share with me intimate details of their lives and how they constantly struggle to make sense of their changing social reality enabled me to write this paper. To each of them, I am eternally grateful. I would also like to thank Professor John Blassingame, Professor of History at Yale University, and Professor Edmund Gordon, John Musser Professor of Psychology and Chair, African and African-American Studies at Yale, for helpful comments and suggestions. Opinions expressed in this paper are solely mine.

perhaps unwittingly, the suppression and degradation of the culture of those groups who are not dominant group members (Fordham, in process).

Peer-proofing Black adolescents' school performance, in the views of many school officials, will empower Black students in ways which are not available to them now. For these officials, peer-proofing Black students' school success has come to mean separating them from other Black students and changing their cultural and racial identity so that they no longer view themselves as Black people. Admittedly, in today's post-civil rights America it is possible to *choose not to be Black*; nonetheless, choosing not to be Black is fraught with conflict, pain, and confusion. There are many reasons to question the appropriateness of structuring the school environment in this manner; there are also many reasons to question why Black teenagers should have to *choose* between their identity as Black Americans and academic success. In light of these untenable options, Black teenagers find themselves on the horns of a dilemma, with consequences which directly and unequivocally affect their futures as adults and as Americans of African descent.

When I began my research on Black adolescents' school success at Capital High,[2] I was primarily concerned with how Black people's social organization—which I described as being characterized by a fictive kinship system (Fordham, 1987, 1988a, 1988b; Fordham and Ogbu, 1986)—affected their children's school behavior, effort, and commitment. Hence, I began by focusing on those aspects of the students' school performance which could be clearly associated with the existing fictive kinship system. As time progressed, however, I became more and more convinced of the holistic nature of the problem of Black adolescents' school performance and saw merit in pursuing the effects of peer influence on academic behavior. Indeed, in response to the poor visibility of Black adolescents' school achievements in the research literature, I was driven to document the existence of Black high achievers in the high school context and to point out, at the same time, some of the factors implicated in their academic success. As I came to view it, the widely acknowledged but infrequently stated goal of peer-proofing Black adolescents' school performance as operationalized at Capital High was a major deterrent rather than an incentive for academic competition among the students.

In light of the fictive kinship organizational structure in the Black community and its implication in the school performance of Black students, I am using this opportunity to explore, for the first time, an alternative way of peer-proofing Black students' academic performance. The peer-proofing I am suggesting here will empower *them* rather than school officials, and will motivate larger numbers of Black students to seek academic excellence. In many ways, my definition of peer-proofing Black adolescents' academic competition is an *inversion* of the practice most frequently used by school officials. Their most prominent practice is to separate Black adolescents who have been identified as academically successful from their age-cohorts and peers, putting them in advanced placement and/or gifted and talented programs. As I shall demonstrate, peer-proofing Black adolescents' academic competition must come to mean immersing them in the fictive kinship system or collective ethos of the Black community, thereby combining their desire to be academically successful and their ethnic and/or racial identity. It also must mean beginning academic instruction with their cultural predisposition to idealize the collectivity and structuring the school curriculum and academic learning in ways which make them feel responsible for each other rather than engaged in one-on-one competition against each other.

The data base for this chapter comes from my two-year ethnographic study of Black students' school success at Capital High School in Washington, D.C. I selected the school as my research site for the following reasons: (1) it is located in a historically Black section of the city of Washington; (2) it attracts both middle-income and low-income students; (3) it has an expanded and well-developed advanced placement program; (4) the principal was eager to have me study school performance at the school; and (5) the faculty did not appear to be unwilling to cooperate with me.

After the District of Columbia Public School System had approved my application to complete this intrusive, long-term study, I then located an appropriate research sample of thirty-three students: twelve high-achieving students (six males and six females) and twenty-one underachieving students (fifteen females and six males). These students were identified and selected in cooperation with the school's counselors, teachers, and administrators. Each of these professionals suggested certain students, and I checked their academic performance and behavior. Having unlimited access to the students' cumulative folders made this verification possible. It also allowed me to document socioeconomic impressions which were frequently bantered about by some school officials. I paid close attention to school officials' suggestions regarding who could be accurately labeled a high or underachieving student, but ultimately I made the decision regarding which of the identified students would become a participant in the study. Much to my surprise, more students than I needed and/or had originally planned for—especially females—were interested in being participants in the study. These students' parents were also very supportive and/or the students were able—individually—to convince them that this was a worthwhile research study.

Students who participated in the first year of the study agreed to (1) in-depth interviews, which were completed in three or more sessions; (2) classroom observations and visitations; (3) observations of their non-classroom activities, including after-school and weekend activities; and (4) home visitations and interviews with their parents. During the second year of the study, I returned to Capital High and administered an extensive research questionnaire to about 650 students from the ninth through the twelfth grade. This questionnaire was developed in situ, based on the data obtained from the thirty-three eleventh-grade students observed during the first year of the study.

Let me state at the outset that I am not claiming that the findings emerging from this one research site are generalizable to all Black adolescents. The data were derived from a small segment of a larger group of Black adolescents. Moreover, although Capital High School's student population reflects the socioeconomic heterogeneity of the Black community at large, it was physically located in a poor Black community. Obviously, data from other research sites are needed to validate the claims I am making regarding this research context and to formulate a general theory of Black adolescent school achievement.

Theoretical Framework:
Fictive Kinship and Black Peoplehood

Initially, I sought to build my explanation of Black adolescents' school success on Ogbu's (1978) cultural ecological model. Essentially, Ogbu theorized that the existence of a "job ceiling," or set of barriers in the opportunity structure, affects Black students' perception of the careers and opportunities available to them, which negatively affects their academic effort. As it was originally constructed, Ogbu's theory focused almost exclusively on Black students' school failure. Since I was interested in determining what factors influence school success among Black adolescents, I became more and more conscious of this theory's inability to explain *intragroup* differences in school. Working with Professor Ogbu to modify his cultural ecological theory (see Fordham and Ogbu, 1986), I was able to move beyond the original focus on instrumental exploitation (limitations in opportunity structure, such as "job ceilings") and instrumental responses to examine the expressive dimension of the relationship between the dominant culture and the indigenous culture of Black Americans. More specifically, in studying the expressive dimension of Black-White relations in America, I was able to isolate two additional factors which are obviously implicated in its unique texture. These two factors, an oppositional collective or social identity and an oppositional cultural frame of reference (Fordham, 1981, 1982, 1985, 1986, 1988a, 1988b; Ogbu, 1980, 1981, 1984), which I described as "fictive kinship," enabled me to explain, to some extent,school performance differences *within* the Black American population.

Anthropologists and other social scientists who have been studying the unique texture of dominant-nondominant relationships in both traditional and contemporary urban societies argue that conflicts and oppositional processes often lead the subordinate members to develop oppositional social identities and oppositional cultural frames of reference. This leads ultimately to what they unanimously identify as the emergence of a *people*, or *peoplehood*, which is not to be equated with a racial or ethnic group. Whereas a *people* may share with racial or ethnic groups the idea of distinctiveness, designation as *a people* is much more inclusive and broader in scope (see Castile and Kushner, 1981; Spicer, 1971, 1980). The unique nature of the historical experiences to which a group attaches significant meaning enhances the possibility of its designation as a *people*. This is possible, Spicer (1980) argues, because each human population has a "historical experience which no other group has undergone" (p.327). For example, the Jews experienced the Holocaust; Black Americans experienced slavery. Even though one social group may share a human experience with another social group (e.g., other social groups have been enslaved at various times in the history of the world), no other social group has had a particular historical experience in the same way. Hence, both the uniqueness of the historical heritage of a particular social group and the meaning it attaches to these common identity symbols influence the group's emergence as *a people*.

Negatively affecting the school performance of Black adolescents at Capital High are the competing pressures of (1) their identity as Black Americans, that is, their sense of peoplehood as I have described it ; (2) their desire to be academically successful; and (3) the hegemony of the organizational structure in place at the school. Since they value or respect these forces equally, they struggle constantly with what they perceive to be unacceptable options: (1) denying their emerging peoplehood by suppressing issues of identity or, alternatively, (2) camouflaging their desire to be academically successful by pretending not to be doing as well in school or putting forth as much effort as they need to, in order to retain their identity as Black Americans. Neither of these "choices" is appealing to most of the students at Capital High, primarily because their identity is anchored in the fictive kinship system.

Fictive kinship indicates a kinshiplike relationship between persons not related by blood or marriage, who also have some reciprocal social or economic relationship. To capture the essence of the oppositional process within the Black community and between Black and White Americans, I have broadened the anthropological definition of fictive kinship to encompass the self-definition of an entire human population: all Black Americans. This wider definition of fictive kinship conveys the sense of peoplehood or collective social identity evident in the numerous kinship and pseudo-kinship terms that Black Americans use to refer to one another. It is also evident in the unique way Black people structure and define their relationship to one another.

In fact, some scholars, including Abrahams and Gay (1972, p. 204), argue that the use of the Black vernacular among Black students in the school context , for example, is "simply another way of communicating a feeling of identity and brotherhood and thus a substitute for 'Brother', 'Sister', 'Man' or 'Dude'" (see also Holt, 1972). Others, including some anthropologists (see Fordham, 1981, 1988a; B. Williams, 1988), see the use of the vernacular as merely another expression of the fictive kinship system as I am describing it here. Williams, for example, does not label the social organization which she found in the Black community as a fictive kinship system. Nonetheless, her description of the interactional patterns of the people she studied on Elm Street in Washington, D.C., documents the kind of human interactions which I postulate are characteristic of people who are intensely involved in the fictive kinship system.

The fictive kinship system which exists in the Black community does not separate a personal and nonpersonal self. Indeed, a striking feature of it is its participants' almost unilateral focus on density in their interactions. This suggests that a valued component of group life in the Black community is knowing the members of the community at many levels. In other words, members of the group are judged in "the round" (see Bailey, 1977). Also, as B. Williams (1988) notes, there is a decided passion for "texture . . . preference for depth over breadth, an interest in rich, vivid, personal, concrete, tangled detail" (p.58). Furthermore, human interactions are replete with "repetition, density, [and the] mining [of] a situation from many facets and angles" (p.58).

This kind of social interaction contrasts sharply with what is expected of students in the school context, where a strong separation of the personal and nonpersonal is expected and rewarded. This kind of separation also fosters an individualistic ethos and a greater attention to breadth rather than depth, competition rather than cooperation, and noninvolvement rather than deep, tangled engagements. Consequently, when Black adolescents move from elementary to secondary school, they find themselves increasingly involved in an institution which rewards behaviors and an interactional style which is essentially an inversion of their indigenous cultural pattern. In some instances, the student's social class and/or personal sense of identity mutes the visible effects of the fictive kinship system on academic performance. Nonetheless, fictive kinship affects the academic performance of all Black students, with the working-class segments of the population more likely to be adversely affected by the oppositional features of Black and White Americans' cultural behaviors. The pervasive influence of the dominant group's individualistic ethos is implicated in the students' tendency to highlight the oppositional features of their indigenous culture in the school context. Some scholars have identified this phenomenon and attributed it to the students' need to reinforce and affirm that they are still legitimate members of the Black community (see Weis, 1985). Ironically, however, in the students' attempts to reinforce their indigenous culture in the school context, they unwittingly ensure their academic "failure," primarily because most aspects of the culture of Black Americans are stigmatized and assigned a negative valence in both the school context and the larger American society. On the other hand, those students who minimize their connection to the fictive kinship system or the oppositional cultural frame, that is, develop a sense of racelessness (see Fordham, 1988a, 1988b), enhance the possibility of their school success.

Because fictive kinship symbolizes Black Americans' sense of peoplehood in opposition to White American social identity, it is closely tied to their various boundary-maintaining behaviors and attitudes toward White people, that is, behaviors which are culturally patterned and which tend to separate "us from them." An example is the tendency for Black Americans to emphasize group loyalty in situations involving conflict or competition with White Americans. Furthermore, Black people have a tendency to disapprove of behaviors and attitudes they consider to be at variance with their group identity symbols and criteria for membership. Since only Black Americans are involved in the evaluation of group members' eligibility for membership in the fictive kinship system, they control the criteria used to judge one's worthiness for membership, and the criteria are totally group specific. This is in stark contrast to White people's determination and control of the criteria for earning grades in school or promotion in the mainstream workplace. Fictive kinship means a lot to Black people because they regard it as the ideal by which members of the group are judged; it is also the medium through which Black Americans distinguish "real" from "spurious" members (M. Williams, 1981a, 1981b).

Black children learn the meaning of fictive kinship from their parents and peers while they are growing up. And it appears that they learn it early and well enough so that they more or less unconsciously, but strongly, tend to associate their life chances and "success" potential with those of their peers and members of their community. Group membership is important in Black peer relationships; as a result, when it comes to dealing with White people and White institutions, the unexpressed assumption guiding behavior seems to be that "my brother is my brother regardless of what he does or has done" (Haskins, 1975; Sargent, 1984) or, as one Black politician put it recently, a "culture of forgiveness" is the norm in the Black community. The ways in which school officials have traditionally peer-proofed Black adolescents' achievement efforts are discussed in the next section of this chapter.

Peer-Proofing Black Adolescents' Academic Competition: The Traditional Approach

The existing literature contains many examples of how school officials' tendency to peer-proof Black adolescents' school achievement patterns by separating them from their peers and other Black people negatively affects their identity as Black people. Major negative consequences are spliced into the practice of placing Black students who perform well on school measures of success into contexts which are dominated by their White peers. Or, alternatively, if they are unable to remove them from a predominantly Black school context, school officials put them in classes which are homogeneously structured, separating them from peers who might benefit from their tutelage were the school's curriculum organized differently. The mere act of separating Black adolescents from those who are racially similar suggests to them that they are, in some important intellectual and nonintellectual ways, different from other Black people and, with the possible exception of phenotypical (or racial) features, clones of their White peers. Separating Black adolescents and other non-dominant-group children—both spatially and psychologically—from their peers and other adult members of their communities, regardless of its benign intentions, appears to exacerbate the conflict such students experience around academic achievement and school success. This appears to be especially traumatic for Black students born and/or schooled during or immediately following the civil rights movement . The following examples illustrate this claim.[3]

In a strikingly revealing article published in *Newsweek*, Sylvester Monroe (1987), now a successful journalist, describes the pain, frustration, and loneliness he felt when he was sent away to school so that his academic performance would be peer-proofed.

> One of the greatest frustrations of my three years at St. George's [a predominantly White private school in New England] was that people were always trying to separate me from other black people in a manner strangely reminiscent of a time when slave owners divided blacks into "good Negroes" and "bad Negroes". Somehow, attending St. George's made me a good Negro, in their eyes, while those left in Robert Taylor [the housing project where he and his parents lived in Chicago] were bad Negroes or, at least, inferior ones . . . Another St. George's teacher was surprised at my reaction when he implied that I should be grateful for the opportunity to attend St. George's, far away from a place like the Robert Taylors. How could I be, I snapped back, when my family, everyone that I cared most about were still there? *But you're different* (my emphasis), he continued. That's why you got out . . . I'm not different, I insisted. I'm just lucky enough to have been in the right place at the right time. (p.57)

Gray (1985) offers an equally compelling description of how she internalized the peer-proofing efforts of her schooling. Like many Black students who were born during the transition period, Gray vividly describes the Herculean efforts of her "successful" parents to ensure the academic success of their children and the school's complicity in their efforts. Moreover, she notes her overcompensation, her efforts to minimize her Blackness in a social setting where Blackness is devalued and stigmatized:

> During my pompous period, I dealt with my insecurities by wearing a veil of superiority. Except around my family and neighbors, I played the role—the un-black . . . To whites, I tried to appear perfect—I earned good grades and spoke impeccable English, was well-mannered and well-groomed. Poor whites,

however, made me nervous. They seldom concealed their contempt for blacks, especially "uppity" ones like me . . . To blacks,
I was all of the above and extremely stuck up. I pretended not
to see them on the street, spoke to them only when spoken to
and cringed in the presence of blacks being loud in front of
whites. The more integrated my Catholic grammar school
became, the more uncomfortable I was there. I had heard white
parents on TV, grumbling about blacks ruining their schools; I
didn't want anyone to think that I, too, might bring down
Sacred Heart Academy. So I behaved, hoping that no one
would associate me with "them" [other Black Americans]. (pp.
E1, E5)

Examples of the high cost incurred by those students who were
seeking school success but were unable to "escape" the Black community in which they were physically ensconced are equally striking in their
implications. It is clear that, in these instances, school officials' efforts at
peer-proofing Black students' academic dreams produce even greater
conflict and ambivalence because Black adolescents are expected voluntarily to separate themselves from their peers, choosing school norms
and standards instead. In the book *Brothers*, Monroe and
Goldman(1988) describe the case of several friends whose efforts at academic achievement were often unsuccessful. Their description of Billy's
problems with school officials and his personal sense of unworthiness is
illuminating.

[Billy] was good at school, even exceptional when he tried, but
he didn't like going . . . Billy was a dreamer, and ghetto schools
were not about dreaming; they seemed to him designed to discourage hope and freeze the black poor where they were, living
in public housing and subsisting on welfare.

Billy stayed [in school] in part to please his mother, though
he did not have much faith in success through study. You had
to believe in the system to go for that, he thought, and Billy was
a precocious unbeliever. He saw cats he knew going crazy
because some honky gave them a B instead of an A, when A's
never got them anywhere anyway; they don't put articles in the
paper about your last test score, he thought , and they don't
reward you in the end for cloistering yourself and being the
class egghead that nobody likes no F'ing way.

You could see brothers like that years later down on Thirty-
ninth Street, the walking wounded, stoned on wine, dope and

disappointment. They had been hellacious students once, guys who really thought they could be doctors or lawyers if they worked hard enough. (pp.45-46)

Likewise, in a discussion of his painful attempts to live in a public housing project in New York City and attend an elite, unidentified preparatory school, Christian Neira (1988) admits that his sense of who he was seriously damaged his struggle to live in both worlds concurrently. Indeed, in an effort to peer-proof his academic achievement, the preparatory school rendered him a foreigner in both communities:

When trying to live in two different worlds, one is in peril of not belonging to either of them . . . Being put in a position of changing one's character every morning and afternoon to adapt to two different worlds endangers one's identity . . .

Each of the two cultures considered me a foreigner, one who did not belong. Where my allegiance resided was their question. Neither world [the housing project nor the prep school] fully understood me because these two cultures almost never meet, when they meet on the street, violence and suspicion are their common language. (p.337)

A common theme in each of the above examples is conflict and ambiguity. Each of these "successful" adults acknowledges that peer-proofing their school performance was internally disconcerting, forcing them to question the value of their racial identity and leading them to question the value of what they were doing and being asked to do even though they continued to do it. At the same time, it is equally clear from their discussions that this separation—either spatially or psychologically—was implicated in their academic success. The following examples from my research site validate the findings reported in the research literature: frequently, Black adolescents' school success is a pyrrhic victory.

Peer-Proofing Black Students' School Success at Capital High: Some Case Studies

Like many high schools in the United States, Capital High School has a tracking system in place. This is the case despite the Wright Decision in 1967, Which outlawed tracking as a means of schooling students in the District of Columbia Public School System. Tracking has been found to have serious undesirable consequences on all students' academic performance (see Oakes, 1985; Lauter and Howe, 1970; Rosenbaum, 1976; Rosenfeld, 1971). Still it persists, both formally and informally. Its existence at Capital is structurally sanctioned in that the school's curriculum is divided in ways which support the placement of students with similar scores on school measures of success in the same classes. Grouping by homogeneous ability is widely sought by Capital's teachers and other school officials. It is also idealized by many parents in the Capital community.

I came to understand the Capital High School organizational structure and its hegemony in peer-proofing Black students' academic behavior in great detail during my two-year study at the school. The school has a four-tier curricular structure consisting of (1) advanced placement, (2) humanities, (3) the regular curriculum in which most of the students are placed, and (4) a program for students in need of special education. The two special programs were the advanced placement and humanities programs. In those instances when the curriculum areas overlapped, students assigned to the regular, advanced placement, and humanities programs at the school were grouped according to their performance on standardized measures of academic success and were either permitted or required to take the appropriate courses for their skill levels.

One of the major problems confronting the five school counselors was how to convince the students whose test scores and other indicators of academic excellence showed them to be well suited for the advanced placement courses that they should forswear other options and choose that one instead. Given the nature and structure of the fictive kinship system which exists in the Black community and the Capital community as well, I was not surprised to find school officials lamenting their inability to convince most of the students to take the advanced placement option. The following cases show how the existing track system undermines the students' sense of collectivity and solidarity, acting as a barrier to the desired goal of peer-proofing Black students' willingness to pursue academic excellence.

Among the male students at Capital High School, the traditional means of peer-proofing their academic achievement were striking in their failure. They were also striking in their lack of efficacy in changing these students' perceptions of the value of high academic performance. My first example comes from a high-achieving male; I shall also present an example from the high-achieving females at the school to show the commonalities of their responses.

Wendell is a high-achieving student. He was the valedictorian of his junior high school class. He lives with his mother and sister in a public housing project in the Capital community. His mother and father have been separated since before his first birthday. She is not able to work full-time at this point in her life; therefore, in order to support herself and her two children, she depends on the existing welfare system. Wendell's mother's dependency and the stigmatized housing they live in, as well as the welfare funds they receive from the state, have all made him keenly aware of the devalued status he occupies, both as an individual in the society and as a Black American. At the elementary and junior high school levels, he sought to minimize or negate these influences on his individual aspirations and the status of Black Americans by working very hard in school. More recently, however, he has begun to rethink his commitment to academic excellence and the values he has lived by to this point in his life. This is readily apparent in his denial of the designation imposed upon him by school officials: Wendell is smart and therefore he is different from his peers. This is best manifested in his assertion that "I got academic [through schooling]—not smart, you know. I don't consider myself smart" (March 23, 1983).

His growing sense of alienation and resistance to school officials' efforts to peer-proof his academic performance were clearly manifested in his unwillingness to become a part of the advanced placement program which existed at the school. It was also evident in his refusal to participate in the ritual making him a member of the school's honor society during the second semester of his junior year. He linked his reluctance to participate in the honor society ceremony to the distinction he now makes between being smart and being academic. He also views school officials' efforts to get him involved in the advanced placement (AP) program as a veiled attempt to reinvent him, making him, in his view, a non-Black person.

> When people think of smart, like, they know everything. I think people who are academic know some things, but, you know, to a certain point. That's how I think. I would have been in AP, but they kept pressing me ... They kept on—like, almost begging me to be in AP ... I wouldn't do it 'cause they kept ... pressing. They kept on. They almost was trying to make me get in AP. I would have got in, too. Like, when I was doing my grades, they looked, and my grades checked. "Oh, he goin' be in AP," they was telling me I was going to be in [advanced placement]. I was in junior high [school]. And they was telling

me. All through the summer, they kept calling me, "You want
to be in AP?" "No, that's all right." "You want to be in AP."
"No, that's all right." So that's why I didn't get in AP. And
they—some things they don't let you do in AP, either. You
know, like sports-wise and stuff. I don't like that. They almost
run your life. (March 23, 1983)

Many of the female students respond in the same or similar ways.
Lisa, for example, refuses to become a member of the advanced placement program. However, unlike Wendell, she takes most of the courses
that are supposed to be limited to students who are registered in the
advanced placement sequence at the school. Lisa loves school and clearly wants to be successful academically. However, like most of the students at Capital High, she perceives the school curriculum and its officials as asking her to make a choice between her identity as a Black
American and her desire to be successful academically. These traditional peer-proofing strategies are not productive in her case. Fortunately
for her, she has been allowed to compromise the existing track programs: to remain with her peers as a participant in the regular school
curriculum while taking courses from the academically more challenging advanced placement component of the curriculum.

Lisa lives with her mother, maternal grandmother and grandfather,
and four siblings in a three-bedroom apartment in the Capital community. All of these adults are gainfully employed: her grandmother works
as a domestic for a "rich white lady"; her grandfather is a construction
worker; her mother is a cashier at one of the major grocery stores in the
Washington area. Her mother earns a decent income, but with five children she is barely able to make ends meet. Lisa's mother and father are
divorced. Her father lives in Richmond, Virginia, with his new wife.
Since her parents' divorce, her father has been able to return to school to
obtain the advanced degree he desperately wanted all of his life. He is
now an accountant. Lisa insists that despite his good fortune, however,
he contributes virtually nothing to his children's support and survival.
His lack of attention has left her with ambivalent feelings about him.
She admires his school achievements and she now wants to become an
accountant like him. On the other hand, she laments his lack of involvement in their (his children's) lives. His response to them has affected her
perception of men, making her far more cautious and wary of the
motives of the young men she meets.

Like most of the students at Capital High, Lisa is convinced that the
way out of the pervasive, sticky poverty which characterizes her life is

academic success. Her family's impoverished living conditions have made owning a house a top priority in her life. In many ways, she equates success with the ability to own a house. Like most of the high-achieving females in the ethnographic component of the study, her family's impoverished lifestyle is at the base of her motivation for academic excellence. Consequently, more than many of her peers, she is severely torn between her desire to achieve success as defined by the larger society and her efforts to retain her identity as a Black American. At the same time, however, she criticizes her peers for refusing to immerse themselves in the academic programs offered at the school, noting that the biggest problem at Capital High is the almost complete absence of "competition" at the school. "'Cause, you know, everybody—nobody study. You know, if you have somebody to compete with, that's what I want. I'm serious! I mean, you know, they study a little bit. I'm talking about, like, everybody, you know, you're competing real hard, you'll want to do it. But I want to do it, 'cause I want to get out of here" (March 10, 1983).

Ironically, however, when Lisa observed this desired competitive spirit in Mr. McGriff, the principal at Capital, she described him as being too preoccupied with work.

> All he think is work, work, work. I mean, you know he won't give no breaks. You know, I'm sitting at the lunch—I mean, at the cafeteria, breakfast time, I'm just getting in, he's going to say, touching me, "You could be studying there!" I think he cares about [the students], but in a way, you know, he be comparing [us to White folks]. Like he'll say—when I was in the library, he said, "You all should be in class. That's why you all don't know nothing now. You see White folks are already ahead of you." I mean, he don't have to throw them in there, he could just say, "You're always behind." I mean, he don't have to throw that in there. (March 10, 1983)

Mr. McGriff's decision to "throw that in there," that is, "You see White folks are already ahead of you," was virtually all Lisa heard. Comparing Black people with White people in 1983 at Capital High was totally unacceptable. Unarguably, if an individual desired to lose all credibility among the students at Capital, comparing Black people with White people in an unfavorable manner was the ultimate faux pas. Mr. McGriff and many of the other school administrators appeared to be completely unaware of how totally debilitating this strategy was. They frequently resorted to this unfavorable racial comparison in an effort to peer-proof the students' academic performance. Because most school officials use their own high school experience to guide their behaviors, they refuse to consider or acknowledge that today's teenagers are coming to adulthood in a cultural context which is drastically different from the one they inherited as young adults.

Lisa's anger at Mr. McGriff's insensitivity was unbridled. Her facial features became distorted and her beautiful brown eyes brimmed with tears as she recalled the painful incident, more than six months later. Her voice thick with emotion, she continued: "In a way, I mean, but, you [we] know, you [we] already know they're ahead. But why rub it in? I mean, you [he] could say—he could have left that "white folks already ahead of you" out. He could have said, "You're already behind. It's time for us to catch up," or something like that. He didn't have to—he threw them . . . [in there]" (formal interview, March 10, 1983).

Lisa's recollection of how denigrated she felt when the principal of the school compared the students with White people typifies most of the students' response to school officials' efforts to reinvent them. However, unlike many of the other students—high- and underachieving, Lisa is an extremely mild-mannered person. Her ability to endure abusive and unkind treatment from her peers, who often teased her because her desire to succeed in school was repeatedly "discovered," was unparalleled. For example, she bravely withstood their efforts to dissuade her from the long bus ride she took every Saturday morning to George Washington University, where she participated in vocabulary-building class and accounting classes, under the auspices of the Upward Bound Program. They also teased her about the number of hours she spent studying every evening. She appeared unfazed by their behaviors and endured their teasing good-naturedly. However, in reporting her reaction to what Mr. McGriff said to her, it was transparently clear that she shared her peers' concerns regarding the school's efforts to reinvent them. Furthermore, the intensity of emotions displayed in recalling the incident suggests a passionate disavowal of this approach in trying to motivate Black adolescents to increase their academic effort in school.

Regrettably, many of the teachers and administrators at the school discount the students' strong resistance to established school policies and practices, frequently attributing the observed dissonance to personal inadequacies shared by the students rather than to institutionally induced responses caused by the desecration and denigration of African American people, their beliefs and values. Moreover, because the students' reaction to schooling differs substantively from the response which was prevalent among Black students during the historical periods predating the civil rights movement, it is judged to be inappropriate. Moreover, school officials tend to see these student responses as merely the reactions of adolescents who are behaving in ways that are uniquely adolescent. By accepting this view of the students' behavior, they are able to discount their reactions without feeling that to behave in this way is professionally irresponsible. Also, by responding in this manner, school officials are able to deny cultural or racial significance in the patterned responses they observe and can then act as if it is just "natural" for all adolescents—Black, White, Purple, or whatever—to behave in this manner.

Peer-Proofing the Academic Curriculum: Some Alternatives

Given the limitations of the existing organizational context, how might school officials at Capital High School increase the number of Black adolescents who are willing to seek school success? In other words, how might school officials peer-proof school success at Capital High in a way which motivates the students to stretch their capabilities? As an anthropologist, I first sought answers to this question from the fieldwork in which I was engaged. I then sought to buttress my emerging answers by looking at several case studies at the secondary and postsecondary levels.

First, however, it is important to emphasize that Capital High is not now, nor was it at the time of my study, engaged in innovative curricular modifications which would likely expand the number of achievers at the school. Rather, as in most high schools in America, a traditional curriculum with some minor modifications is the modus operandi. Since this was and is the reality at Capital, large numbers of Black students at the school are less academically successful than they could be if the school's curriculum were arranged differently and Black students' life and culture were incorporated into the seams of the schooling process.

My findings suggest that the following elements might enhance Black adolescents' school performance if they were included in the school curriculum and revised organizational structure: (1) repetition as an important element in school learning,[4] (2) density in school-sanctioned interactional styles, (3) a general concern for texture in classroom interactions and the structuring of schooling outcomes, and (4) group-sanctioned learning.

As I have suggested in my discussion of the fictive kinship system in the Black community, Black Americans appear to value knowing each other in what Bailey (1977) has labeled "the round."[5] His use of the term suggests that a strong value is attached to knowing the individual at many levels, that in order to understand the individual, one must possess information in excess of that which is publicly known. Knowing only that a particular individual is the principal of Capital High School, for example, is woefully inadequate for understanding him or even sparking the students' interest in him as an object of interest. If students knew other, less visible aspects of his life, their willingness to study Mr. McGriff would be enhanced. Requiring that they know other aspects of his persona—for example, that he was a track star in college, that he broke several college records, that he is married and the father of several children—would enable them to make use of their cultural propensity to value subjects and objects in "the round" (Bailey, 1977).[6]

One could extrapolate from this orientation a way of presenting school subject matter. As B. Williams's (1988) analysis indicates, attention to detail or background is one way of getting Black adolescents more interested in school-sanctioned learning. For example, Black students' interest in math might be enhanced by broadening the focus on algebraic formulas to include information about who invented the particular formula and also aspects of that individual's life that might have led to the person's willingness to risk going beyond the then extant knowledge boundaries. There might also be a greater emphasis on animate rather than inanimate materials in order to fuel the students' interest. The most important goal in teaching any subject matter should be increasing the students' willingness to put forth effort in order to master it. Consequently, if biographical details and other personal aspects of the inventor's life will inspire or motivate students' interests, these strategies should be sanctioned by school officials.

This is also a way of incorporating what I am labeling "texture" into the existing school curriculum.[7] In many ways texture in Black people's interactions is responsible for the density in human interactions which was discussed above. As I view it, *texture* suggests the existence of an organizational composition which is multi-dimensional in its valuative feature. Indeed, in Black Americans' fictive kinship system, *texture* implies a multilayered approach to life, emphasizing many stops and starts, beginnings and endings. It minimizes attention to linearly defined realities and breadth. What it emphasizes instead is attention to the structure and vivid detail of human life, consistently marking and analyzing minute inconsistencies and contradictions.

The efficacy of group-sanctioned learning as a way of peer-proofing Black students' achievement ethos can be illustrated with two examples from both the precollege and college contexts. The findings reported by Mr. Green in New York (see Bishop, 1986) and Professor Treisman at the University of California at Berkeley (see Treisman, 1985) indicate how powerful a tool peer pressure can be in promoting academic achievement among Black adolescents.

Green changed the identity of Jordon Mott Junior High School from one well below the norm on standards of academic achievement to one of the few schools where Black students outperformed most of their peers in comparable schools in New York City.

He was able to do this by organizing and implementing a collective or group-centered ethos in the classroom context. His curricular modifications enabled him to peer-proof academic achievement at the school. Essentially, the changes Green adopted at Mott Junior High support "self-realization through personal effort in service to the group," a latent yet powerful component of Black Americans' idealized cultural norms.

This approach is not widely stressed in the American public school system, but, as Green so astutely observes, it is the predominant ideal in the status mobility system within the Black community, at least among school-age children. Consequently, in order to raise the school achievement pattern of the students at the urban school where he is the principal, Green defied the conventional wisdom which appears to be operating in the larger society: success is gained by destroying ligatures or social attachments to family and other subdivisions within the Black community.

According to Green, "You have to make the kid want to be good" (cited in Bishop, 1986, p. 43). In other words, schools have to build on Black students' culturally learned predisposition to seek "self-realization through personal effort in service to the group" in order to raise their level of interest in school as well as to motivate them to put forth greater effort. Mr. Green insists that the most important prerequisites in getting Black students to put forth greater effort in school (it is patently clear that he believes that lack of effort is what is at the base of Black students' underachievement in the school context) are, first, a willingness on the part of school officials , including classroom teachers, to recognize students' achievement efforts and, second, empowering the students so that they are willing to display what they learn in the school context. None of these responses is likely to occur in a context like Capital High, where students are pitted against each other in one-on-one competition

One author described how Mr. Green's curriculum modifications were influential in peer-proofing academic achievement at Jordon Mott:

The student player is given rewards based on the performance of the class/team . . . Each of Green's classes must earn a certain number of points academically before any of its members are allowed to even attend a basketball game much less compete in one. Class trips and parties are similarly earned on the basis of academic performance and attendance . . . A complex master schedule is drawn up at the beginning of each term, pitting all of the classes in each grade against one another in good old head-to-head, in-your-face competition. Reading and math are the games, and the desk-to-desk combat is fierce. The won-lost results and the standings are posted and followed keenly. (Bishop 1986, p. 43)

Bishop (1986) insists that Green would have been dismissed from his job as principal of the school were it not for the "astounding results achieved from this approach to learning at Mott Junior High School":

[Green's] students were drawn from two ordinary [elementary] schools that are ranked near the bottom of the barrel (Nos. 574 and 614 out of 623 public schools) in reading skills. By the time his students leave (after eighth grade) they are reading a full grade above their own level, a reflection of Jordon Mott's impressive ranking—in the top 11% of all city public schools. (p. 44)

Bishop's discussion of how Mr. Green was able to improve the academic performance of Black students at Jordon Mott School argues well for the importance of both incorporating the cultural history of the students in the school curriculum and minimizing a perception on the part of the students that they must "choose" between their identity as Black people and their desire for academic success.

In a telephone interview, Mr. Green assured me that what I had read about his school was accurate: the students at Jordon Mott are outperforming students in schools similar to Mott in socioeconomic factors; they are also outperforming students in schools that are dissimilar in socioeconomic factors. He went on to tell me that his major problem is limiting the excitement of the students and their teachers. At Mott, each class is divided into four teams, with each team balanced for ability. What Green is interested in promoting is academic motivation and effort on the part of the students. The best way to accomplish this goal, he maintains, is to have the curriculum materials structured in such a way that the students come to view what is taught in school and their racial identity as inseparable. If Black students come to see schools and schooling in this way, they also see academic achievement and effort as unavoidable without, at the same time, violating their sense of who they are as Black people. On the other hand, if curriculum materials are structured in such a way that Black students come to see the materials as designed to separate them from other Black people, academic effort and motivation will suffer. Unfortunately, in Green's view, this is how most Black students view the traditional academic structure. Consequently, instead of viewing the school curriculum as supporting and promoting their identity as Black people, many contemporary Black students perceive it as attempting to strip them of that identity.

A second, even more powerful, example of how it is possible for school officials to peer-proof academic learning comes from the Mathematics Department at the University of California at Berkeley. Professor Uri Treisman is intervening in the lives of Black freshmen students who indicate by taking calculus their desire to be involved in "name professions." He is currently reporting the results of an extensive six-year study of these students' response to group-centered learning. Treisman (1985) has the data to support his claims:

> Most of the students I interviewed in 1975 and 1976 did not succeed at the University [of California at Berkeley]. Among those who had come from predominantly minority, inner city high schools, there were valedictorians and leaders of church and youth groups, individuals who were the pride of their communities. Their decision to pursue advancement through schooling had placed them in the limelight, separating them from the majority of students around them. Their rejection of non-academic routes to advancement had been so clear, their reinforcement from both family and community for their decision to pursue an elite higher education so strong, that once at the University they felt there was no turning back. (p. 21)

Professor Treisman repeatedly notes that the Black students who came to Berkeley during this time period did not lack academic motivation and high expectations from their parents and home communities. Indeed, he insists that there was tremendous pressure to succeed. Nevertheless, most of these students failed the prerequisite math and science courses mandated by the university for those persons seeking careers in the natural sciences. He attributes their massive failure to (1) a hostile environment—the university; (2) the lack of a supportive, academically focused peer group; and (3) an unwillingness on the part of these former high school achievers to seek help when they needed it.

Surprisingly, Treisman notes that this failure rate was not limited to Black students who had come to Berkeley from inner-city schools. "Even for many black students who had attended academically reputable, predominantly white high schools" (p.27), failure in the freshman year math and science courses was the rule rather than the exception.

> Even though these students were relatively well-prepared academically, the pace and intensity of competitive first-year mathematics and science courses coupled with the unexpected social isolation they encountered prevented many of them from getting their bearings or developing adequate study habits; thus, few did well in these courses. (p.22)

In a concerted effort to reverse this dismal retention rate, in 1976 the University of California at Berkeley developed the Professional Development Program (PDP) for minority students. PDP is a "faculty-sponsored honors program for minorities and women, designed, in the words of one of its founders, 'to produce a Nobel Prize winner'" (p.23). The success of the program is embedded in its focus on the strengths of the students rather than remediation of their apparent weaknesses. Hence, the students are taught to view PDP as an honors program, with success being dependent upon their willingness to collaborate with each other. This was the critical strategy necessary to change the achievement pattern of Black math and science students at the University of California-Berkeley. More importantly, Treisman's findings suggest that, when Black students are taught using a group-centered approach to school learning as the backdrop, their performance on school measures of success rises. Indeed, when this approach was utilized at UCB, Treisman reports that the Black student participants outperformed a similar group of Asian students. This is revolutionary! He indicates that he is now transplanting this approach to the teaching of calculus at other universities, including Stanford and UCLA. He is also looking at how other practitioners at the high school level who are willing and able can use the cultural orientation of Black and other nondominant students to enhance the academic effort of such students at that level.

Noting that Black students who are selected to attend the University of California at Berkeley are obviously among the best prepared in the country, Professor Treisman goes on to point out that at predominantly White schools—like UCB—with a minuscule Black student population,

Black high achievers, like the ones studied at Capital High in Washington,D.C., come with a distorted sense of individualism or self-reliance as the way to make it in college. Indeed, in a conversation with Professor Treisman, he assured me that his observations and study of Black students at UCB over the past six years indicate that these very bright Black adolescents' sense of self-reliance has gone awry, leading to a stronger tendency on their part to work in isolation, because they view this as the way to "make it." They have internalized and distorted the peer-proofing messages supported by their high school teachers and other school officials. This is especially true among the male students. In short, his findings at UCB parallel the findings of my study at Capital High in that the high-achieving students worked without the total support and sanction of their peers. Indeed, as many of the high achievers at Capital High erroneously envisioned it, people who are successful in America achieve that status primarily because of some unique ability they have, and therefore if they desire to duplicate this feat, they must demonstrate that they too possess unique skills or at least skills which are commonly shared with others like themselves, but at a unique level. Hence, they become enamored of the notion of individualism and independence and working to prove that they are not dependent on someone else for advancement. Because the Black students at Berkeley were generally the high achievers in their classes at the high school level, they had accepted, wholesale, the individualistic ethos promulgated as the way to achieve school success in America. Consequently, it was difficult to convince them of the value of group-centered learning, of the value of depending on their peers for support and collaboration.

However, at a predominantly White institution like UCB, Professor Treisman found that this approach to schooling and achievement was dysfunctional for Black high achievers. Their unwillingness to seek support from either their White peers, whom they did not trust, or their Black peers, with whom they socialized but with whom they did not study, was disastrous for academic achievement.

Essentially, what each of these two examples suggests is the impact and power of the group-centered ethos in Black students' school performance, with the group being the most important variable in both academic excellence and in underachievement. But since there are virtually no school-sanctioned efforts to peer-proof academic performance at schools like Capital High, it is not surprising to learn that when students from other academically similar schools enter college (e.g., Berkeley), they are extremely leery of a reversal of what has been drummed into them for most of their precollege schooling: "Don't worry about what other students are doing in school. Outperform them and you will be successful." Ironically, what the New York, Capital High, and Berkeley examples demonstrate, however, is that policymakers and school officials might begin the effort to peer-proof Black adolescents' school performance by teaching them to work in collaboration with each other in order to maximize their human potential.

Conclusions

School officials' traditional efforts to peer-proof Black adolescents' school performance have been largely unsuccessful primarily because in seeking to peer-proof the Black child to fit into the culturally different world of the larger society, school people tend to make him or her a misfit in both contexts. Documentation of these outcomes was presented in the case materials of Gray, Neira, and Monroe, and in the Capital High case study data of Wendell and Lisa. All of them acknowledge that they have experienced some overt and covert pressure to separate themselves from their less successful peers. As case studies, Wendell and Lisa are typical of how high-achieving Black adolescents at Capital High respond to school officials' efforts to peer-proof their academic performance. They are unquestionably torn between their desire to be successful as defined by the larger society and their desire to retain their sense of who they are as Black people. These ambivalent feelings are evident in their refusal to become official members of the advanced placement program. Although there are many ways in which they are similar, it is important to stress briefly that there are also many gender-specific differences in the students' response to school officials' efforts to peer-proof their academic performance, differences which enable a larger number of the female students to achieve school success.

Nevertheless, as the data from the research studies at Berkeley and the junior high school in the Bronx show, it is possible to greatly improve the academic performance of all Black students in ways which are unparalleled in the history of Black people in America, without a major overhaul of the existing school structure. These cases in the research literature also indicate a need to revise and modify the existing school curriculum in a way which demonstrates to Black adolescents that they are living up to the idealized norms of Black people in America. As each of these programs suggests, making Black students dependent upon each other for success and survival is the best way to peer-proof their academic performance. Moreover, as I view it, by peer-proofing Black students' academic competition in this manner, we are strengthening not only the Black community but also America at large, an outcome which is not to be casually dismissed during this period in American history.

Chapter 4

Disempowering White Working-Class Females: The Role of the High School

Lois Weis

This chapter will explore the way in which one working-class high school in a deindustrializing area of the United States serves largely to disempower females despite an apparent connection between young working-class women's identity and aspects of feminism. I will, in this chapter, address two issues: (1) the emerging identity of females and the way in which it is linked with aspects of feminism; and (2) the way in which the school fractures the beginnings of a critical moment of critique of gender relations in the working class. Specifically, I will suggest that this fracturing is linked to the nature of teacher identity, which is reflective of an ethos of White male dominance, and the way in which this identity offers a frame of reference which translates into practice. In so arguing, I do not mean to suggest that the school is the only institution which fractures these feminist glimmerings, nor that they would necessarily flourish if not for the school. This may or may not be the case, as I have argued extensively elsewhere (Weis, 1990). My task here is to discuss the school's role in contributing to female disempowerment. It is also not my task here to discuss all ways in which schools might accomplish this end. Rather, I will raise points which emerged as exceptionally significant in an ethnography related to White working-class identity formation in the context of deindustrialization.

Dorothy Smith (1987) and others have argued that the working-class family is historically characterized by a marked subordination of women to men. Working-class women live out a discipline which almost totally subordinates their lives to the needs and desires of males. There is, in this class fraction, an implicit contract between husband and wife by which she provides household and personal services demanded

95

by him in return for which he provides for her and her children whatever he deems appropriate. Thus, according to Smith,

> the household is organized in relation to his needs and wishes; mealtimes are when he wants his meals; he eats with the children or alone, as he chooses; sex is when he wants it; the children are to be kept quiet when he does not want to hear them. The wife knows at the back of her mind that he could take his wage-earning capacity and make a similar "contract" with another woman. As wages have increased, the breadwinner's spending money has enlarged to include leisure activities which are his, rather than hers—a larger car, a motorcycle, a boat. Even a camper often proves more for him than for her, since for her it is simply a transfer from convenient to less convenient conditions of the same domestic labor she performs at home. (pp. 46-47)

Numerous scholars attest to the conditions of working-class womens' lives and focus on the notion of the "family wage" as being a contributing factor. Martha May (1987, pp. 111-131) suggests on the basis of a study of the Ford Motor Company that the family wage as ideology became and remained important because it appeared advantageous to all participants. For the working class, for instance, it held out the possibility of an adequate income. A family wage meant that an adult male worker could support his family and enable his children to attend school. To achieve this goal, however, the family wage ideology both employed and maintained existing gender distinctions in work roles. For employers, the family wage ideology held out the possibility of lowered wages for some workers (mainly women), and a stable work force whereby industry could amass long-term profits.

The family wage, however, did not benefit working-class women. By linking gender roles and subsistence for the working class, the family wage ideology successfully reinforced the notion that women should receive lower wages than men and/or stay at home. In the final analysis, the consequence for women of the family wage ideology is that it severely limited their work force participation because women could not earn enough money to make it worth their while. The demand for subsistence among the working class thus became articulated in the form of a request for a family wage—a wage that reinforced a particular role for women and children, thus reinforcing patriarchy in the home. As May states, however, ironically, that family wage was not widespread or long-lived enough to benefit more than a small segment of the working class, and it dovetailed neatly with the concerns of employers for profits. In this sense, the family wage, as ideology, served to divide the working class for a temporary gain, at the great expense of its female members. (p. 126)

The fact that women could earn relatively little in the work force thrust wage-earning women back on families as a primary means of emotional and physical support. Thus, although many working-class women historically were in the wage labor force before marriage, their wage work experiences failed to alter their dependence on the family since nearly all jobs available to women offered less security and status than did the role of wife and mother. Leslie Woodcock Tentler (1979), on the basis of an extensive investigation of working-class family life from 1900 to 1930, concludes as follows:

For the working class women, then, life outside the family was apt to be economically precarious and very lonely. It was not a life of freedom and autonomy. This was so because the great majority of unskilled women earned less than subsistence wages. They needed the economic protection of family, and without it they lacked the resources to experiment with new styles of life. Yet the price of family economic protection was, as we have seen, a surrender of considerable personal autonomy. Life outside the family, moreover, was difficult for women because extrafamilial institutions did not offer them the emotional security, the social status, the easy personal identity of family membership. Ultimately the family provided the only world in which working class women were secure and fully acceptable. (p. 135)

It is in the context of the above arguments that the current study of Freeway High youth becomes so interesting. Given the demise of the industrial economy which enabled the family wage to be at least an envisioned possibility (not necessarily a reality, of course) for some segments of working-class America, and the very real fact that male industrial workers are now unable to locate jobs that pay anywhere near what industrial jobs once paid, the family wage as even a *possible* reality for the working class is undermined. In addition, as Smith (1987, pp. 23-54) reminds us, the economy has changed in that the demand for *certain* types of womens' labor has increased because corporate capitalism requires clerical, service, and sales workers at low cost. The implicit "contract" which restricts the employment of a married woman and reinforces her role in the domestic economy controlled by her husband has been weakened because women are being called upon to participate more and more in the paid labor force. In addition, inflation and the demise of the industrial economy mean that more and more women *must* enter the paid work force in order to fulfill their traditional home-based responsibilities.[1] Thus, the demand for female labor, coupled with the decline of the industrial economy, provides the structural basis for an erosion of the particular form which patriarchy has taken in the working-class family.

Given these radical changes in the economy, the time is indeed ripe for gender consciousness to change in the working class (Weis, 1990; Eisenstein, 1984). However, structural change of this sort does not necessarily mean that the male dominant family will decline appreciably. The question is, how are females and males envisioning their lives and to what extent does this exhibit a challenge to current arrangements? Although the time might be ripe for a change in gender consciousness in the White working class, institutions such as schools may be working against such change in some rather powerful ways. It is these issues which I will explore here.[2]

Data were collected as part of an ethnographic study of Freeway High. I spent the academic year 1985-86 in the high school, acting as a participant-observer for three days a week. Data were gathered in classrooms, study halls, the cafeteria, extracurricular activities, and through in-depth interviews with over sixty juniors, virtually all teachers of juniors, the vice-principals, social workers, guidance counselors, and others.

Freeway, the site of the investigation, is located in the heart of the American Rust Belt—a place where heavy industry has moved out, thereby eroding the occupational base upon which the White working class has rested historically. Gone are many of the jobs in heavy industry, automobiles, and manufacturing. The largest growth sector in the economy is now service, not production. Jobs in the evolving service sector demand retraining, pay less, provide less security and benefits, and often demand relocation. Deindustrialization means a less secure, generally lower standard of living for working-class Americans, and residents in Freeway are no exception. The eroding of the traditional proletariat is even more stark in Freeway given that Freeway Steel shut down seven years ago, leaving in its wake approximately 18,500 lost jobs. It is within this broader economic context that an investigation of female identity formation and the partial fracturing of such identity through schooling becomes important.

Freeway Females

As I have argued at length in *Working Class Without Work* (1990), female identity in Freeway is moving in a more emancipatory direction than male identity. Specifically, while males are rigidifying a virulent form of White male dominance in their identity, females exhibit what might be called a *critical moment of critique* of male dominance and patriarchy. This incipient critique, however, is not, at the moment, reflective of a collective struggle around the issue of gender. Rather, these girls pose individualistic and private solutions to their felt notions that the old forms of male dominance will not work for them and are, at the same time, somewhat unjust. As I will suggest later, the school contributes to the fragmentation of this incipient critique in some rather powerful ways. I will, at this time, discuss briefly aspects of female identity in Freeway. Here I present just the bare outline of their identity; extensive data to support this description are presented elsewhere (Weis, 1988; Weis, 1990).

Previous studies suggest that working-class high school females elaborate, at the level of their own identity, a public-private dichotomy which emphasizes the centrality of the private and marginalizes the public. During adolescence, home and family life assume a central position for girls and wage labor a secondary position. As many studies have shown, White working-class girls elaborate what Angela McRobbie (1978) calls an "ideology of romance," constructing a gender identity which serves, ultimately, to encourage woman's second class status in both the home and workplace. The studies of McRobbie and Linda Valli (1986), in particular, have been important in helping us understand how these processes work upon and through the identity of young women.

Data from Freeway suggest clearly that these females do not marginalize a wage labor identity; rather, they affirm it.[3] Unlike previous studies, in which an "ideology of romance" is elaborated, this study shows that students, both in the "advanced" and "regular" classes, think first of continuing their education and establishing themselves in a career or job.[4] Some of these young women are thinking of nontraditional jobs such as marine biologist, engineer, or psychologist. The following are representative comments from both advanced and nonadvanced students to a question about post-high school plans.

Judy: I'm thinking of [state university] for electrical engineering. I know I'm going to go into that.

Lois Weis: How did you pick electrical engineering?

Judy: Cuz my brother is an electrical engineer . . . He works for General Electric. He has a BA.

(an advanced student)

. . .

Rhonda: (I'll) probably go into medicine.

LW: Any particular area?

Rhonda: Medical technician, maybe.

LW: Would you consider being a nurse or doctor?

Rhonda: I considered being a nurse. But with all the strikes and them saying they're underpaid. I read a lot about the job.

(an advanced student)

. . .

Jessica: My mother wants me to be in engineering like my brother cuz he's so successful . . . I have an interest with the behavior of marine animals. Which is kind of stupid cuz we don't live anywhere near an ocean so I was thinking of going to Florida State. My parents don't want me to go to any other school but [State University] so I haven't brought this up yet. I figure we can wait awhile.

(an advanced student)

. . .

Lorna: Well, I go to [a cooperative vocational education program] for food service and I think I want to be a caterer. I don't want to be sitting down all the time. I like to be on my feet moving [she does not wish to go into business even though her shorthand teacher says she has "potential"]. I like to cook and stuff [but] you get to do everything, not just stay in the kitchen.

. . . [Suburban community college] has got a two-year course and then if I want to, I can transfer my credits and stuff and go to a four-year college. My mother's got a friend, she teaches food service in a college, and she was telling me about it. Like what to do and stuff.

(a nonadvanced student)

. . .

LW: When you leave high school, what do you want to do?

Carol: A lot of things. I do want to go to college for fashion design. I don't know how good I'll do.

LW: Where do you want to go?

Carol: I haven't thought about it. But as soon as I graduate [from high school] I want to get my New York State license [for hairdressing] and get a job, and then save money so that I have money when I want it . . . I want to have my own salon but first of all, I want to start off in somebody else's salon so I get the experience.

(a nonadvanced student)

The fact that Freeway students do not marginalize a wage labor identity contrasts sharply with data collected by Valli (1986), McRobbie (1978), Jane Gaskell (1984), and others. Ann Marie Wolpe (1978), for example, argues that

> by the time teenage girls reach school leaving age, they articulate their future in terms of family responsibilities. They reject, often realistically, advice about pursuing school subjects which could open up new avenues; the jobs they anticipate are not only within their scope, but more importantly, are easily accessible to them and in fact in conformity with their future familial responsibilities. (p. 326)

The girls in Valli's study similarly had notions of the primacy of family responsibilities, raising children and possibly working part-time. As Valli notes, "By denying wage labor primacy over domestic labor they inadvertently consented to and confirmed their own subordination, preparing themselves for both unskilled, low-paid work and unpaid domestic service" (p. 232).

The Freeway youth are markedly different in this respect. As I have argued at length elsewhere, although some assert that they wish to have some form of home or family identity, it is never asserted first, and generally only as a possibility "later on," when their own job or career is "settled." A small number of girls reject totally the possibility of marriage and children, but the vast majority want to wait "until I am at least thirty," which is, to teenagers, a lifetime away. The primary point, however, is that they assert strongly that they must settle themselves first (go to school, get a job, and so forth) before entering into family responsibilities; in other words, the construction of a home or family identity is secondary, rather than the reverse. Only one girl interviewed elaborates a romance ideology, and this girl is, in fact, severely criticized by the others (Weis, 1990, Chapter 3). The following representative comments support this point.

> Judy: I want to go to college for four years, get my job, working for a few years, and then get married . . . I like supporting myself. I don't want my husband supporting me. I like being independent.

> LW: You're doing something very different from your mother. Why? [Mother was married at nineteen; went back to work when Judy was in grade three.]

> Judy: I think I have to . . . What happens if I marry a husband who is not making good money? My dad works at Freeway Steel. He's switching jobs all the time [although the plant is closed, there is still pieceworking going on and workers are called back according to seniority rules at much lower pay than they formerly earned]. He used to work at the strip mill; now he's not. Now everything is gone, benefits and everything.

> . . .

> LW: Do you hope to get married? Do you hope to have children?

> Liz: After college and everything's settled.

> LW: What do you mean by "everything's settled"?

> Liz: I know where I'm going to live. I know what I'm going to be doing; my job is secure, the whole thing. Nothing's open. Everything's going to be secure.

> . . .

> Carla: Oh, I'm going to do that later [get married; have children]. I'm going to school to get everything over with. I wouldn't want to get married or have kids before that.

> LW: Why not?

Carla: It'd be too hard. I just want to get my school work over with, get my life together, get a job . . . I want to be independent. I don't want to be dependent on him [my husband] for money. Then what would I do if I got divorced fifteen years, twenty years, you know how people are and marriages. Twenty years down the line you have kids, the husband has an affair or just you have problems, you get divorced, then where is that going to leave me? I want to get my life in order first, with my career and everything . . . Maybe it has something to do with the high divorce rates. Or the stories you hear about men losing their jobs and not having any job skills, and you see poverty and I just don't want that. I want to be financially secure on my own.

The girls' identity in Freeway exhibits a beginning challenge to the domestic code—that code under which home or family is defined as women's place and the public sphere of power and work as men's place. Although I have provided only a sketch of this identity in this chapter, these girls are, in fact, envisioning their lives very differently than girls in previous studies and very differently than investigators such as Lillian Breslow Rubin (1976) and Glen Elder (1974) suggest that their mothers and grandmothers did. *For them, the domestic is not primary; wage labor is.* If patriarchy rests on a fundamental distinction between men's and women's labor and currently the domination of women in both the home or family sphere and the workplace, these girls exhibit the glimmerings of a critique of that. They understand, to the point of being able to articulate, the fact that too many negative consequences result if you depend on men to the exclusion of depending on yourself, and that this means you must engage in long-term wage labor. They do not suggest the part-time work solution and/or flights into fantasy futures offered by girls in many previous studies.

In this sense, then, their identity exhibits a critical moment of critique of an underlying premise of patriarchy, that being the notion that women's primary place is in the home or family sphere and that men will, in turn, take care of them. This glimmer of critique is encouraged both by the women's movement and by economic changes which ensure that women *must* work outside the home (given the loss of well-paying male wage laboring jobs) and that they *can* obtain jobs (given the move to a service sector economy and the need for female labor). Their incipient critique does not necessarily prefigure collective action around issues of gender, however (Weis, 1990). In fact, although the critique is in its very beginning stages in that it is largely individualistic rather than collective in orientation and envisioned action, the school itself currently tends to encourage the disempowerment of females, thus fracturing the potential for the development of a full-fledged critique. It is to these points that I now turn.

Teachers

All teachers of juniors were interviewed as part of this study. In addition, extensive informal interaction with teachers occurred throughout the year. Although 35 percent of the teachers are female, female teachers have little coherent voice in the school. The male voice, on the other hand, is clearly articulated, suggesting a powerful ethos of White male separateness and superiority. This conclusion is based on extensive data analysis which revealed extremely clear categories for male teachers and no such clarity for female teachers. This is not to suggest that female teachers had nothing to say, but rather, that an articulated female voice could not be discerned.

As I will suggest, it is exceptionally clear who the male teachers are and what they see as the positives and negatives of teaching. What makes the voice distinctly male in this case is that it is tied to work in heavy industry—an area in which females did not participate. Although there are no doubt words behind the female silence, it is nonetheless striking that the voice of the teacher in Freeway is that of the working-class White male. Future research, of course, needs to probe more directly into the silences among women in working-class communities.[5]

I will suggest two main points here: (1) many of the teachers were connected to the steel plant at one time in their lives; and (2) both the perceived positives and negatives of teaching are related in large part to direct experiences in the plant or in similar industries. Thus the dominant teacher identity in Freeway is constructed in relation to the steel plant or work in related industries.

Teachers as Steel Workers

A very high proportion of male teachers worked at the steel plant at one point in their lives, whether as college students during the summer or as wage laborers who decided to leave the plant and pursue teaching. Many teachers, then, have direct experience in industry and are themselves from the working class, not unlike their students. Application materials for all teachers indicate that many of them, at one time or another, worked in the plant. Interviews with teachers confirm this, and teachers elaborate reasons why they left. Below, I first present information from application materials. It is significant that many faculty took care, on the application form, to point out that they worked for Freeway Steel, thus alerting hiring committees to the candidates' ongoing connection with Freeway.[6] This is done simply because the Freeway school board has a distinct preference for hiring teachers from the area.[7]

Industrial arts teacher, application 1961. Prior to my preparation for a teaching career, I was employed by the Freeway Steel Company from 1951 to 1958. During this time, I completed an apprenticeship in the machinist trade and worked as a journeyman machinist until I attained my position as Industrial Arts instructor at [a high school in the larger city].

Industrial arts teacher, application 1960. I have had several years of industrial experience at Freeway steel that will help me in trying to teach the students the different processes of industry.

Industrial arts teacher, application 1966. I was entered into the apprenticeship machinist program at Freeway steel in December 1949 but when I had completed only three years of this course, I had enlisted in the Navy where I qualified for Machinery Repairman School . . . I returned to my former place of employment upon completing my enlistment, and subsequently successfully completed my apprenticeship course which entitled me to a classification of 'A machinist'.

Industrial arts teacher, application 1968. I have lived in this city all my life and attended Freeway schools. I know how many things are done within the system. I have some industrial background, having worked five summers and the last eight months for Freeway Steel.

Social studies teacher, application 1960. I have lived all my life in Freeway and for the past seven years I have been employed by the Freeway Steel corporation. Because I have shared many of the same experiences as other Freeway parents I feel I know what they want for their children. Also, because of my experiences, I feel I can better understand the attitudes and the problems of the children.

Math teacher, application 1962 (on resume). 7/66-9/66 Steelworker, Freeway Steel. Worked in billet yards as a laborer and loader.

> *Business teacher, 1971* (on resume). General Laborer,
> Freeway Steel, full-time summer employment, 1968 and 1969.
>   Main duties: Piled and banded steel, hooker; straightener
> machine operator; roller operator.

In fact, a high proportion of male teachers worked in the plant at one time or another, as interviews and informal interactions throughout the year made clear. At my initial meeting with the social studies department, for example, I was struck by the fact that every male there had some experience in the plant, and the women had fathers, brothers, uncles, or husbands who had worked there. It is not, therefore, only the industrial arts teachers who are former plant workers, although potential industrial arts teachers, not surprisingly, tend to highlight this more frequently in their applications. Many of the academic area teachers also worked in the plant on a full-time basis, or during summers when they were in college. These are not the sons of professionals earning summer money, however. These are sons of factory workers, earning money by working in the plant so they can attend school, thereby escaping having to work there forever like their fathers, uncles, and grandfathers. As a number of men point out in the following excerpts, working in the plant during the summer was one way of convincing themselves that they wanted to go back to college so as not to have to spend their entire lives there. The following comments are most revealing in this regard.

> Paul Pelly: I've lived here all my life. When I got out of high school, I had an opportunity to go to college and I took machine shop in high school and I said, "Oh, I'll go to Freeway Steel and get hired as a machinist for apprentice"; so I went to the apprenticeship program and I started there in '49. In March of 1951 I went into the Navy for four years . . . came back to finish my apprenticeship and I kept working at Freeway Steel . . . And then I had some radical surgery done on my hip, and then the whole socket had to be rebuilt—and I saw where I wasn't going anywhere. Looked at the people coming in with the buckets over the years that I was there and looking at myself at the age of sixty, "I'm going to be doing this?" You had to get a lot of seniority to get a summer vacation. I always had to get odd days. You couldn't get holidays. You couldn't get Christmas; you couldn't get Easter; you couldn't get something.
>
> . . . So, at the age of thirty-seven, I decided to go back to school . . . So, anyway, I came here [Freeway High] around Thanksgiving of

'66 and I didn't know if I was going to like teaching, and I didn't want to give up my job at Freeway Steel. I had eighteen years. But eventually it was getting hectic. I was teaching during the day and working nights at the plant, and going to school. There was a time when I had two days of three hours of sleep. Really a drag on my wife . . . So I decided I'm either going to do one or the other so I quit the plant.

(a vocational education teacher)

. . .

Bob Pritcher: I was a machinist at Freeway Steel and machine repair at Chevy. Just to give you a little background, I made $12,800 at Chevrolet and went down to about $4,400 teaching here. It was a disaster. For the first three years of my life [here], I didn't think I was going to make it.

LW: Why did you do it [switch jobs]?

BP: For numerous reasons. Number one, I wasn't very happy with the steel plant because I was working the night shift; and, number two, I was at Chevrolet, I was working and it didn't seem like I had any time off at all. I was working thirteen out of fourteen days, and I was working twelve hours a day or ten hours a day. I had four children.

LW: So you never saw them?

BP: I never saw daylight to be honest with you. I used to go to work at 5:00 in the morning and I would get home at 7:30-8:00 in the evening. By the time I had supper, it was 9:00—back to bed. The first one on the streets to cut tracks in the snow.

(a vocational education teacher)

. . .

Tony Torcivia: My father worked at the steel plant here . . . And I appreciated what I saw when he came home from work. How hard he worked, how tired he was, grimy and what have you. Working on a heavy industry job like that. The money that he made was pretty good. But he encouraged me to go on to college . . . He kind of encouraged me to say, "Look, you see what I'm doing. I don't want you to do that."

... Let me be very honest with you. What happened to me is that I went to [a university out of state]. I really did kind of mediocre the first year—a C average right on the button. I was kind of disillusioned with the whole thing ... Then I decided I wanted to work. So my father says, "They are hiring at the steel plant, why don't you look for a job there?" So I did, and I don't know if he called anybody or what have you, [and he] specifically bugged me to work in the coke ovens.

... [I worked in the coke ovens] for the first summer of my freshman year and I couldn't believe what people did to earn a living in the place ... This grimy old character that was the foreman ... had a bunch of us college kids up there. "All right," he said, "tomorrow you are going to report to this place to work, I want you to wear heavy dungarees, long underwear, a heavy shirt, like a flannel shirt." And, of course, we all figured he was setting us up. So I went in with very light summer clothes working in the coke ovens. And it was an extremely, extremely hot day, and you get on top of the coke ovens where we were working, it was additionally 185 degrees because of the heat coming up from the coke ovens and, of course, the summer weather. And it was brutal. Five out of the six of us didn't wear what he prescribed. And we had a rough day.

So he said, "All right, you guys, tomorrow you'll understand." And he went on to explain that all this heavy clothing trapped all our sweat, and, by the evaporation of our sweat, allowed us slowly to keep cooler. But after four weeks there—this dirty, filthy environment—and I used to shower there, come home and shower again. That's how dirty it was. Soot and grime in my mouth and nose and eyes. It was a continuous thing. The clothes that I wore for work, then, were just black.

... So, after working at it four weeks, probably not even that long, my father was driving me to work one day on his way to work and I said, "I think I'll work about one more week." He says, "No, you won't. You are going to stick it out—finish the week before you're supposed to go back to school." He said, "You made a commitment and you're going to live with it. I don't care if you like it or not." Ok, so I did, and, by the time it was over, I was ready to go back to college. I couldn't *wait* to go back to college and I did a lot better. I took a piece of coke with me and put it on my desk so that if I found any distractions I knew what I had facing me.

(a science teacher)

The teachers at Freeway knew, then, that the alternative to school was a life of heavy industry, and they "chose," either early or late in life, to opt for schooling. Schooling was seen as a way out of the coke ovens, blast furnace, bar roll, and so on. Education represented a way out of the plant, and teachers chose to take it. Many of their relatives worked in the plant, and they envisioned that as a distinct possibility for themselves. Some chose the plant and escaped *back* to teaching. Others chose teaching from the very start. The bottom line, however, is that Freeway teachers are, by and large, people whose own lived experience is that of the working proletariat, the children of whom they now teach.

Positives of Teaching

The fact that so many teachers see themselves as escaping industry is related to the way in which teachers view their job. Although it is fashionable among academics to view teaching as an increasingly proletarianized position, teachers do not necessarily see it this way, especially if they are from the traditional proletariat (Apple, 1983; Carlson, 1985).

In addition to "liking kids," Freeway teachers articulate the positives of teaching largely in terms of the conditions of work as compared with those in heavy industry. This does not mean that faculty are satisfied with everything at Freeway High, and I have suggested elsewhere that there are a number of issues revolving around control over teacher labor that remain points of contention for faculty (Weis, 1990). Nevertheless, on balance, as many of the faculty above suggest, they compare teaching with life in heavy industry and decidedly favor teaching. The following reflect the "positives" of teaching as teachers see them. It is noteworthy that teachers state that they choose teaching, not only because they "like children," but because teaching compares *very* favorably with envisioned alternative ways of earning a living.

> Joan Snapple: I like it [teaching] very much. I just felt that in having your own [beauty] salon [which she had previously and still operates part-time], you really had a lot of responsibility and had to work very long hours. It was excellent money or I would have come into teaching sooner. I only came into teaching because I liked it. I certainly didn't come into it for the money. I had, by this time, been doing hair [for] close to twenty years.
>
> LW: When you say long hours, what do you mean?
>
> JS: Fourteen hours a day, and this would be five days a week because I just wouldn't work the sixth day—I could have, but

wouldn't. And this was when I had the salon here at home and I worked. Fourteen hours were common.

... [As my son grew] I did my traveling to [state college] to get my degree and then I just decided that I really didn't think I would want to go back into hairdressing full-time because of how strenuous it was and that you had to pay for your own Blue Cross, Blue Shield [insurance]. I was responsible for that and responsible for the unemployment insurance [for my employees] ... I felt, too, I could also do hair ... I taught and did the hair, then I realized this was perfectly easy. Of course, now, as I've gotten older, eight hours is enough of it. But when I first started teaching, I would do twenty-five, thirty hours [a week] of hair along with the hours I was in school.

(a cosmetology teacher)

. . .

Sam Mouton: I like the kids. I like the faculty and since I've been here I have had probably more positive situations and things happen to me with faculty and with the students. I enjoy working with the age groups; I enjoy working in the courses I'm teaching—criminal justice and consumer economics—two fabulous courses.

(a social studies teacher)

. . .

Bob Pritcher: Well, from the positive standpoint, teaching, you have Saturdays and Sundays off plus the fact that you've got ten weeks out of the year for golf. At that particular time [when I left the steel plant], I played baseball and a lot of golf and that was very appealing to me.

... I [also] can walk the streets, as I do live in the town, I walk the streets and the kids are on the streets—former students of mine with kids—with their wives, and when I get a good introduction or I don't get ignored, or I [don't] get snubbed or something, I know I'm doing a good job.

... When I was in industry, I remember going to work and I'd think out of a six-day week, which was always a six-day week, I think I would dread going to work four or five out of the six. Probably the only time I wouldn't was payday. Get paid; that was a gut feeling I always had. But in teaching, I still like coming to school nine out of ten days. Not ten out of ten, but nine out of ten . . . My wife always says, "I don't see how you can be that cheerful in the morning." . . . Basically, I would say 95 percent of the time I enjoy getting up in the morning.

(a vocational education teacher)

. . .

Dwayne Patrick: The positives of teaching [are] the hours. I prefer to be in a routine; it's endless the hours there [he sold furniture prior to teaching business subjects at Freeway High].

LW: Can you give me an example?

DP: You can work sixty hours, seventy hours a week at the job selling . . . The hours are shorter coming here. Job security would be better [in teaching], the benefits, a pension. [In retailing], you have nothing. You can be let go at any time.

. . . You notice people coming and going almost every week over there [in retailing].

LW: Why do they get fired?

DP: Not selling. There's a lot of pressure on you . . . In fact, one of these stores just went out of business . . . They have, like, fifteen salespeople there. And every month they fire somebody. If you're at the bottom, you're out . . . These guys [the successful ones] make really good money . . . $40,000 or $50,000 maybe. The top salesman. But if they don't [sell] and they get down on the bottom, I think, like, two months on low, they are out. They get rid of them . . . So I didn't want to do that all my life.

(a business teacher)

The positives of teaching revolve around working with students as well as the perception that the conditions of work are far more favorable than in industry or the type of businesses in which these people could participate. Numerous teachers cite the benefits of teaching as being associated with being able to work in the daylight and have holidays off, better vacations, and so forth. *The conditions of work are seen as far superior to those in alternative jobs they had or could envision for themselves.* Industry, for example, is grimy and one has to put in long hours, as is the case for retail business and self-employment such as hairdressing. In the case of hairdressing, Ms. Snapple states that she also had to provide for her own health insurance at considerable expense. Teaching is simply seen as *easier* work and also less alienating given that teachers express an attachment to the product of their labor, that is, students.

Negatives of Teaching

It is significant that the biggest private complaint (to me) of teachers is the pay and that many compare their pay with what they used to earn or could have earned in heavy industry, construction, and so forth. Wages, however, are seen as the *only* positive point of work outside of teaching and teachers are well aware that the industrial economy no longer exists for them or their students.

> John Teichler: Another reason why I would think of leaving teaching after twenty-five years here, I'm making probably two-thirds of what I would be making had I chose to go into another profession. You still have the people in the factories making more than the teacher does. I told you, my first year of teaching here. I had a kid sleeping in the back of the room, I woke him up a couple of times, "Hey, you with us?" [He said] "I worked last night at the steel plant. I worked the 11 to 7 shift. Sorry." At the end of that week he came to me and showed me his check. He was making more than I was, and I had been teaching three years and he'd just gotten a job a month or two months before that!
>
> (a social studies teacher)

· · ·

> Bob Pritcher: From the negative standpoint, the money situation was by far number one. I remember coming in here [Freeway High], this is the honest to God truth, I remember coming in here and I used to clear for the first year . . . one week I was bringing home $118.00 clear and [two weeks later] $122 clear. And my mortgage payment was $120 a month. So two weeks of my pay went towards my mortgage.
>
> . . . I was in the hole . . . So in the summer time, I sold beer; I did all kinds of things. I worked as a machinist, a tool and die maker—those kinds of things.
>
> (a vocational education teacher)

· · ·

Paul Pelly: [When I left industry] I took a $6,000 cut in pay . . . Actually the starting salary was less, but they had previous teachers in vocations. For experience in industry, they gave them two additional steps. So the superintendent told me, he said, "Hell, I have to recommend you for the first step, but I think the board would give you two additional steps like they did the other people." And here I am.

(a vocational education teacher)

. . .

Tom LaPorte: At one time, with a master's degree, I was the lowest paid on the street. It was nothing for guys on my street to be making $40,000, $50,000 at the steel mill. That's good money plus all your benefits and everything else. The big thing was then they took pride in the fact that they made more money than the educated people.

LW: Did they say that to you?

TP: Oh, sure. They were making the bucks.

(school social worker)

. . .

Tony Torcivia: I made good money [in the steel plant].

LW: Like how much were you making?

TT: Going back down to 1968-69, I was probably making a couple of hundred dollars or more a week, depending [on] whether I worked holidays; of course, we got the bottom of the barrel, so we got double time and a quarter on holidays, so you made lots of money. But the thing is, socially, I did nothing. I was exhausted from the shift. Most of the time I worked from three to eleven, which is a horrendous shift to work. What do you do after you get home at eleven o'clock, and what do you do early in the morning?

. . . I came into teaching and pretty much took a pay cut. My first paycheck here was, turned out to be something like $90 a week in 1967. I would have been better off working in the steel plant. A lot of the faculty members here have that attitude. "You know, we could be making more; why are we treated like this professionally when we could be making more in the steel plant?" . . . A lot of the kids went on right to Freeway [steel] and made a good living.

LW: Did faculty at the time talk about that?

TT: Oh, yeah. Definitely. The benefits. You are always comparing benefits and salary with people who are working in the Ford plant, for example, and the steel plant.

(a science teacher)

Teachers make it clear, then, that conditions of teaching compare favorably with those in other work which they feel they would be doing if not teaching. These are not people who compare their own conditions of work with those of lawyers, doctors, or university professors. They are comparing themselves with their fathers or uncles who worked in the industrial sector, and/or with what they themselves used to do in industry or business. Teaching, in this sense, compares favorably, except for the pay.

The voice described here is that of the White working-class male. As a group, teachers relate to the steel plant, in particular, or more generally, to a life of heavy industry. They are pleased to be teaching in that it is better than a job in heavy industry in all ways except pay. *The articulated teacher voice in the school is a White, male, working-class voice.* Female teachers have no competing, organized voice. The male voice is loud and clear; the female weak, fragmented, and unarticulated by comparison.

Within the School—Separatist Spheres

The working-class White male voice provides a framework for practice within the school. In other words, although voice does not determine action in any simple sense, it does offer a frame or reference from which teachers construct how to relate and interact with other people. In the case of Freeway, one of the most powerful sets of messages to emerge from the ethnography of White working-class youth identity formation revolves around the appropriateness of separate gender and race spheres, and the normalcy of certain types of behaviors and attitudes related to this separation. Although such separation is part of the youth identities themselves (Weis, 1990, Chapter 2), the school legitimates and reinforces it through its own sets of routines. These routines stem logically from the working-class male voice of teachers as detailed above. This separation is true for both gender and race, although there are countervailing tendencies within the school related to gender, in partic-

ular. My intention in this chapter, however, is to deal only with separatist gender spheres and the White male dominance associated with
this legitimation. The topic of race is treated elsewhere (Weis, 1990).

To begin with, it is important to note that separate gender space
exists in the school and that men invade female space, whereas women
never invade male space. This parallels within the school the traditional
allocation of space whereby men come and go from the domestic scene
(women's space) but women are expected to remain in this sphere and
are not welcome in public male places. This use of space within the
school was apparent to me when I made initial contacts with teachers in
the spring of 1985 and was reinforced at the faculty in-service on
September 3. Men and women simply occupy different space within the
school. The faculty lounges [not simply bathrooms] are physically separate, in that one very large room is partitioned so as to have one lounge
for females and one for males, and the faculty lunchroom is separated
by virtue of where people choose to sit.

Field Notes: May 21, 1985 [on entering the field]

Meetings with Ms. Hartle and Ms. Jones, both of the business
department. Meeting separately with Ms. Hartle at 1:15 and Ms.
Jones at 2:20. The meetings were set up by Mr. Jackson, coordinator of the business department, since they could not attend
the general meeting for business faculty.

This is the first time I was in the faculty lounge [located down
the hall from the principal's office]. The lounge is separate for
men and women. The women have their side and the men
theirs. When I inquired about this, Ms. Hartle said, "Yeah, that
gives us more privacy. We have a rest room on each side." I
asked if people ever go into the other side and she said, "The
guys sometimes come here if they want to see someone, but we
never go to the other side. They come in and talk." [The men
are using the door to the womens' side of the lounge even
though they have their own door.]

This same segregated pattern was apparent at the first orientation
meeting in the fall.

Field notes: September 3

The orientation was scheduled to begin at 9:00. I arrived at 8:45
and there was coffee and donuts in the cafeteria. Many people
were already there. Personnel tended to be gender segregated.

Men were at their own tables, and women theirs. It was immediately apparent that this was the case.

Throughout the school year, these patterns persisted. Although there were separate spaces for women and men, it was seen as acceptable that men invaded women's space. Men constantly walked into the women's side of the lounge and sat and talked, for example. I never saw a woman in the men's lounge, and it would have been seen as highly unacceptable. I myself was made to feel that the men's lounge was not my space, although the women's lounge was theirs. The lunchroom, although ostensibly a shared gender space, once again became divided. This partially corresponded to discipline taught, but not entirely. Only one female, a math teacher, regularly sat with men, and only one male, a social studies teacher, regularly sat with women. The one Black female teacher in the lunch period I joined on a regular basis, sat with the monitors, some of whom were Black and some White. The White females always sat at one end of the table, and the women of color and all monitors and aides sat at the other end of the "female table." This was a stable seating pattern throughout the entire year and tended to be reflected in all other lunch periods, although I spent most of my time in one of them.

Interactions within the spaces tended to be stereotypically gender specific. Women, for example, often discussed recipes, food, cosmetics, and so forth. Men discussed, on the other hand, computers, football, and betting pools. Significantly, little of the lunchroom talk revolved around students, although there was talk about the administration. The stereotypical nature of female discussion is evident in the field notes reproduced below:

February 6, 1986 [in the lunchroom]

I just realized how much of the time women teachers discuss recipes. One woman had the school lunch of chili.

Ms. Fletcher: There is too much meat in it.

Ms. Butcher: Everyone makes chili differently, I put a lot of celery and beans in it. Some people don't.

Ms. Fletcher: I do too. This chili has too much meat in it.

Ms. Butcher: My husband likes chili soup. He likes it so thin it's like soup. My kids call it hamburger soup. "When are you going to make hamburger soup, Mom?"

Ms. Sanford: You know, [a restaurant in town] has something like a chili soup with cheese on top of it. It's good. I don't make a good chili; my daughter-in-law does. She adds a can of tomato soup at the end to thicken it. It's really good. No water, just tomato soup.

Ms. Butler: I use a can of tomatoes in mine.

At another point during the year, Ms. Snapple, the cosmetology teacher, handed out a clipping to the women in the lunchroom entitled, "Your Refrigerator Holds Worlds of Cosmetics." In this article were recipes for Avocado Dry Skin Mask, Cucumber Refresher Mask, Banana Mask, Herbal Sauna, Tomato Compress, and so forth. A great deal of time was spent by the women teachers discussing these homemade cosmetics, including what to do if you are allergic to certain fruits. Ms. Snapple pointed out that you should use the cosmetics "within a relatively short period of time, before rancidity or spoilage sets in."

In addition to recipes and related elements of traditional female culture, there are elements which exist within this separate sphere that are directly critical of men. These range from a discussion of how sloppy men are to the fact that women still do not experience equality with males. The issue of unequal pay received quite a bit of attention from a certain group.

Field notes: Lunch, October 23

Nancy [a business teacher] was talking about the salaries of secretaries. "Starting salaries in business are $4,000, $9,000, or $10,000. You just can't live on that. Men come in as management trainees at $17,000. Secretaries, just because they are women, don't make $17,000 after fifteen years. It used to make me so mad [she was a secretary]. These men in the department at [state university, where she used to work] used to make so much money. I was eighteen [years old] and making $3,900. Men couldn't survive if it weren't for female secretaries."

Many other times throughout the year this conversation surfaced among female teachers. Jan earlier said, with respect to talk about the difficulties associated with photocopying materials for teaching, "Yeah, and they wonder why they have teacher shortages. We have no say over anything. They make it impossible to do our job. The only reason that things are as good as they are is that they've exploited bright women in the past." Nancy, a business teacher, took up the issue of gender inequality rather vociferously during numerous lunch conversations and in a later interview which I conducted with her. Below, she offers a feminist analysis of why pay for secretaries is low, for example.

> I [have had] male students say to me that they do intend to be secretaries and they've asked, "How much do they [secretaries] make?" Now, that's the disappointing factor since it is basically, out there in the real world, dominated by women and [it] is a traditional woman's occupation. Its traditional pay is low because it is not considered equal to male work and that is a very poor perception of the males that control the corporate world because they couldn't function without those well-trained secretaries who sometimes may not have a college degree but have to take more specialized courses in their area than some people at the college level and have to prove mastery. They [secretaries] are not paid for mastery in these difficult skills: the language arts and other communications skills; the manual dexterity you need for typing and shorthand; and just the basic decision-making skills that they have to have to be able to handle the responsibility. They do not get their just dessert at all.

There is, therefore, discussion among women faculty of gender inequality and, particularly, of low pay for women. The second point of sustained criticism among female teachers revolved around the perception that men want female servants. This is clarified in the two sets of field notes below:

September, 1985

In the teacher's lunchroom three women were complaining that it is the men [from the previous lunch period] who leave their dishes and napkins on the tables [the place is always a mess from the previous period].

Nancy: They have maids at home.

All the women were complaining that the men are slobs and don't even have the "courtesy to clean up after themselves."

Susan: They expect us to clean up after them.

May 6, 1986

In the teacher's lunchroom, 11:00.

Paul [running the in-school suspension room today] is getting lunch for three students there. He is holding one tray and drops the tater tots [potatoes] on the floor. He proceeds to walk out.

> Nancy: Did you ever notice how these guys expect someone to clean up after them?

> Susan: Yeah, they really do. They leave the tables in here a mess.

> Jan: I feel sorry for the girls here who get married young. They don't know what they're getting into.

> Nancy: They have this knight on a white charger crap. They think they'll get a knight on a white charger, and they get a horse's ass.

Susan and Jan get up and clean up the tater tots from the floor.

It is noteworthy that the separatist spheres are maintained, and, at the same time, that the female sphere contains emerging elements critical of men within it. Some of the women constantly criticize both the fact that women earn less than men and that men expect to be picked up after. However, it is important to note that the women do, in fact, pick up after the men. Thus, when Paul spills the tater tots, Nancy and Jan, although critical of male behavior, proceed to clean up. They do, in some sense, then, see that as their role.

Men also invade women's space, whereas the reverse is not true, as I noted earlier. This extends to the classroom itself, where, as I noted on many occasions throughout the year, male teachers walk in and out of female classrooms to check equipment, grade papers, and so forth. It is seen as perfectly appropriate to invade women's space in this way. Conversely, I never saw a female teacher invade male space, either public in the sense of teaching space, or private in the sense of the faculty lounge.

The way in which space is used in the school reinforces both a notion of separateness by gender and male dominance. Whatever progressive elements exist within the female identity structure tend to be only minimally encouraged by comparison. There are, however, some glimmerings of gender challenge among the faculty themselves, reflective of the same social movement and economic changes that are encouraging the beginnings of gender challenge among female students. Female teachers, although existing within a separate sphere, partially defined and certainly invaded by men, do, in fact, render problematic certain elements of female existence. Furthermore, there are some active attempts on the part of the school to encourage challenges to traditional gender identity. In the guidance office, for example, an article entitled "Message to Daughters—Learn to Go it On Your Own" is prominently displayed. The article suggests that women should carve an economic niche for themselves and not simply be a wife and mother. This also represents the beginnings of a challenge to gender identity in this working-class high school. By and large, however, the school tends to encourage separatism and the inequality which, in a concrete setting, accompanies such separatism. It does not, in any large measure, encourage the girls to explore their emerging identity.

The Disempowerment of Females

I have argued here that young women in Freeway exhibit the beginnings of a challenge to traditional gender relations in the White working class. They do not, in fact, envision their lives with men in the same way as their mothers and grandmothers did, and they hold out the possibility of feminist leanings in the future. It is, therefore, important that the school fractures these glimmerings rather than encourages them. White male teachers dominate articulated voice and space in school, reinforcing an ethos of White male separateness and superiority. Female teachers have no coherent voice, nor do they challenge the dominant male use of space within the school. Although certain women teachers themselves exhibit the glimmerings of feminism, they do not suggest a sustained or organized challenge to the dominant male framework of voice or action. Although this does not mean, of course, that female students are totally controlled by the male framework, it does suggest that there will be little organized challenge to such a framework. Rather than encourage young working-class White women to explore their identities as women, thus nurturing the glimmerings of critique, the school serves to fracture these beginnings by reinforcing gender separation and White male dominance.

Given the radical changes in the economy which at least lay the structural basis for change in gender consciousness, it is significant that the school does its part to fracture and squash this movement, although perhaps unintentionally. The role of the school is largely to constrain an important moment of critique among young working-class girls, although, as noted throughout this chapter, there are aspects of the school which, in a nonorganized fashion, partially promote it. At the moment, however, the school is acting as a repressive apparatus in relation to the development of a feminist consciousness in the working class. The glimmerings of change already exist within female youth identity; the school is currently undermining these glimmerings. This need not be the case, however. The chapter in this volume by Bell illustrates how the school can work on and develop these glimmerings by encouraging female students to talk about that they see, feel, and experience.

PART II

Strategies for Empowerment Through Education

Chapter 5

A Curriculum for Empowerment, Action, and Change

——————————————— *James A. Banks*

When students are empowered, they have the ability to influence their personal, social, political, and economic worlds. Students need specific knowledge, skills, and attitudes in order to have the ability to influence the worlds in which they live. They need knowledge of their social, political, and economic worlds, the skills to influence their environments, and humane values that will motivate them to participate in social change to help create a more just society and world.

This chapter describes the nature of knowledge and the dominant canons, paradigms, and perspectives that are institutionalized within the school and university curriculum. I contend that the knowledge that is institutionalized within the schools and the larger society neither enables students to become reflective and critical citizens nor helps them to participate effectively in their society in ways that will make it more democratic and just. I propose and describe a curriculum designed to help students to understand knowledge as a social construction and to acquire the knowledge, skills, and values needed to participate in civic action and social change.

The Nature of School Knowledge

Students are usually taught school knowledge as a set of facts and concepts to be memorized and later recalled. They are rarely encouraged to examine the assumptions, values, and nature of the knowledge they are required to memorize or to examine the ways in which knowledge is constructed. Knowledge in the school curriculum is usually viewed as objective, neutral, and immune from critical analysis. Popular writers such as Hirsch (1987) and Ravitch and Finn (1987) have contributed to the school conception of knowledge as a body of facts not to be questioned, critically analyzed, and reconstructed. Hirsch (1987) writes as if knowledge is neutral and static. His book contains a list of important facts that students should master in order to become "culturally literate." Ravitch and Finn (1987) identify and lament the factual knowledge that U.S. high school students do not know. Neither Hirsch nor Ravitch and Finn discuss the limitations of factual knowledge or point out that knowledge is dynamic, changing, and constructed within a social context rather than neutral and static.

I agree with Hirsch, Ravitch and Finn that all U.S. citizens need to master a common core of shared knowledge. However, the important question is: *Who will participate in the formulation of that knowledge and whose interests will it serve?* We need a broad level of participation in the identification, construction, and formulation of the knowledge that we expect all of our citizens to master. Such knowledge should reflect cultural democracy and serve the interests of all of the people within our pluralistic nation and world. It should contribute to public virtue and the public good. The knowledge institutionalized within our schools and colleges and within the popular culture should reflect the interests, experiences, and goals of all of the nation's citizens and should empower all people to participate effectively in a democratic society.

Knowledge and Empowerment

To empower students to participate effectively in their civic community, we must change the ways in which they acquire, view, and evaluate knowledge. We must engage students in a process of attaining knowledge in which they are required to critically analyze conflicting paradigms and explanations and the values and assumptions of different knowledge systems, forms, and categories. Students must also be given opportunities to construct knowledge themselves so that they can develop a sophisticated appreciation of the nature and limitations of knowledge and understand the extent to which knowledge is a social construction that reflects the social, political, and cultural context in which it is formulated.

Participating in processes in which they formulate and construct various knowledge forms will also enable students to understand how various groups within a society often formulate, shape, and disseminate knowledge that supports their interests and legitimizes their power. Groups without power and influence often challenge the dominant paradigms, knowledge systems, and perspectives that are institutionalized within society. Knowledge and paradigms consistent with the interests, goals, and assumptions of dominant groups are institutionalized within the schools and universities as well as within the popular culture. A latent function of such knowledge is to legitimize the dominant political, economic, and cultural arrangements within society.

The Attempt to Reformulate the Canon

The ethnic studies and women studies movements, which emerged from the civil rights movement of the 1960s and 1970s, have as a major goal a reformulation of the canon that is used to select and evaluate knowledge for inclusion into the school and university curriculum (Banks, 1989). The demand for a reformulation of the curriculum canon has evoked a concerted and angry reaction from established mainstream scholars. They have described the push by ethnic and feminist scholars for a reformulation of the canon as an attempt to politicize the curriculum and to promote "special interests." Two national organizations have been formed by established mainstream scholars to resist the efforts by ethnic and feminist scholars to reformulate the canon and to transform the school and university curriculum so that it will more accurately reflect the experiences, visions, and goals of women and people of color. They are the Madison Center and the National Association of Scholars (Heller, 1989). The mainstream scholars who have labeled the curricular goals of women and people of color "special interests" view their own interests as universal and in the public good and any claims that challenge their interests as "special interests." Dominant groups within a society not only view their own interests as identical to the public interest but are usually able to get other groups, including structurally excluded groups, to internalize this belief. The school and university curricula help students to acquire the belief that the interests, goals, and values of dominant groups are identical to those of the civic community.

School Knowledge and the Dominant Canon

To develop a sense of the need for social change, a commitment to social participation, and the skills to participate effectively in social action that eventuates in change, the knowledge that students acquire must have certain characteristics. It must describe events, concepts, and situations from the perspectives of the diverse cultural and racial groups within a society, including those that are politically and culturally dominant as well as those that are structurally excluded from full societal participation. Much of school knowledge as well as knowledge in the popular culture presents events and situations from the perspectives of the victors rather than the vanquished and from the perspectives of those who control the social, economic, and political institutions in society rather than from the points of view of those who are victimized and marginalized.

School and societal knowledge that presents issues, events, and concepts primarily from the perspectives of dominant groups tends to justify the status quo, rationalize racial and gender inequality, and to make students content with the status quo. An important latent function of such knowledge is to convince students that the current social, political, and economic institutions are just and that substantial change within society is neither justified nor required.

The ways in which the current social, economic, and political structures are justified in the school and university curricula are usually subtle rather than blatant. These justifications are consequently more effective because they are infrequently suspected, recognized, questioned, or criticized. These dominant perspectives emanate from the canon that is used to define, select, and evaluate knowledge in the school and university curriculum in the United States and in other Western nations. This canon is Eurocentric and male dominated. It is rarely explicitly defined or discussed. It is taken for granted, unquestioned, and internalized by writers, researchers, teachers, professors, and students.

The Western-centric and male-centric canon that dominates the school and university curriculum often marginalizes the experiences of people of color, Third World nations and cultures, and the perspectives and histories of women. It results in the Americas being called the "New World," in the notion that Columbus "discovered" America, in the Anglo immigrants to the West being called "settlers" rather than "immigrants," and in the description of the Anglo immigrants rush to the West as the "Westward Movement." Calling the Americas the "New World" subtly denies the nearly forty thousand years that Native Americans have lived in this land. The implication is that history did not begin in the Americas until the Europeans arrived. From the perspectives of the Lakota Sioux, the Anglo settlers in the West were invaders and conquerors. The "Westward Movement" is a highly Eurocentric concept. The Lakota Sioux did not consider their homeland the West but the center of the universe. And, of course, it was the Anglos who were moving west and not the Sioux. From the perspective of the Lakota Sioux it was not a Westward Movement but the Great Invasion.

Concepts such as the "New World," the "Westward Movement,"

"hostile Indians," and "lazy welfare mothers" not only justify the status quo and current social and economic realities, but also fail to help students understand why there is a need to substantially change current social, political, and economic realities or help them to develop a commitment to social change and political action. These Anglocentric and Eurocentric notions also fail to help students of color and female students to develop a sense of empowerment and efficacy over their lives and their destinies. Both the research by Coleman (1966) and the research on locus of control (Lefcourt, 1976) indicate that people need a sense of control over their destiny in order to become empowered to achieve or to act. Many students of color and female students are victimized and marginalized by the knowledge that results from the Eurocentric canon because they are made to believe that problems such as racism and sexism either do not exist in any substantial way or that such problems result from their own actions or shortcomings. In his book, *The Closing of the American Mind,* Bloom (1987) states that African American students are not well integrated into the structure of predominantly White university campuses because of their own resistence to social integration. This is a classic example of "blaming the victim" (Ryan, 1971) and contradicts the scientific findings by Fleming (1984). Fleming attributes the structural exclusion of African American students on predominantly White campuses to an inhospitable environment that fails to meet the needs of African American students .

The Dominant Canon and the Popular Culture

The popular culture frequently reinforces and extends the dominant canon and the paradigms taught in the school and university curriculum. An example is the popular film *Mississippi Burning.* This film presents several dominant-group perspectives on the civil rights movement of the 1960s that are notable. In actual history, African Americans were the real heroes of the civil rights movement. They were the primary architects of the movement, led the first demonstrations and sit-ins, and showed tremendous efficacy in the movement. The FBI (Federal Bureau of Investigation), under the leadership of J. Edgar Hoover, was at best a reluctant protector of civil rights and played a major role spying on and undercutting the civil rights movement and civil rights leaders. Martin Luther King was a frequent victim of Hoover's tactics and undercover agents (Garrow, 1986). Despite these realities, *Mississippi Burning* presents African Americans as shadowy figures who were primarily victims and two FBI agents as the real heroes and defenders of Black rights in the civil rights movement. The depiction of the civil rights movement in *Mississippi Burning* is a travesty on history but is a popular film that is believable and credible to many Americans because it is consistent with the canon that is institutionalized and taught within the school and university curriculum.

A Transformative Curriculum for Empowerment

In the above section of this chapter, I described the nature and goals of the dominant Eurocentric curriculum in the nation's schools and colleges. This curriculum reinforces the status quo, makes students passive and content, and encourages them to acquiescently accept the dominant ideologies, political and economic arrangements, and prevailing myths and paradigms used to rationalize and justify the current social and political structure.

A transformative curriculum designed to empower students, especially those from victimized and marginalized groups, must help students to develop the knowledge and skills needed to critically examine the current political and economic structure and the myths and ideologies used to justify it. Such a curriculum must teach students critical thinking skills, the ways in which knowledge is constructed, the basic assumptions and values that undergird knowledge systems, and how to construct knowledge themselves.

A transformative curriculum cannot be constructed merely by adding content about ethnic groups and women to the existing Eurocentric curriculum or by integrating or infusing ethnic content or content about women into the mainstream curriculum. When the curriculum is revised using either an additive or an infusion approach, the basic assumptions, perspectives, paradigms, and values of the dominant curriculum remain unchallenged and substantially unchanged, despite the addition of ethnic content or content about women. In such a revised curriculum, the experiences of women and people of color are viewed from the perspectives and values of mainstream males with power. When the meeting of the Lakota Sioux and the Anglos from the East is conceptualized as the "Westward Movement," adding content about the Lakota and about women neither changes nor challenges the basic assumptions of the curriculum or the canon used to select content for inclusion into it. The Lakota and women heroes selected for study are selected using the Western-centric, male-dominated paradigm. When the dominant paradigm and canon are used to select ethnic and women heroes for inclusion into the curriculum, the heroes selected for study are those who are valued by dominant groups and not necessarily those considered heroes by victimized and nonmainstream groups. Ethnic heroes selected for study and veneration are usually those who helped Whites to conquer or oppress powerless people rather than those who challenged the existing social, economic, and political order. Consequently, Sacajawea and Booker T. Washington are more likely to be selected for inclusion into the mainstream curriculum than are Geronimo and Nat Turner.

Critical Thinking and Multiple Voices

A curriculum designed to empower students must be transformative in nature and help students to develop the knowledge, skills, and values needed to become social critics who can make reflective decisions and implement their decisions in effective personal, social, political, and economic action. In other words, reflective decision making and personal and civic action must be the primary goals of a transformative and empowering curriculum.

The transformative curriculum must help students to reconceptualize and rethink the experience of humans in both the United States and the world, to view the human experience from the perspectives of a range of cultural, ethnic, and social-class groups, and to construct their own versions of the past, present, and future. In the transformative curriculum multiple voices are heard and legitimized: the voices of textbook, literary, and historical writers, the voices of teachers, and the voices of other students. Students can construct their own versions of the past, present, and future after listening to and reflecting on the multiple and diverse voices in the transformative classroom. Literacy in the transformative curriculum is reconceptualized to include diverse voices and perspectives and is not limited to literacy in the Hirsch (1987) sense, that is, to the mastering of a list of facts constructed by authorities. Writes Starrs, (1988), "In the new definition literacy should be seen as a struggle for voice. As such the presence of different voices is an opportunity and a challenge. All students will deal with the fact that their voices differ from one another's, from their teachers', from their authors'. All learners will somehow cope with the issue of translating their many voices, and in the process they will join in creating culture—not simply receiving it."

The transformative curriculum teaches students to think and reflect critically on the materials they read and the voices they hear. Baldwin (1985), in a classic essay, "A Talk to Teachers," states that the main purpose of education is to teach students to think: "The purpose of education . . . is to create in a person the ability to look at the world for himself, to make his own decisions, to say to himself this is black or this is white, to decide for himself whether there is a God in heaven or not. To ask questions of the universe, and then to live with those questions, is the way he achieves his identity" (p. 326). Although Baldwin believed that thinking was the real purpose of education, he also believed that no society was serious about teaching its citizens to think. He writes further: "But no society is really anxious to have that kind of person around. What society really, ideally, wants is a citizenry which will simply obey the rules of society. If a society succeeds in this, that society is about to perish" (p. 326).

The transformative curriculum can teach students to think by encouraging them, when they are reading or listening to resources, to consider the author's purposes for writing or speaking, his or her basic assumptions, and how the author's perspective or point of view compares with that of other authors and resources. Students can develop the skills to critically analyze historical and contemporary resources by being given two accounts of the same event or situation that present different perspectives and points of view.

A Lesson with Different Voices

In a lesson I developed for a junior high school U.S. history textbook (Banks and Sebesta, 1982) entitled, "Christopher Columbus and the Arawak Indians," the students are presented with an excerpt from Columbus's diary that describes his arrival in an Arawak community in the Caribbean in 1492. These are among the things that Columbus (Jan,1930) writes about the Arawaks:

> They took all and gave all, such as they had, with good will, but it seemed to me that they were a people very lacking in everything. They all go naked as their mothers bore them, and the women also, although I saw only one very young girl . . . They should be good servants and quick to learn, since I see that they very soon say all that is said to them, and I believe that they would easily be made Christians, for it appeared to me that they had no religious beliefs. Our Lord willing, at the time of my departure, I will bring back six of them to Your Highnesses, that they may learn to talk. I saw no beast of any kind in this island, except patrons.

The students are then encouraged to view Columbus's voice from the perspective of the Arawaks. The Arawaks had an aural culture and consequently left no written documents. However, archaeologist Fred

Olsen studied Arawak artifacts and used what he learned from them to construct a day in the life of the Arawaks, which he describes in his book, *On the Trail of the Arawaks* (Olsen, 1974). The students are asked to read an excerpt from Olsen's account of a day in the life of the Arawaks and to respond to these questions:

> Columbus wrote in his diary that he thought the Arawaks had no religious beliefs. You read about Arawak life in the report by Fred Olsen. Do you think Columbus was correct? Why?
> Accounts written by people who took part in or witnessed (saw) an historical event are called primary sources. Can historians believe everything they read in a primary source? Explain. (Banks and Sebesta, 1982, p. 43)

Key Concepts and Issues

In addition to helping students to view events and situations from diverse ethnic, gender, and social-class perspectives, a transformative curriculum should also be organized around key concepts and social issues. The conceptual, issue-oriented curriculum facilitates the teaching of decision making and social action skills in several important ways. First, a conceptual curriculum helps students to understand the ways in which knowledge is constructed, to formulate concepts themselves, and to understand the ways in which the concepts formulated reflect the values, purposes, and assumptions of the conceptualizers. In an inquiry-oriented conceptual curriculum, students are not passive consumers of previously constructed knowledge, but are encouraged to formulate new ways to organize, conceptualize, and think about data and information.

The conceptual approach also allows the teacher to rethink the ways that topics, periods, and literary movements are structured and labeled. Periodization in history, literature, and art tend to reflect a Eurocentric bias, such as the Middle Ages, the Renaissance, and the Westward Movement. When content is organized around key interdisciplinary concepts such as culture, communication, and values, the teacher can structure lessons and units that facilitate the inclusion of content from diverse cultures as well as content that will help students to develop the knowledge, values, commitments, and skills needed to participate in effective personal, economic, and civic action.

In the U.S. junior high school textbook I authored that was cited earlier (Banks and Sebesta, 1982), I used a key concept, 'revolution', to organize a unit rather than focus the unit exclusively on the revolution in the English colonies in 1776. By organizing the unit around the concept of revolution rather than a particular revolution, the students were able to examine three American revolutions, to study each in depth, and to derive generalizations about revolutions in general. They were also able to identify ways in which these three revolutions were alike and different. They also used the definition and generalizations they derived about revolutions from this unit to determine whether events such as the civil rights movement of the 1960s and 1970s and the women rights movement of the 1970s could accurately be called "revolutions." The three American revolutions they studied were (1) the Pueblo Revolt of 1680, in which Pope led a resistance against the conquering Spaniards; (2) the revolution in the British Colonies, 1776; and (3) the Mexican Revolution of 1810, whose aim was to acquire Mexico's independence from Spain.

The Moral Component of Action

After students have mastered interdisciplinary knowledge related to a concept or issue such as racism or sexism, they should participate in value or moral inquiry exercises. The goal of such exercises should be to help students to develop a set of consistent, clarified values that can guide purposeful and reflective personal or civic action related to the issue examined. This goal can best be attained by teaching students a method or process for deriving their values within a democratic classroom atmosphere. In this kind of democratic classroom, students must be free to express their value choices, determine how those choices conflict, examine alternative values, consider the consequences of different value choices, make value choices, and defend their moral choices within the context of human dignity and other values of the American creed. Students must be given an opportunity to reflectively derive their own values in order to develop a commitment to human dignity, equality, and other democratic values. They must be encouraged to reflect upon value choices within a democratic atmosphere in order to internalize them (Banks and Clegg, 1990).

I have developed a value inquiry model that teachers can use to help students to identify and clarify their values and to make reflective moral choices. It consists of these steps (Banks and Clegg, 1990, p. 445):

1. Defining and recognizing value problems
2. Describing value-relevant behavior
3. Naming values exemplified by the behavior
4. Determining conflicting values in behavior described

5. Hypothesizing about the possible consequence of the values analyzed
6. Naming alternative values to those described by behavior observed
7. Hypothesizing about the possible consequences of values analyzed
8. Declaring value preferences; choosing
9. Stating reasons, sources, and possible consequences of value choice: justifying, hypothesizing, predicting

I will illustrate how Mr. Carson, a junior high school social studies teacher, used this model while teaching a unit on the civil rights movement. Mr. Carson wanted his students to acquire an understanding of the historical development of the civil rights movement, to analyze and clarify their values related to integration and segregation, and to conceptualize and perhaps take some kinds of actions related to racism and desegregation in their personal life, the school, or the local community. Mr. Carson is a social studies teacher in a predominantly White suburban school district near a city in the Northwest that has a population of about 500,000.

Mr. Carson used the Banks value inquiry model to help his students analyze the value issues revealed in Chapter 8 of *The Long Shadow of Little Rock* by Daisy Bates (1987). In this excellently written and moving chapter, Mrs. Bates describes the moral dilemma she faced when serving as head of the National Association for the Advancement of Colored People (NAACP) in Little Rock when Central High School was desegregated by nine African American high school students. The desegregation of Central High School began during the 1957-58 school year.

Mrs. Bates was the leading supporter and organizer for the nine students. Her husband, L. C. Bates, was a journalist. They owned a newspaper, *The States Press*. In Chapter 8 of *The Long Shadow of Little Rock,* Mrs. Bates describes how a middle-aged White woman came to her home at 3:00 in the afternoon and told her to call a press conference and announce that she was withdrawing her support for the nine students and advising them to withdraw from Central High School and return to the Negro schools. The woman said she represented a group of "Southern Christian women." Mrs. Bates asked the woman what would happen if she didn't do what she told her to do. She looked at Mrs. Bates straight in the eye and said,"You'll be destroyed—you, your newspaper, your reputation . . . Everything."

During her long, anguished night, Mrs. Bates wondered whether she had the right to destroy sixteen years of her husband's work—the newspaper. Yet she felt that she could not abandon a cause to which she and many other African Americans were deeply committed. By morning Mrs. Bates had made her difficult and painful decision. She called her visitor and said, "No." Later, she told her husband, L. C. what she had done. He said, "Daisy, you did the right thing." Mrs. Bates's visitor kept her promise. *The State Press* was closed because advertising from it was withdrawn by all of the major stores and businesses in Little Rock. The Bates family suffered financial and personal turmoil because of the closing of *The State Press* and because of threats and attempts on Mrs. Bates's life.

Using the Banks value inquiry model, these are some of the questions Mr. Carson asked his students:

Defining and Recognizing Value Problems
1. What value problem did Mrs. Bates face after she was visited by the woman?

Naming Values Exemplified by Behavior Described
2. What did the visitor value or think was important? What did Mrs. Bates value? What did Mr. Bates value?

Hypothesizing about the Sources of Values Analyzed
3. How do you think Mrs. Bates's visitor developed the values she had? How do you think Mr. and Mrs. Bates developed the values they showed in this selection?

Declaring Value Preferences: Choosing
4. Try to put yourself in Mrs. Daisy Bates's place on October 29, 1959. What decision would you have made?

Stating Reasons, Sources, and Possible Consequences of Value Choice
5. Why should Mrs. Bates have made the decision you stated above? What were the possible consequences of her saying "no" and saying "yes" to her visitor? Give as many reasons as you can about why Mrs. Bates should have made the decision you stated above.

Keep in mind that Mrs. Bates knew that if she said yes to her visitor she would probably have been able to keep her property but that the nine students would have probably had to return to Black schools and that segregation would have been maintained in Little Rock. On the other hand, by saying no, she risked losing all of her property and her husband's property, including his newspaper. Also, consider the fact that she did not involve him in making her decision.

Decision Making and Citizen Action

After Mr. Carson's students had derived knowledge about the civil rights movement of the 1950s and 1960s and had clarified their values regarding these issues, he asked them to list all of the possible actions they could take to increase desegregation in their personal lives as well as in the life of the school and the community. Mr. Carson was careful to explain to the students that action should be broadly conceptualized. He defined action in a way that might include a personal commitment to do something, such as making an effort to have more friends from different racial and ethnic groups, making a commitment to see the videotape *Roots* and to discuss it with a friend, as well as to read a play or book that would better one's understanding of another racial or ethnic group, such as *A Raisin in the Sun* by Lorraine Hansberry or *Beloved* by Toni Morrison. Among the possible actions that the students listed that they could take were these:

1. Make a personal commitment to stop telling racist jokes.

2. Make a commitment to challenge our own racial and ethnic stereotypes either before or after we verbalize them.

3. Compile an annotated list of books about ethnic groups that we will ask the librarian to order for our school library.

4. Ask the principal to order sets of photographs that show African Americans and other people of color who have jobs that represent a variety of careers. Ask the principal to encourage our teachers to display these photographs on their classroom walls.

5. Observe television programs to determine the extent to which people of color, such as African Americans and Asian Americans, are represented in such jobs as news anchors and hosts of programs. Write to local and national television stations to express our concern if we discover that people of color are not represented in powerful and visible roles in news or other kinds of television programs .

6. Contact a school in the inner city to determine if there are joint activities and projects in which we and they might participate.

7. Ask the principal or the board of education in our school district to require our teachers to attend in-service staff development workshops that will help them learn ways in which to integrate content about ethnic and racial groups into our courses.

8. Share some of the facts that we have learned in this unit, such as that by the year 2000, one out of three Americans will be a person of color, with our parents and discuss these facts with them.

9. Make a personal commitment to have a friend from another

racial, ethnic, or religious group by the end of the year.

10. Make a personal commitment to read at least one book a year that deals with a racial, cultural, or ethnic group other than my own.

11. Do nothing, take no actions.

The Decision-Making Process

After the students had made a list of possible actions they could take regarding the issues studied in the unit (including no actions), Mr. Carson asked them to consider the possible consequences of each of the actions identified, such as the following:

If I Take No Actions

> *Then* I will be doing nothing to improve race relations in my personal life, in my school, my community, or nation.
>
> *But* I will not risk trying to do something that could fail. I will also be indicating to others, by my behavior, that I am not concerned about improving race relations in my personal life, my family, school, or community.

If I Make a Personal Commitment to Tell No More Racist Jokes

> *Then* I will be improving my personal behavior that relates to other racial, ethnic and cultural groups. I will also demonstrate to others that I am concerned about improving race relations in my personal life.
>
> *But* I will be doing little directly to improve the behaviors of other people in my family, school, and community.

After the students had worked in groups of five to identify and state the possible consequences of various courses of actions, Mr. Carson asked them to continue working in their groups and to select one or two personal or group actions they would like to take related to the problems they had studied in the unit. Mr. Carson also asked the students to be prepared to defend and/or explain the course of action or actions they chose, to tell whether it was feasible for them to carry out the action or actions, and to provide a timeline for initiation and completion (if possible). These are among the actions the students chose:

• Kathy and Susan decided to read the play *A Raisin in the Sun* by Lorraine Hansberry to try to get a better understanding of the experience of African Americans in the United States.

• Clay's group, which included Clay, Pete, Tessie, Rosie, and Maria, decided that they would prepare a list of books on ethnic cultures and ask the school librarian to order them for the school library. Clay's group planned to ask Mr. Carson to help them find resources for the preparation of the annotated list of books.

• Roselyn decided that she wanted to improve her understanding of ethnic cultures by reading. She decided to read these books during the year: *Let the Circle Be Unbroken* by Mildred D. Taylor, *A Jar of Dreams* by Yoshiko Uchida, and *America Is in the Heart* by Carlos Bulosan.

• Aralean's group, which included Juan, James, Angela, and Patricia, decided that they wanted to develop a proposal that would require teachers in the district to attend multicultural education workshops. They will develop their plan with Mr. Carson and present it to the principal and then to the board of education for possible adoption.

The Role of the Teacher in an Empowerment and Transformative Curriculum

An effective transformative and empowerment curriculum must be implemented by teachers who have the knowledge, skills, and attitudes needed to help students to understand the ways in which knowledge is constructed and used to support power-group relationships in society. Teachers are human beings who bring their cultural perspectives, values, hopes, and dreams to the classroom. They also bring their prejudices, stereotypes, and misconceptions to the classroom. Teachers' values and perspectives mediate and interact with what they teach and influence the way that messages are communicated and perceived by their students. A teacher who believes that Christopher Columbus "discovered" America and one who believes that Columbus came to America when it was peopled by groups with rich and diverse cultures will send different messages to their students when the European exploration of America is studied.

Because teachers mediate the messages and symbols communicated to the students through the curriculum, it is important for them to come to grips with their own personal and cultural values and identities in order for them to help students from diverse racial, ethnic, and cultural groups to develop clarified cultural identities and to relate positively to each other. I am hypothesizing that self-clarification is a prerequisite to dealing effectively with and relating positively to outside ethnic and cultural groups. An Anglo-American teacher who is confused about his or her cultural identity and who has a nonreflective conception of the ways that Anglo-American culture relates to other groups in the United States, will have a very difficult time relating positively to outside ethnic groups such as African Americans and Mexican Americans.

Effective teacher education programs should help pre- and in-service teachers to explore and clarify their own ethnic and cultural identities and to develop more positive attitudes toward other racial, ethnic, and cultural groups. To do this, such programs must recognize and reflect the complex ethnic and cultural identities and characteristics of the individuals within teacher education programs (Banks, 1988). Teachers should also learn how to facilitate the identity quest among students and help them to become effective and able participants in the common civic culture.

Effective teachers in the transformative curriculum must not only have clarified personal and cultural identifications; they must also be keenly aware of the various paradigms, canons, and knowledge systems on which the dominant curriculum is based and those that it eschews. Because teacher education students attain most of their knowledge without analyzing its assumptions and values or engaging in the process of constructing knowledge themselves, they often leave teacher education programs with many misconceptions about culturally and racially different groups and with conceptions about their national history and culture that are incomplete, misleading, and chauvinistic. Consequently, the knowledge that many teachers bring to the classroom contributes to the mystification rather than to the clarification of social, historical, and political realities. This knowledge also perpetuates inequality and oppression rather than contributes to justice, liberation, and empowerment.

In order to educate teachers so that they will convey images, perspectives, and points of view in the curriculum that will demystify social realities and promote cultural freedom and empowerment, we must radically change the ways in which they acquire knowledge. We must engage them in a process of attaining knowledge in which they are required to analyze the values and assumptions of different paradigms and theories. Teacher education students must also be given the opportunity to construct concepts, generalizations, and theories so that they can develop an understanding of the nature and limitations of knowledge and comprehend the extent to which knowledge reflects the social and cultural context in which it is formulated.

Participating in processes in which they formulate and construct knowledge forms will also help teacher education students to understand how various groups in society who formulate, shape, and disseminate knowledge often structure and disseminate knowledge that supports their interests and legitimizes their power. This knowledge often legitimizes dominant institutions and helps to make victimized groups politically passive and content with their deprived status. Teachers must not only understand how the dominant paradigms and canon help keep victimized groups powerless but also must be committed to social change and action if they are to become agents of liberation and empowerment.

Chapter 6

Empowerment Through Media Literacy: A Multicultural Approach

Carlos E. Cortés

In her 1989 article, "Education for Citizenship: New Dimensions," Professor Wilma Longstreet of the University of New Orleans wrote the following:

> We spend years teaching reading and remedial reading while we hardly glance at these newer, more powerful media. Our young are literally at the mercy of television, besieged by far greater amounts of information on each screen than was ever possible on the pages of a book, and we give them no help in sorting and analyzing that barrage of data or in defending themselves from the high level of stimuli that accompany the barrage. (p. 44)

Barrage, yes. But the media barrage comes from more than television. It emanates from all media—television and motion pictures, radio and recorded music, newspapers and magazines. And the barrage consists of more than data. The media provide fictional as well as nonfictional images and messages, from media presumably made just to entertain (and make money) as well as from programs and publications intended to provide information. Although some members of the so-called entertainment media proclaim that they merely offer diversion, in fact they simultaneously teach, whether intentionally or incidentally. Let's reverse the equation. Whatever the stated or unstated goals of the media, people learn from both fictional and nonfictional media sources, although they usually do not realize that such media-based learning is occurring (Jowett, 1976; Sklar, 1975; Singer and Kazdon, 1976).

Likening television to schools and television programs to school courses, sociologist Herbert J. Gans (1967) argued that

> almost all TV programs and magazine fiction teach something
> about American society. For example, *Batman* is, from this van-
> tage point, a course in criminology that describes how a super-
> human aristocrat does a better job eradicating crime than do
> public officials. Similarly, *The Beverly Hillbillies* offers a course in
> social stratification and applied economics, teaching that with
> money, uneducated and uncultured people can do pretty well
> in American society, and can easily outwit more sophisticated
> and more powerful middle-class types . . . And even the
> innocuous family situation comedies such as *Ozzie and Harriet*
> deal occasionally with ethical problems encountered on a
> neighborhood level . . . Although the schools argue that they
> are the major transmitter of society's moral values, the mass
> media offer a great deal more content on this topic. (pp. 21-22)

In her 1980 testimony to the House Select Committee on Aging, actress
Janet MacLachlan referred to her ten-year-old daughter as a "TV
junkie." Expressing special anxiety about stereotyping in children's programs, MacLachlan described her daughter as someone whose "attitudes about people, the relationship between them and about herself are
skewed by the medium—by the unrealistic and stereotyped portrayals
of the elderly, of black people, of Asian, Latin-Hispanic, American
Indian people," to the point that she "equates age with tragedy, and
skin color with negativity and failure" (Shaheen, 1984, p. 22).

As formal or informal teachers, then, the media participate in the
complex process of educating society. That process contributes to the
empowerment of some people (and groups) and the disempowerment
of others by disseminating images and ideas about different societal
groups—for example, ethnic, racial, gender, religious, age, and of varying physical and mental characteristics. Reporting that there had been
more than 2,300 research papers on television and human behavior,
social psychologist George Comstock (1977) addressed the relationship
of media to empowerment:

> Several writers have argued that television is a powerful rein-
> forcer of the status quo. The ostensible mechanisms are the
> effects of its portrayals on public expectations and perceptions.
> Television portrayals and particularly violent drama are said to
> assign roles of authority, power, success, failure, dependence,
> and vulnerability in a manner that matches the real-life social

hierarchy, thereby strengthening that hierarchy by increasing its acknowledgement among the public and by failing to provide positive images for members of social categories occupying a subservient position. Content analyses of television drama support the contention that portrayals reflect normative status. (pp. 20-21)

The learning impact of media manifests itself throughout American life. It can be found in visceral individual responses to varying stimuli. Take the following dramatic example of how the constant media reiteration of one theme has created a nearly reflexive, virtually mindless ethnic stereotype. On September 18, 1986, the popular daytime television game show, *The $25,000 Pyramid*, was being shown. In *Pyramid*, competition involves two pairs of contestants. For each pair, words appear on a screen in front of one contestant, who then gives clues to guide the partner into identifying the correct words. On that day the word *gangs* popped up on the cluer's screen. Without hesitation, he fired out the first thing that came into his mind: "They have lots of these in East L.A." (a heavily Mexican American section of Los Angeles). Responding immediately, the guest celebrity partner answered, "Gangs." Under competitive pressure, two strangers had instantly achieved mental communion, linking East L.A. with gangs and retransmitting their ethnic stereotype to a national audience.

Where had they developed this identical vision of a Chicano community as being synonymous with gangs? Obviously and unfortunately, East Los Angeles does have gangs. But it also has a multitude of far more prevalent elements, like families, schools, businesses, churches, and socially contributing organizations. Yet the media fixation with and sensationalizing of Latino gangs—from news reports and documentaries to TV series and feature films—have elevated and reinforced gangs into *the* quintessential popular vision of East L.A. (and many other Latino communities), as demonstrated on *Pyramid*. The media, in short, have created a gang-featuring public curriculum on Latinos.

Take another example of media teaching power, an example that reflects begrudging media recognition of its educational power and potential. Prior to the 1977 national television showing of Francis Ford Coppola's *The Godfather Saga* (a revised and expanded version of the two theatrical motion pictures, *The Godfather* and *The Godfather: Part II*), the following words appeared on screen, simultaneously intoned by a solemn voice: "*The Godfather* is a fictional account of the activities of a small group of ruthless criminals. It would be erroneous and unfair to suggest that they are representative of any ethnic group." Forewarned that the characters were not "representative of any ethnic group," a nationwide television audience then watched the violent, multigenerational saga of the Corleone family. The early part of the film took place in Sicily, large segments of the film were spoken in Italian with English subtitles, and most of the characters bore such names as Barzini, Clemenza, Brasi, Fanucci, and Tattaglia. No problem. The disclaimer had guaranteed that viewers would not think of them as members of any specific ethnic group.

Moreover, those worthless words became the model for future media disclaimers, being copied and only slightly modified in later controversial films that similarly presented other ethnic groups as criminally violent, such as the 1983 *Scarface* (Cuban Americans) and the 1985 *Year of the Dragon* (Chinese Americans). Did these words mitigate the image-influencing impact of these films? Dubious! However, the disclaimer did serve as a media admission that entertainment films do, in fact, teach . . . that they possess the power to create, reinforce, and modify public images about ethnic groups.

Therein lies the problem. The media, both fictional and nonfictional, teach. They have a powerful influence on popular group images, including public perceptions of ethnic and racial groups. Often these images become so widespread and reflexive that they achieve the status of stereotypes. Through their multicultural image-making educational power, the media have the capacity for contributing to the empowerment or disempowerment of persons of different ethnic backgrounds.

But what can educators do about it? Obviously, any "solution" to the problem of media multicultural empowerment would have to include structural, personnel, and content changes within the media—for example, greater racial, ethnic, and gender diversity at all levels of media decision making and image creation, greater sensitivity in fictional media portrayals of diverse groups, and better balance (as well as less sensationalism) in media coverage and treatment of stories involving ethnic and racial groups. Just as obviously, educators have limited direct and immediate influence on those aspects of a "solution." Although we as educators might choose to become involved in such quests, we lack the power to transform these goals rapidly into realities. But this does not render teachers powerless. We have the power to empower—or at least contribute to empowerment—*within* the educational system.

As Christine Sleeter correctly argues in the introduction to this book, multicultural education should help empower students by assisting them to become more active and effective participants in addressing their own problems, including societal inequities. When applied to the mass media, this school multicultural empowerment would include strengthening student knowledge about the media, developing student skills in critically analyzing the media, and helping students become more action oriented when dealing with the media. All students need to achieve a more analytical and activist stance toward the media. Moreover, given the structural inequities in contemporary U.S. society, the empowerment of minority students becomes of particular importance (Cummins, 1989). But before proceeding further with a discussion of the media, I would like to place the media within a larger educational framework, a framework that I have labeled the "societal curriculum" (Cortés, 1981).

Media as a Component
of the Societal Curriculum

Discussions of education often, and mistakenly, use schools and education as synonymous concepts. Certainly schools constitute an important part of education. However, they do not monopolize education, nor could they even if they wished.

Students learn through schools, but people, including students, also learn outside of schools through the societal curriculum—that massive, ongoing, informal curriculum of families, peer groups, neighborhoods, churches, organizations, institutions, mass media, and other socializing forces that educate all of us throughout our lives. Through the societal curriculum students learn language. They learn culture. They learn attitudes and patterns of behavior. They learn about themselves and others. They learn about our nation and about other nations and cultures of the world.

Most important for the issue of multicultural empowerment, they learn about the many types of groups that make up our society. Much of the societal curriculum educates multiculturally, for better and for worse, thereby contributing to empowerment and disempowerment. Through the multicultural societal curriculum people learn about such empowerment-related themes as race, ethnic diversity, religion, the significance of gender, the implications of age, and the potential of persons of different physical and mental attributes. They also learn about relations involving individuals, groups, and institutions.

Moreover, the temporal range of nonschool learning far exceeds that of schools. Young people learn *before* they ever begin school. While they go to school, students continue to learn in society. Finally, for most of us school days will end, but societal learning will continue as long as we live. To help empower students for life, schools should prepare them to deal effectively and analytically with the societal curriculum, the process of lifelong nonschool learning, of which the media function as a powerful central element.

The societal curriculum may be viewed as operating in four general, overlapping, and interacting curricular sectors:

1. *The immediate curriculum*—the educational influences emanating from family, home, peer group, neighborhood, and community
2. *The institutional curriculum*—the formal and informal educational curriculum that resides within such diverse institutions and organizations as religious institutions, youth groups, social organizations, professional associations, and special interest entities
3. *The serendipitous curriculum*—the incidental, sometimes accidental, teaching that occurs through individual experiences in each person's life
4. *The media curriculum*—the educational messages disseminated intentionally and unintentionally through the various media, like newspapers, magazines, motion pictures, television, and radio.

The media curriculum has been my special research interest, with an emphasis on the teaching role of motion pictures. (I am currently working on a three-volume study of the multicultural implications of motion pictures: the first volume on the history of the U.S. feature film treatment of ethnicity, the second volume on the movie depiction of foreign nations and cultures, and the third volume on the film treatment of interracial love.)

The teaching power of the mass media has long drawn the attention of scholars and concerned societal groups. The educational impact of motion pictures, for example, has been debated since the early part of this century. Studies have shown that movies influence intergroup attitudes and perceptions, sometimes reinforcing them, other times modifying them (Raths and Trager, 1948). One pioneering study (Peterson and Thurstone, 1933) revealed that when students viewed the classic 1915 silent film, *The Birth of a Nation*, which included a degrading portrayal of southern Blacks, in the post-Civil War Reconstruction Era, an increase in student prejudice toward Black Americans resulted. In contrast, another study (Rosen, 1948) found that the 1947 anti-anti-Semitism film, *Gentleman's Agreement*, actually improved student attitudes toward

Jews, even though most of the surveyed students stated that the film *had not* influenced their attitudes!

Television, including cable, has dominated recent analysis. Although the extent of television viewing defies precise verification, experts concur that it has been growing around the world. Average household TV viewing time in the United States has climbed from five hours per day in 1956 to six hours per day in 1971 and to seven hours per day in 1983. As early as 1961, scholars reported that young Americans between the ages of three and sixteen devoted one-sixth of their waking hours to television (Schramm, Lyle, and Parker, 1961). According to another estimate, by the time of high school graduation, the average student will have spent 11,000 hours in the classroom and 22,000 hours in front of the television set (Shaheen, 1984). Sometimes movies and television overlap, particularly as TV, cable, and videocassettes become prime recyclers of theatrical motion pictures.

However, in examining the media curriculum—in fact, all aspects of the societal curriculum—we need to remain aware that teaching and learning are not synonymous. If they were, teachers would never have to give examinations. We would only have to evaluate teacher presentations and textbook content to assess learning. Yet we teach—in the classroom and through assignments—and then discover great variation in the extent, content, and quality of student learning.

This teaching-learning gap also applies to the societal curriculum. Research has demonstrated conclusively that people learn about societal diversity from the media. But when scholars have examined the nature and content of media impact, they have encountered varying learner responses (Pingree and Hawkins, 1982). Three landmark television presentations—Norman Lear's popular comedy series, *All in the Family*, the highly acclaimed *Cosby Show*, and the powerful 1977 docudrama, *Roots*—demonstrate the phenomenon of variable learning and contrasting viewer interpretations.

Inaugurated in 1971, *All in the Family* portrayed Archie Bunker as the classic bigot—racist, sexist, and just about every other kind of anti-"ist" imaginable. By making Bunker's views appear comically absurd, the show attempted to critique bigotry. It succeeded . . . for some viewers. But others identified with him, seeing Bunker's beliefs and prejudices as a confirmation of the validity of their own (Leckenby and Surlin, 1976). For example, one study (Vidmar and Rokeach, 1974) confirmed the "selective perception hypothesis" by determining that "high prejudiced viewers" tended to admire Bunker and condone his racial and ethnic slurs.

Even the far less controversial *Cosby Show*, which presents a positive portrayal of a well-educated, cerebral, financially successful African American family, has drawn its share of concerned reactions. Some viewers have expressed reservations on the grounds that the show's concentration on well-heeled African Americans might unintentionally encourage viewers to ignore the tremendous social and economic problems still faced by the majority of American Blacks. As media scholar Paula Matabane wrote recently (1988):

> "The Cosby Show," for example, epitomizes the Afro-American dream of full acceptance and assimilation into U.S. society. Both the series and Bill Cosby as an individual represent successful competitors in network television and in attaining a high status. Although this achievement is certainly not inherently negative, we should consider the role television plays in the cultivation of an overall picture of growing racial equality that conceals unequal social relationships and overestimates of how well blacks are integrating into white society (if at all). The illusion of well-being among the oppressed may lead to reduced political activity and less demand for social justice and equality. (p. 30)

Responses also varied concerning the eight-night January, 1977, showing of Alex Haley's *Roots*, the epic television docudrama on the experience of Black slaves in America. The series attracted numerous scholars (Hur, 1978; Surlin, 1978; Howard, Rothbart, and Sloan, 1978), who discovered a variety of audience reactions when assessed along group lines, although viewers did not polarize as sharply as with *All in the Family*. For example, one study (Balon, 1978) in Austin, Texas, reported that Mexican Americans and Anglos, far more than Black viewers, considered *Roots* to be an accurate presentation of slavery, and Mexican Americans, far more than Blacks and Anglos, found the depiction of southern whites to be accurate.

Some scholars have come to broader conclusions about how entertainment media learning varies among societal groups. For example, based on an examination of the perceived reality of television, one study (Greenberg and Reeves, 1976) concluded that "economically disadvantaged homes, black children, younger children, female children, and those with a higher frequency of watching have all indicated more belief in the true-to-life nature of TV entertainment" (p. 88). This raises serious issues for the relationship of the media to multicultural empowerment.

Media, then, constitute a central, powerful element of that

omnipresent public educational process, the societal curriculum. Developing a sharpened capacity to analyze the media can help empower; the failure to develop such a capacity contributes to disempowerment. Given the lifelong significance of the media as an educational force, media empowerment should be an integral part of all students' education. Schools should help students develop an empowering media literacy that includes at least two basic dimensions. First, schools need to help students become more effective media analysts. Second, schools can help students to understand how they can influence the media.

Empowerment Through Media Analysis

In her introduction, Sleeter emphasizes the importance of schools for increasing students' ability to analyze as a basis for empowerment. This should include the capacity for analyzing the media. Moreover, beyond general media literacy, teachers should be certain to bring a multicultural dimension to this media empowerment. This includes the development of an understanding of the ways in which the media treat different ethnic groups, as well as the sensitizing of students to patterns of ethnic treatment that have become media standards, sometimes clichés.

Analytical skills can be honed from the time students enter school. In the early elementary grades, as Pang in this volume suggests, teachers can help students learn to analyze the content of a variety of sources—children's stories, photographs, printed cartoons, film strips, drawings, animated films, even comic strips. Advertisements on television, in magazines and newspapers, and even on billboards and bumper stickers can be stimulating sources for different age groups in their study of the process of public image formation. High school students can examine newspapers, magazines, national newscasts, feature films, and television series for their treatment of different subjects, including ethnic, gender, and religious groups as well as foreign nations.

For many teachers, development of their own media analysis skills may be a personal challenge, since most have never been exposed to such training. Teachers can increase their own media awareness by keeping a media curriculum journal. In my multicultural and media analysis courses and long-range workshops, I begin by giving teachers the assignment of keeping a journal documenting what media teaching they observe concerning ethnicity, foreign cultures, genders, religions, age cohorts, and other societal groupings—whether that teaching is intentional or unintended, whether fictional or nonfictional. This helps teachers develop an awareness of the extent and content of the media curriculum, as well as the habit of thinking analytically about the media curriculum to which their students are exposed. Teachers can engage in this exercise first by formally keeping such a journal, later by remaining constantly alert to this media teaching.

Beyond awareness come classroom strategies for media analysis. Fortunately, an increasing number of materials that provide suggestions for both pedagogy and social action are becoming available. For example, the quarterly magazine *Media & Values* provides in-depth discussions of basic media issues, as well as pedagogical suggestions for teachers, counselors, and others working to empower youth. Some of the journal's special issues are devoted to societal diversity, and I write a column on minorities and the media for each issue.

Moreover, the growing availability of books that address specific aspects of media analysis should prove of great value to teachers. Take, for example, recent strides in the use of moving-image media (motion pictures and television) to study history. Historian John J. O'Connor (1989) has identified four basic uses of such media for historical scholarship and historically related classroom teaching:

1. *As factual evidence*—how to extract and evaluate information carefully and subtly from a variety of moving-image media sources, ranging from newsreels and documentaries to feature films

2. *As historical recreations*—how to examine historical films and television docudramas for their authenticity, factual accuracy, and validity

3. *As sociocultural documents*—how to analyze film and television in order to gain insights into the eras in which specific moving-image media were created

4. *As evidence for the development of the moving-image media art and industry*—how to study the ways in which film and television have developed both as art forms and as products of an increasingly complex industry

We should never underestimate how the media have influenced our students' vision of the past as well as of the present. As Steven O'Brien (1989), a teacher at Hamilton-Wenham High School in Hamilton, Massachusetts, wrote recently:

> My son finished his homework on the Progressive Era by reading only what was necessary to answer the questions his teacher had assigned. I asked whether he wasn't even slightly inter-

ested in knowing the context in which the events he had just read and written about occurred. He patiently explained that movies and television were the ways he preferred to learn about the past. (p. 100)

To involve students in the multicultural aspects of our nation's history, the media can be used to stimulate thinking and to humanize ongoing historical dilemmas. For example, the 1988 feature film *Mississippi Burning* and the 1989 television docudrama *Unconquered* can lead students into an analysis of the civil rights movement of the 1960s. Moreover, students should consider the manner in which these two shows emphasized the role of Whites in the movement while at the same time deemphasizing the role played by Blacks in the struggle for their own liberation—with implications for how this media treatment might influence the historical perceptions of young people who did not live through that era. Both productions have received justifiable criticism because of their overemphasis on the role of Whites in the civil rights movement. Yet the very controversy over these two presentations heightens their potential as teaching devices—when used critically—and can motivate students to engage in further study of the movement.

Media can also be used to stimulate students to consider multiple perspectives on current and historical multicultural dilemmas. For example, the opening sequence of the 1987 motion picture, *China Girl*, dramatizes the dilemma of changing urban neighborhoods. In this sequence a proud Chinese American family opens a restaurant in an Italian American section of New York City while local residents watch with emotions ranging from the nostalgic sorrow of the elderly to the barely restrained bitterness of young people. This brief sequence could be used to provoke consideration of the multiethnic implications and challenges of immigration and demographic change.

The media themselves are making it easier for teachers to carry out instruction in media analysis. The Discovery Channel, for example, has announced plans for *Assignment: Discovery*, hoping that teachers will tape and make classroom use of the program, which will cover a different topic each day. Whittle Communications of Knoxville, Tennessee, has gone even further with its *Channel One*, a daily twelve-minute news and general information program created specifically for direct broadcasting to junior and senior high schools throughout the nation. Having completed a twenty-five-show pilot test in six schools, Whittle hopes that *Channel One* will be reaching six to seven million teenagers (double the estimated teenage viewing audience for any prime-time show) in eight thousand schools by the fall of 1990. To attain this ambitious goal, Whittle says it will provide $50,000 worth of satellite dishes, television sets, and videocassette recorders to each school that guarantees that its students will watch the show every day.

There is a catch, of course. Along with the twelve minutes of news come two minutes of advertising targeted at this very susceptible and malleable teenage audience. For just this reason, *Channel One* has encountered considerable educator opposition (as well as support) from such groups as Action for Children's Television and the National Parent-Teachers Association.

However, educators have an option that goes beyond either rejection or simple dissemination of these or other programs to students. Teachers could use *Channel One* (as well as other media material) to teach analytical thinking. Along with general instruction in critical thinking, teachers could train students in specific media analysis strategies, using *Channel One* as a source for analysis. This would include, of course, the analysis of its advertisements. In this way students could become more empowered both by sharpening their ability to analyze news presentations critically and by developing an understanding of techniques used by advertisers to sell products. Teachers could then create additional assignments so that students would apply these analytical skills to news and advertising in nonschool media.

The foregoing should not be viewed as an endorsement of the use of *Channel One* or any other specific program. The ethical issues raised in opposition to *Channel One* by alarmed educators deserve serious consideration. However, if adopted, these programs should definitely not be presented simply for the rote consumption of information or the uncritical viewing of advertisements. Rather, teachers interested in the empowerment of students should use these programs as source material for strengthening critical thinking and the skills of media analysis.

Empowerment Through Media Activism

Beyond becoming more literate as media users, students can also learn how to have a greater influence on the media. Education for empowerment should help students learn to become effective advocates of social justice, in this case the fair and equitable treatment of all groups by the media. For example, teachers can have students examine how various individuals and groups have responded to the media in general or to specific media examples in an effort to influence the media.

Individuals, ethnic organizations, and associations concerned with multicultural equity have generally focused on media content, usually how media have depicted specific groups. Increasing public awareness of the teaching potential of the media and growing efforts to influence their content can be found in various forms: awards presented to media-makers who have contributed to "positive images" of specific groups; protests against what some perceive to be "negative images" or distortions of various multicultural topics; boycotts of targeted movies, television shows (including their sponsors), magazines, or music videos; and efforts by some groups to work with the media to improve images or mitigate negative treatment. Students could assess the reasons for such efforts, the kinds of content that different groups find positive or negative, the types of activities carried out by media-oriented groups, and the relative successes and failures of different media-oriented strategies.

Take, for example, recent responses to the media portrayal of people with disabilities. In January, 1989, the California Governor's Committee for the Employment of Disabled Persons presented the Media Access Award for the year's best feature film to *Gaby*, the inspiring story of renowned Mexican author Gabriela Brimmer, who wrote an acclaimed autobiography, although paralyzed by cerebral palsy. In addition, the committee gave a special merit award to the television series *L.A. Law* for its sensitive portrayal of Benny Stolwitz, a mentally retarded young man who demonstrates competence and dignity as a messenger for a Los Angeles legal firm, in the process overcoming the reservations of some firm members. Other groups representing mentally retarded Americans commended actor Larry Drake, who brilliantly portrays Benny, for his contributions to improving the image of mentally retarded persons.

Contrast this with the uproar from the hearing-impaired community over the 1989 movie hit, *See No Evil, Hear No Evil*. Made as a comedy involving a deaf man and a blind man, the film struck many deaf people as more demeaning than funny. As signed by Tony Award-winning actress Phyllis Frelich, "Being deaf and blind, they think those are funny handicaps . . . It's an inaccurate portrayal. They'll do anything to sell a movie, at the price of making us suffer with the insults" (Lopez-Johnson, 1989, p. 8).

By studying different group and organizational reactions to the media, students can assess what types of action have been most effective in influencing media content. Based on their own analysis of media content, students might even decide to engage in some kind of action related to the media, possibly focusing on local news coverage. For example, they could compare local newspaper and television coverage of chosen events or groups, and then write to the various local media explaining their conclusions, encouraging those media that seem most responsible and responsive in their coverage, and making recommendations for improved and more sensitive coverage.

But action should not dwell only on ways of responding to the media. Action could also include participation in the creation of media presentations. Students could write articles or columns on multicultural themes and about multicultural issues for school newspapers. Some students might write multiculturally oriented articles for local newspapers and seek opportunities for helping to create more multiculturally responsive local radio and television programs. The national antiprejudice project, A World of Difference, has made effective use of local television stations and newspapers in its public educational activities. Involvement in such projects as A World of Difference could teach students how they can become involved with the media as a means for improving intergroup understanding.

Participation in media-oriented action also gives students the opportunity to test how effective or ineffective their media-influencing strategies and media-creating efforts turn out to be. They can evaluate the different media's responses to their actions, as well as reader and viewer responses to their own media contributions. In this way students can learn more about the possibilities and the obstacles to bringing about media content change, including the strength of working together collectively as a means of empowerment. Most important, they should realize that people do not have to remain passive concerning the media.

Conclusion

Schools play a critical role in creating opportunities for or obstacles to student empowerment. This includes helping them to become more empowered through media literacy, able to deal more effectively with that omnipresent lifelong educator, the mass media. Schools should help students develop the capacity to deal with the multicultural implications of the media, both as analytical consumers and as participants in collective action in an effort to make the media more sensitive to racial and cultural issues.

Teachers should continually be cognizant of the content of the media curriculum. They can bring it into their classrooms to enrich, motivate, provide social context, and heighten the significance of school subjects. They can help prepare students to be more enlightened learners and influencers within the media curriculum.

In short, the multicultural analysis of the mass media can be a major step toward the empowerment of all students. In a world in which they will be enveloped by the media, in which they will be bombarded with information, images, and messages in both informational and entertainment form, the ability to engage the media consciously and effectively is a necessary aspect of greater control over one's own destinies. As one avenue to empowerment, students must learn to use, not be used, by the media.

Chapter 7

Cooperative Learning as Empowering Pedagogy

Mara Sapon-Shevin
Nancy Schniedewind

The teacher is standing at the board and has asked a question of the group of students at her feet. Six or seven students wave their hands wildly, begging the teacher to call on them. The rest of the class—which includes two students mainstreamed from a special education classroom, two recent immigrants from Vietnam, and four Hispanic students for whom English is a second language—watch the drama unfolding. Several of them actually know the answer but are still shy in front of the group, one child is desperately afraid that someone will laugh at her if she gets it wrong and so remains silent, several didn't really understand the question, and one boy is convinced that the teacher doesn't like him and won't call on him and so simply doesn't bother to try. The teacher calls on the waving hand which belongs to Michael; the other children groan and hope that he will get it wrong so that they can have a chance. He does, and they cheer. One child snickers to her neighbor, "He's always wrong." The teacher calls on Nicole, who gives the right answer, and the teacher says "Great." The other children who had had their hands up now put them down, deflated and disappointed. One child mutters, "Nicole thinks she's so smart," and Nicole blushes and looks embarrassed.

What has this lesson taught children? Although the official subject matter was prepositions, there were many other lessons as well. Powerful messages and values have been communicated by the teacher's interactions with the children. The children have learned that although it is good to be right, it is more important to be fast. They have learned that only one child can get the teacher's approval, and that other children are what stand in the way of them receiving recognition and praise. They have confirmed that Michael is "stupid" and not worthy of their attention, and that Nicole is "smart" and should be scorned for being a "show-off." Nicole has learned that she may have to choose between "doing well" and "having friends," since the two often seem incompatible. Some of the children have been reinforced in their belief that academic success is outside their realm and that it doesn't even pay to make the attempt, lest they risk embarrassment and disdain. Witnessing the silence or slowness of their classmates who do not speak English well, the native English-speaking children have had confirmed their suspicion that "those" kids aren't capable of full participation or achievement in their classroom, and the Spanish-speaking children have learned that their language and skills are not of value and certainly will not help them attain success.

Not bad for a short lesson! Although none of the above messages were listed in the teacher's lesson plan, they did, nonetheless, flow predictably and consistently from her teaching and management strategies. Children learned that some people are "winners" and others "losers," that children who are different are not as capable or worthy, and that success is a scarce commodity, not available to all, and accessible only by pleasing the teachers. What was there about the structure of the interaction that promoted these outcomes, and what are the alternatives? Although many factors influence classroom interactions and practice, the major feature of the above teaching episode was *competition*. Students were placed in a situation in which they had to demonstrate to the teacher that they were better or faster or smarter than the other children in order to win her approval and praise. Not all children were called on to demonstrate what they knew or had learned, and the teacher created a situation in which a highly valued commodity—teacher praise and attention—was limited and not available to all.

Because all of us, students and teachers, are products of a highly competitive educational system and other competitive cultural institutions, it is often difficult to step back and examine the alternatives to this pattern of teaching and interaction. Alfie Kohn (1986) argues in his book, *No Contest: The Case Against Competition*, that "precisely because we are so enmeshed in it, competition can easily escape our notice. A fish doesn't reflect on the nature of water. He cannot imagine its absence, so he cannot consider its presence" (p. 1). Our culture—its schools, media, and ideologies—does not help people jump out of the water to look at the sea of competition.

In order to begin the process of altering our vision and our practice, we must first question some assumptions that we have about competition, specifically that competition is simply "human nature" and the inevitable way in which people must or even should interact. We must understand how we have become indoctrinated in these beliefs and how we can free ourselves from their control over our teaching and our lives. After examining some of these popular beliefs and assumptions, this chapter will explore the basic principles of cooperative learning, drawing the connections between the implementation of these principles and the development of classrooms which nurture and support multicultural education and student and teacher empowerment. We conclude by suggesting that cooperative learning can be linked to raising critical consciousness about the sources and forms of inequality and to helping students and teachers become empowered to create the changes necessary for multicultural classrooms, schools, and society. Teachers can structure their classrooms so that students learn to *cooperate* rather than compete, and teachers can also teach *about* cooperation so that students are aware of the myriad ways in which cooperation can be applied as a central organizing principle in their lives both inside and outside of school.

Competition and Oppression: The Critical Link

In order to understand how cooperative learning can be an empowering pedagogy which moves us toward a more equitable society, we must see clearly how the pervasiveness of competition and competitive structures leads to oppression. By understanding the extent to which we are all victims of the structures created and fueled by competition, we can begin to consider how cooperative structures can provide different models for human interaction, empowerment, and learning. One way of examining the extent to which we have all been shaped by our competitive schooling experience (embedded within a competitive society) is to examine some of the myths concerning competition which have guided the behavior of many of our teachers and leaders [1]

Competition is the inevitable result
of the struggle for scarce resources.

In his book, *No Contest*, Kohn (1986) documents some of the relationships between competition and inequality. Anthropological studies point to the positive correspondence between competitive societies and those with the existence of haves and have-nots. Although cultural beliefs in our society reinforce the notion that competition is inevitable, the research which Kohn documents reveals that there is no evidence to support that notion. Those who are served by such an argument are those who benefit from the status quo, not subordinate groups. Psychological perspectives also reinforce connections between competition and inequality. The psychological motivation to compete, Kohn suggests, comes from low self-esteem, creating the need to better others. Among social groups such "bettering" reinforces oppression. Competition inhibits security and creates anxiety which, among social groups, catalyzes stereotyping and discrimination.

It is indeed true that when there isn't enough to go around, or there is the *perception* that there isn't enough for everyone, people who engage in aggressive, competitive behaviors often seem to have the advantage. Another glance at schools, however, demonstrates that the scarce resources that are being competed for by students are largely artificial, created by teachers or school structures. When a teacher announces that the first child who reads ten books will receive a sticker, the *teacher* has created the situation of scarcity. The teacher might just as well give every child who completes ten books a sticker, or might structure book reading as a more cooperative, communal activity, encouraging reading partners, shared book reports, and other such practices. In reality, there is no need for a shortage of praise or success within any classroom, other than the creation of that condition by the teacher or the broader school system (often a function of the "broader" function of schooling as a sorting mechanism). If our schools were structured differently and teachers prepared with a different vision, all students could be successful, all could learn, and all could "win." Like the Peace Corps poster which asked, "Is this glass of water half empty or half full?" we come to realize that the way in which we frame situations has a critical effect on the solutions which we are able to consider. Although there are, in the world, situations of actual scarcity, these too can be seen either as calling for competition or as demanding sophisticated problem solving, negotiation, and compromise.

Competition is motivating.

Many teachers encourage competition in the hope that students will be motivated to work hard and do well. In actuality, competition is often *not* motivating to the majority of students. According to Johnson and Johnson (1975), competition is only motivating when three conditions are met; one of these conditions is that all students perceive themselves as having an equal chance of winning. In most classrooms, of course, this is patently untrue. Students come to school with vastly different backgrounds and preparation, and both students and teacher are generally aware of who will win long before the competition begins. Thus, although several students in the class may be spurred on to do more or to work harder, the majority of students will not be so motivated. Secondly, competition is a cultural value which is not held in high esteem by many groups. Cross-cultural studies have revealed incidences in which Hawaiian and Native American children have rejected group contingencies and reward structures which would place one student above another or would embarrass any of the participants (Gallimore and Howard, 1968; Kohn, 1986). Thus children of color may *not* be motivated by competition, further increasing their alienation from the majority culture. When students are engaged in learning which they find personally meaningful and rewarding, they require neither external rewards nor competitive prizes in order to pursue these activities. In fact, competition is often used as a way of motivating students to do things that they do *not* want to do or find boring or distasteful. The need for competition to motivate students to learn should be cause for the serious reexamination of the nature and specific content of the curriculum and the work required.

All the world loves a winner.

In fact, competition takes its toll on both the winners and the losers. The damage to losers is often far more obvious; the child last chosen for the team, the child first eliminated in the spelling bee, and the child who has no stars on his or her star chart are often ostracized, devalued, and isolated from the other students. Students who consistently lose are rarely motivated to continue to try, but often remove themselves from the competition entirely, deciding that sports, or school, or music, or whatever, are simply not for them.

But "winners" are also damaged by competitive structures. Many children who do well in school are isolated from their peers, labeled as "eggheads" or "brains," and often feel they must choose between peer group acceptance and academic achievement. The extent to which girls and women often "fear success" and self-limit their own achievement in order to avoid this social sanction has been well documented.[2] For many students of color, as Fordham's chapter in this book shows, "winning" at the cost of solidarity with one's classmates is also particularly damaging to interpersonal relationships. Within many native cultures, calling attention to oneself is considered extremely poor form, and students will often go out of their way not to draw this kind of individual attention to themselves (Kohn, 1986).

Competition builds camaraderie and friendships.

Rather than drawing people closer together, competition usually serves to push people away from one another. Although members of the same team may feel liking and warmth for other team members, this feeling is engendered only by a process of disassociation from and dehumanization of the opponent or the competitors. It is difficult to get close to people with whom you are about to compete; it is easier to feel good about winning if one ignores the feeling and human qualities of one's opponents.

Although schools are not the only sources of socialization and political inculcation, it is at least partly within the competitive environment of schools that people learn to be oppressors, others to be oppressed. Men learn to oppress women, Whites to oppress people of color, the able-bodied to oppress the disabled, and the majority culture to oppress minority groups. Consider, for example, the game of musical chairs, in which there are more people than chairs, and any one who doesn't have a chair when the music stops is out of the game. In playing this game, children typically push and shove one another, often insisting "I was here first" and doing whatever is necessary to remain in the game. Children who decide not to push or shove or who are unable to do so adequately are out of the game. There is no impetus for students to brainstorm alternative solutions to the chair "scarcity," such as sharing chairs, getting more chairs, and so on. Children who are smaller, weaker, or not clear on the instructions are eliminated immediately, thereby being denied not only participation but the chance to "learn the game" as well.

In playing musical chairs, children are systematically taught (by the game) that it is all right for some people to "get" while others don't, and that it is "fair" to structure situations which result in vastly inequitable outcomes. Because such games are generally organized and managed by adults, who are assumed to be smarter and to "know better" than children, these messages have social sanction and the stamp of authority and authenticity. This teaching process is recreated millions of times throughout our educational histories, and is directly tied to the maintenance of many related forms of oppression, such as racism, sexism, and ageism.

Competition encourages people to survey other people's differences for potential weak spots of vulnerability—How can I maximize the opponent's weakness in order to win? From our competitive interactions with people whom we perceive as "different" from us, we learn to ascribe winner or loser status based on certain perceived overt characteristics, such as boys are better at math, girls have neater handwriting, little kids aren't as capable as big kids, older people are feeble and incapable. In physical competitions, girls are often scorned for their "inferior" muscle strength (or isolated if they violate stereotypes and *are* strong), and people who accomplish the same task differently are not likely to be valued unless their strategy leads to victory, generally narrowly defined and determined by speed rather than outcome or product. Thus, the race is often to the swift rather than to the artistic, the dramatic, the creative, or the innovative. This framework clearly interferes with celebrating individual variation or recognizing areas of commonality and shared goals.

The interpersonal outcomes of competition—rivalry, envy, and contempt—all encourage blaming the loser and justifying their "deserved" fate. Socially this dynamic plays itself out when dominant groups blame subordinate ones for their problems rather than examining the structure of inequality. Finally, competition mitigates against collective action for change. Kohn aptly notes that people don't embrace collaborative action when they're in a race.

The typical classroom is framed by competition, marked by struggle between students (and often between teacher and students), and riddled by indicators of comparative achievement and worth. Star charts on the wall announce who has been successful at learning multiplication tables, only children with "neat" handwriting have their papers posted for display, the class-three reading groups are homogeneously composed (with all students aware of which is the "low" group), and the teacher cajoles good behavior by saying "I like the way Noreen is doing her work" and by choosing the "quietest table" to go to lunch first. As described above, this competitive orientation leads to isolation and alienation.

But there are alternatives. Both the reward structure of the classroom and the content of the curriculum can be altered so that students see each other as sources of help and support, and learn about solidarity, ally building, and the tremendous power of combined effort and strength.

Cooperative learning can be used as a strategy for achieving social equity and justice in classrooms and for helping students understand how such a model can be applied in broader, societal contexts as well. Cooperative structures create the conditions for reversing inequality, producing egalitarian social structures and caring relationships where diverse people can work together toward common goals. Students and teachers need opportunities to reflect on these connections.

Cooperative Learning and the Multicultural Classroom

Cooperative learning is a pedagogical approach in which a teacher structures learning so that heterogeneous groups of students work together to achieve a shared learning goal. Each student is responsible not only for her or his learning, but for other group members' learning as well. The key to cooperative learning is positive interdependence and individual accountability. While working together toward a group goal each group member knows that she or he is individually responsible for the material and that her or his contribution will be essential for the group to complete its task. In the process students learn that "all of us are smarter than any one of us" (Johnson, Johnson, and Holubec, 1986; Kagan, 1988; Slavin, 1983).

The principles implicit in cooperative learning, as we define it, are similar to those needed for an effective multicultural classroom.

Cooperatively-structured learning is democratic.

All students are active group participants and have equal access to learning opportunities and to resources. Within a cooperative classroom, democracy is not something which is studied about, but something which is lived. Activities are utilized to encourage and provide skills to the tentative student. Teacher time and educational resources are provided equitably to all students regardless of ability, gender, or race. For example groups are heterogeneous and mixed by ability, race, or gender. The teacher structures learning carefully so each student in a group has an important task. Students are taught skills to help others who are having difficulty so that all can succeed.

Students in cooperatively structured learning activities
take responsibility for both themselves and others.

An ethic of care pervades their group as students pay sensitive attention to each other. They give help when asked for it, and are generous with encouragement and support. Cooperative classrooms create communities of caring in which students see themselves as having specific responsibilities to one another regardless of race, age, class, gender, or disability. Teachers not only model this kind of caring behavior, but they encourage students to help one another in many contexts.

For example, an English-speaking student might be paired with an ESL (English as a second language) student to work together on an open-ended story. The English-speaking student would be responsible for helping the ESL student with vocabulary work and comprehension questions relating to the passage. The ESL student would be responsible for teaching some vocabulary to his or her partner. If academically appropriate, both would work together to develop a conclusion to the story, with each contributing definable ideas or segments.

Heterogeneity and diversity are valued
in cooperatively structured learning activities.

In cooperative classrooms heterogeneity and diversity are not simply tolerated, they are nourished and valued. Classroom teachers go to great lengths to ensure that all students are aware of the rich diversity in the classroom, and the teacher is careful to organize instruction and activities in such a way that children who are not from the majority culture are not made to feel like "outsiders." Children from different family structures or ethnic backgrounds, those who celebrate different religious holidays, and those who have unique skills are all encouraged to share these with the group. When conflict around difference emerges in their groups, students learn skills to manage them nonviolently and attempt to find a win/win resolution.

For example, in a jigsawed cooperative lesson (Aronson, 1978) in which students were investigating the meaning and origin of various holidays, those commemorating White persons, European traditions, or Christian holy days would not be the focus of the lesson. Those commemorating people of color, African and Asian traditions, and Jewish and other religious holy days would be equally included. Or, for example, in a cooperative lesson on families and the variety of family forms, information about a Black student's experience in an extended family would enrich the understanding of the group and better enable them to complete their task.

In addition to the common principles shared by cooperative learning and multicultural education, research supports the premise that working in cooperative groups fosters more positive student interaction among diverse students. Most of this research has focused on race. It has been found that all students, particularly minority students, learn more than in traditional classrooms, and that liking of school and liking of others of different racial backgrounds increase (Johnson, Johnson, and Maruyama, 1983; Miller and Brewer, 1984; Sharan, 1984; Slavin, 1983). Slavin (1982) found that student friendship choices outside of their own ethnic groups increased after involvement in cooperative learning activities. The structure of cooperative learning itself is conducive to positive intergroup relations. When the *Brown vs. Board of*

Education school desegregation case was being decided, social scientists submitted a statement that emphasized that positive intergroup relations would arise from school desegregation if, and only if, students were involved in cooperative, equal-status interaction structured by the schools (Johnson, Johnson, and Maruyama, 1983). Cooperative learning embodies many of these conditions.

Too often educators have assumed that interracial contact, in and of itself, will create positive interracial attitudes and behavior. This is not the case. Johnson, Johnson, and Maruyama, (1983, p. 37) put this well:

> When majority and minority students are placed in the same classroom, they carry with them prejudices and stereotypes prevalent in our society. There is considerable evidence the negative attitudes exist among heterogeneous students prior to their interacting. When heterogeneous students are placed in the same school and classroom these negative attitudes may become more extreme, or positive attitudes may develop, depending on how instruction is organized . . . The key is how interaction is structured. There are ways of structuring interaction between majority and minority students so that constructive and supportive peer relationships result, or so that destructive and rejecting peer relationships result.

Cooperative learning experiences, compared with competitive and individualistic experiences, result in greater interpersonal attraction because of students' sense that others are encouraging and supporting their efforts to achieve (Johnson, Johnson, and Maruyama, 1983). Constructive relations among diverse students necessitate students having the ability to take the perspective of others, recognizing that there are multiple ways of perceiving and understanding an event or situation. Being able to see another perspective challenges rigid stereotypes and contributes to an appreciation of individual differences. The higher self-esteem produced by cooperative learning is also associated with decreases in prejudice (Johnson, Johnson, and Maruyama, 1983).

Allport (1954) has postulated that Whites have mixed feelings about multiracial situations and accept desegregated situations best when they don't have to initiate interpersonal contact. With cooperative learning, students don't have to take that first, and, for some, difficult step to initiate contact with students of other races. The teacher provides the structure and format through cooperative learning groups. Perceptions of similarity between oneself and others also is an important determinant of friendships. When educators structure cooperative groups, dissimilar students gain a new basis of perceived similarity—their common, assigned group identity (Slavin, 1983).

Furthermore, Kagan (1988) has gone on to suggest that there are cultural differences among students in their valuing of cooperation and competition. Black and Mexican American students favor cooperative situations, whereas Anglo students favor competitive ones. Aronson (1978) found, in evaluating a cooperative learning program in the Austin, Texas, public schools, that Black and Mexican American students learned much more in jigsawed, cooperative classrooms than in competitively structured ones. They liked school more than students of similar racial backgrounds in traditional classes (Slavin, 1982). In explaining these and similar findings, Kagan (1980) writes the following:

> It appears quite likely that traditional classrooms are systematically biased against certain minority and low-income groups who are more cooperative in their social orientation . . . The structure of [traditional] classrooms may well fit the motivational structure of majority children far better than of minority and low-income children . . . Traditional classrooms may be culturally irrelevant for children with other than mainstream competitive values; if so it is no wonder that achievement of minority and low-income students falls below that of majority children in traditional classrooms. (p. 210)

Given the possibility of such structural bias, it is critical that multicultural classrooms provide opportunities for learning through cooperation.

Although less research has been done on the effects of cooperative learning on gender relationships and the learning of female and male students, we speculate that many of the points discussed above regarding race will prove to be applicable to gender as well. Just as cooperative learning groups promote cross-racial cooperation, an investigation of students using Sharan's group investigation technique found increases in cross-sexual cooperative behaviors after completing the task (Raviv, 1982). Some studies have suggested that just as cooperative learning takes the pressure off students to initiate cross-racial interaction by doing it for them, cooperative groups also enable females and males to name cross-sex classmates as "friends" and increase their willingness to work with each other by removing the romantic implications of doing so (Best, 1983).

Although cooperative learning can provide a significant impetus to improving cross-sex interactions, patterns of inequality still persist and must be addressed in order for cooperative learning to function to address sex inequalities. Research by Webb (1984), for example, demonstrated that achievement and interaction results for cooperative learning groups depended on the ratio of females to males in the group. In groups with two females and two males, the achievement of females and males was nearly identical, but in majority-female groups and majority-male groups, the males showed higher achievement than the females. In both instances (of unequal numbers of males and females), more attention was focused on males (they were asked for help more frequently and were responded to more often), whereas the females' attempts to receive help were often ignored. Related research by Lockheed and Harris (1984) confirms the finding that simply placing students in cooperative learning groups is not sufficient to overcome other deeply entrenched patterns of social inequality among males and females.

Just as Kagan found differences in how students from various racial and cultural groups value competition and cooperation, there is evidence to suggest that girls generally express greater preference for cooperative learning than do boys at all grade levels (Owens, 1980, 1982). Applying Kagan's argument about race to the gender issue, it can be argued that the predominance of competitively structured learning in American schools may be a form of structural bias that impedes not only the learning of minority-group members, but also the learning of female students. More research on cooperative learning and gender is sorely needed if we are to be effective in removing all forms of inequality from our teaching and our classrooms.

How Cooperative Learning Is Implemented:
Decisions for Empowerment

Cooperative learning comes in many forms. The choices educators make about *how* to implement cooperative learning will determine its potential as an empowering pedagogy. Such decisions are not merely educational, but can detract from, or contribute to, the creation of multicultural schools and society. Our vision of a cooperative, multicultural classroom is democratic, one in which students take responsibility for themselves and others, and one in which heterogeneity and diversity are highly valued. Our vision is that a multicultural society would be marked by the same qualities. The following challenges may help educators consider if the forms of cooperative learning they employ contribute to a multicultural present and future.

Consistent competition or intragroup cooperation
with intergroup competition?

In "team"-oriented cooperative learning approaches, students teach
each other in heterogeneous teams and then compete with members of
other teams to earn points for their team based, for example, on their
success in tournaments or on quizzes.[3] Team identity is used to encourage individual accountability, and the possibility of winning is used to
motivate effort. In cooperative classrooms where intergroup competition is *not* used, student cooperative groups are often encouraged to
help other groups, thereby fostering a feeling of total classroom cooperation (Johnson and Johnson, 1975, 1986; Johnson, Johnson, and Holubek,
1986). Intergroup competition in school legitimizes competition in society. To many students, the word *team* connotes athletic competition, and
therefore reinforces the idea that they are cooperating in *order* to overcome another group. Kohn's (1986) research suggests that intragroup
cooperation in the context of intergroup competition fosters negative
views of other groups and does not help develop acceptance within
one's own group. The use of classroom teams, even when these are heterogeneous, still reinforces a "we-they" mentality; students' views of
other groups as threats are easily transferred to other ethnic or racial
groups or to any group different from their own.

Do we want to teach students that there are intrinsic values to cooperation, or to view it as simply another, better, way to get ahead of other
people? Which configuration of classroom cooperation will contribute
best to creating multicultural classrooms and societies with an underlying ethic of care and inclusion?

Extrinsic or intrinsic rewards
to encourage cooperation?

Although cooperative learning educators agree that group goals are
essential, the forms of those group goals vary. Some educators motivate
students with extrinsic rewards such as team scores, certificates, privileges such as stickers, snacks in the room, or extra credit (Kagan, 1980;
Slavin, 1988, 1987); students help others learn and ask for help because
they want their team to win. Other educators believe that students can
be motivated by the equally powerful concern for the learning of all
group members. In classrooms where intrinsic motivation is the goal,
teachers discuss with students the rationale for helping everyone learn
and the values of responsibility for self and others, sharing, and caring.
After this kind of positive cooperative experience and such dialogues
about cooperation and mutual empowerment, students care more for

each other and each other's learning and *choose* to be cooperative in a variety of circumstances (Aronson, 1978; Lickona, 1980; Solomon et al., in press).

We can think ahead to when students will have to negotiate many competitive social situations and institutions in which groups are often set up against each other, difference is used as a sorting mechanism, and there are no extrinsic rewards for cooperating. Will these students-become-citizens adapt to competitive situations, especially where rewards are money and power, or call upon the knowledge, values, and experiences from a cooperative educational experience and pose cooperative alternatives that will benefit a variety of diverse people? Our choices about extrinsic or intrinsic motivation in the cooperative learning classroom may affect the answer.

Teaching collaborative skills in the process
of cooperative learning?

Collaborative skills include such social skills as listening, encouraging others, giving constructive feedback, and checking for understanding (Dishon and O'Leary, 1984; Johnson, Johnson, and Holubek, 1986). If we are concerned about student empowerment in the context of a multiracial classroom, we can ask: If the primary goal of using cooperative learning is increased academic achievement, is teaching skills necessary to work effectively in groups equally important? In the latter case, do we teach social skills so students can function more effectively in their learning groups or to also foster internalization of these skills for use in *all* aspects of their lives?

Tightly structured, cooperative groups focused on knowledge and skill acquisition in teacher-directed classrooms can be effective in raising academic achievement even without teaching social skills (Slavin, 1986). However, academic achievement and increased social skills can and should go hand in hand. Students can learn how to "process" their group, that is, to analyze its functioning, apart from evaluating the task completion. They can discuss, for example, what contributed to or detracted from the smooth working of the group, and what they might do differently next time, reflection that can also increase academic achievement (Johnson and Johnson, 1986; Johnson, Johnson, and Holubek, 1986; Yager et al., 1986).

Educators can also ask students to apply the social skills taught in cooperative groups to other areas of their lives—for example, a conflict between boys and girls over playground space and equipment at recess or a disagreement among groups of racially different students over the themes or music for a dance. In addition to learning social skills, students can gain consciousness of group dynamics and the ability and responsibility for making cooperation work. When students are given opportunities to understand and practice applying cooperative skills beyond the classroom, they can understand that cooperation is a choice and that they have the skills to make that choice a reality.

Who controls the cooperative learning?

Cooperative learning can become a powerful model of empowerment only if students and teachers are able to redefine their roles in the decision-making process, allowing for increasing levels of student *and* teacher autonomy and independence. In some instances, cooperative learning is used as a management tool through tightly structured activities with recognition and rewards for acceptable behavior, sometimes in the context of interteam competition (Kagan, 1980) with the teacher maintaining authority and control. Alternatively, educators can decide to use cooperative learning to help students manage *their own* behavior by teaching students skills to use throughout the year. For example, when girls and boys can't get to work because they're fighting over group roles, a teacher can take responsibility for dealing with that situation. Or, with some practice in the skills of listening, criticizing ideas and not people, and conflict resolution, a teacher can first give students the responsibility for working it out (Aronson, 1978; Johnson, Johnson, and Holubek, 1986; Moorman and Dishon, 1983; Solomon et al., in press). These decisions too have implications for the creation of multicultural environments. If students learn to do as they are told solely because an authority figure expects it, they will be less inclined to challenge and change inequality in society. If they are learning, however, that they can become capable and responsible for cooperatively solving difficult problems affecting their lives, they will know from experience that by sharing power and working together people can make changes.

Cooperative learning as an "activity"
or as a central organizing value in the classroom?

In order for cooperative learning to be fully empowering, teachers need to be encouraged to look at all aspects of their classrooms, not to simply implement "a" cooperative lesson during a portion of the day. It makes little sense to attempt to instill in students the value of cooperation during a specific activity and then to discourage them from talking or helping each other during the rest of the school day. Star charts on the wall, competitive behavior management systems which determine the "row of the week" or the "student of the day," and competitive grading systems are all incompatible with classrooms which truly foster interpersonal communication, creative conflict resolution, and the valuing of differences. Teachers and students should be urged to think carefully about all aspects of their school program—grading, games, seating arrangements, and so on—in order to implement the most comprehensive and consistent approach to forming classroom communities of cooperation.

One impediment to viewing cooperation as a broad-based principle rather than as a technique or a management strategy stems, in part, from the ways in which cooperative learning has been packaged and "sold." When cooperative learning is taught as some expert's "seven-step model" to be followed precisely, then teachers are not encouraged to think about how the model fits in with the rest of what they do. Unfortunately and ironically, cooperative learning has not been immune from entrepreneurial marketing and dissemination. In order for cooperative learning to become fully empowering, teachers must be encouraged to make the principles and practices of cooperation their own, not simply to "buy into" an existing, well-structured, and documented method taught by outside experts.

All of the above considerations must be part of a systematic implementation of cooperative learning. Educators who are thoughtful about their goals and intentions in implementing cooperative learning will be better able to make rational decisions about how their teaching process can facilitate these goals.

Cooperative Learning:
A Path to Consciousness and Change

We have reviewed how cooperative learning as a pedagogy encourages student learning, efficacy, and interpersonal liking, and how specific forms of cooperative learning are more conducive than others to developing awareness and skills for enhancing multiculturalism and student empowerment. Yet more than commitment to process is necessary. It is also necessary to teach content that helps students develop a critical consciousness about the basis of inequality in school and society and the options for change. Simply teaching a lesson cooperatively does not ensure its value; in addition to thinking about *how* we teach, we must pay careful attention to *what* we teach. Teachers may create wonderful cooperatively structured learning experiences in their classrooms, but at the same time they may be working in a school that institutionalizes competition—for example, one that employs a rigid tracking system. As Oakes (1986) has documented, the tracking itself reinforces inequality and runs counter to hopes for true multicultural education. Similarly, although females and males, students of color and Whites may be working well in heterogeneous cooperative groups in the classrooms, unless they are helped to think about how cultural and institutional racism and sexism affect their lives—for example, in their play patterns at recess and friendship choices in general—they'll be less able to understand and change the inequality that will continue to affect them beyond the classroom.

When lessons are devoted to helping students learn about and counteract classroom and societal oppression *and* the lesson is taught cooperatively, the power of cooperative learning is significantly enhanced. Educators can enable students to develop the consciousness to identify the competition and inequality they see, analyze it for what it is, and propose cooperative, fair alternatives to it (Schniedewind and Davidson, 1983, 1987). Teachers can enable students to make connections between the effects of competition and cooperation and the specific forms of inequality on themselves, their classrooms, their community, the nation, and the world. If students are asked to think and talk about the difference in their relationships with others in competitive and cooperative classrooms, they can then become conscious that similar, traditionally competitive situations and institutions can be structured cooperatively with comparable results in social relationships. Students might be asked to consider, for example, why girls express a greater preference for cooperation than boys, and boys greater preference for competition, and what the implications of this are for their interaction and collaboration (Owens, 1980, 1982). They can come to envision, for example, cooperative alternatives in boy-girl rivalry, competitive sports, the organization of work, and the arms race. Understanding the elements of competition and cooperation in many situations provides them the consciousness necessary to make choices about the desirability of competition or cooperation from personal to global realms. Similarly, when students have learned to analyze their textbooks and other media for race, class, age, and sex bias, as both Cortés and Pang in this book suggest, they can then be helped to apply those awarenesses to broader areas of their culture from the media to leadership patterns in institutions.

Attention to building critical consciousness can address the effects of real or perceived inequality among students on their expectations of others, an issue closely related to stereotyping. When students perceive others as unequal because of race, for example, or see that some students have less well developed academic skills, stereotyped views of lower status students can be reinforced. Since equality of status within contact situations has been considered a factor in improving interracial or intergroup attitudes, some educators have devised interventions to deal with this situation. For example, Cohen (1986) trains low-status students in high-prestige skills which they, in turn, can teach their high-status peers. An alternative to such teacher-directed alterations of situations of inequality is to educate students about the *reasons* for the inequality, whether perceived or real, and assist them in contributing to changing that. Using cooperative learning, students can learn about the effects of racism, class bias, and sexism on their lives and educational opportunities. White students can learn how their own stereotypes might play into a situation of perceived inequality. All students can learn how subtle racism in some books and curriculum materials can enhance the learning of White students and detract from that of students of color. Rather than blame the victim, students can come to see the source of inequality (Schniedewind and Davidson, 1983, 1987). Such awareness can diminish stereotyping by students in heterogeneous cooperative groups, motivate privileged students to *want* to help their peers, and provide the consciousness for all students to begin to change inequality.

Practically, how do we raise such awareness? Educators can modify what they already do. One teacher typically assigned an open-ended project in which each student researched and presented information on a famous New Yorker. Another year that teacher adapted that assignment to raise awareness about cooperation and competition, the dynamics of discrimination, and alternatives for change. Students now work in cooperative groups of three. The class must make sure there is an equal distribution of women and men and people of diverse racial groups chosen to research. In doing their research, students are assigned such questions as the following: (1) How did this person's race, class, or sex affect his or her opportunities in his or her life? (2) What types of discrimination, if any, did this person face? How did he or she overcome it? (3) How did she or he work to change injustice toward groups of people, whether her or his own social group or another? (4) In what way did he or she cooperate with others to help create a better world? With this kind of research focus, followed by whole-class discussions comparing findings, students learn the assigned subject matter content. At the same time they reflect on the way broader social factors affect people, as well as consider options for change. Final discussion questions such as, What can we fifth graders do now to carry on the efforts of these people we studied to create a more fair, peaceful world? can stimulate action projects by students.

Because cooperative learning has been promoted because of its utility for *any* and all subject matter, some teachers use cooperative learning to teach the standard curriculum, without working to achieve consistency between the process of cooperation and the *content* of what is being studied. Because the typical curriculum assumes competitive ideas, institutions, and relationships as normative, both students and teachers are denied the opportunity to make important connections. For example, students have studied cooperatively to learn information about wars without ever being asked to consider their inevitability, justness, or alternatives to them. Students have been assigned a cooperatively structured unit on advertising with the goal of teaching them advertising techniques. The competitive, sexist, often exploitive, underpinnings of much advertising were never examined.[4]

Other teachers have developed critical consciousness by reflecting on the standard curriculum, adapting it, and adding supplemental materials; they have used cooperatively structured materials that foster critical thinking *about* competition and cooperation. For example, students solve math word problems that have content about cooperation. Teachers select stories or novels in which it is possible to examine the effects of competition or cooperation on characters; students then discuss the effect of those dynamics. An ecology unit culminates in a booklet about cooperative ecological projects for the community. Historical events are examined for the degree to which competition or cooperation was at work and how that affected people's lives. In addition, students take action to develop cooperative alternatives in their families, communities, the nation, and the world. From making a cooperative community mural, to running a student self-managed enterprise in school, to joining a pairing project with a group in the Third World working for social justice, students can collaboratively take action for change (Schniedewind and Davidson, 1987). Similarly, as students learn more about race, class, sex, and age bias and how it has affected them and others, they also come to see that they can make changes. They can work together to make calendars that celebrate holidays of various religions and cultures and distribute them in school; analyze their school for Title IX compliance and suggest changes; collaboratively write stories that reflect equality and read them to younger students; or work collectively to contribute to the solution to a community problem (Schniedewind and Davidson, 1983). Through such activities students can feel that they too are makers of history.

Conclusion

The process of empowerment involves critical reflection on the nature of oppression; a vision of alternative models of interaction, decision making, and power; and the skills necessary to implement this vision. Cooperative learning is a pedagogy that provides personal power and group support. Educators can build into academic content and ongoing class discussion a critical awareness of the effects of competition and inequality on our lives and ideas for their alternatives—cooperation and multiculturalism. From such pedagogy and content, students then have the skills and consciousness necessary to create changes that empower them personally and that can catalyze social change. This process, which could serve as a focus of schooling, is reflected in the model shown in Figure 7.1 (Bell and Schniedewind, 1987). The challenge before us is clear; with vision, courage, and support and encouragement from others, teachers interested in transforming schools and society into equitable and empowering institutions can begin that task now.

FIGURE 7.1

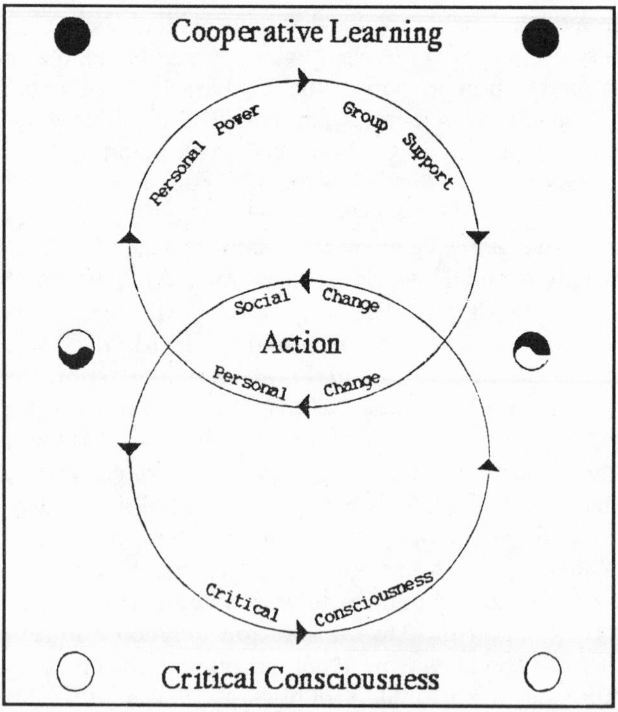

Cooperative Learning

Personal Power   Group Support

Social Change
Action
Personal Change

Critical Consciousness

Critical Consciousness

Chapter 8

Teaching Children About Social Issues: Kidpower

——————————————— *Valerie Ooka Pang*

Our most valuable natural resource is our children. The stability of the United States lies in the deliberate development of an active and participatory citizenry. Children can be empowered to use their minds, enthusiasm, creativity, and skills to contribute to their communities.

Empowerment of children has been defined as a four-part process: children should become confident in their abilities "to make a difference" in society, become confident in making sound decisions, become secure in their judgments, and believe in their interconnectedness with others (Hahn, 1984). Opportunities to use those skills occur every day. Children have been instrumental in placing animals on the endangered species list. They have also lobbied for new streetlights at busy intersections. The lives of many Americans have been affected by the efforts of younger Americans. Citizenship does not consist solely of voting rights of adult citizens; children can learn about and develop their capability to make changes. Schools can provide opportunities for them to exercise their knowledge and skills right now and not in some distant future. This chapter will discuss how we can empower our younger citizens to examine their environment for justice and for stereotypic misconceptions, and to challenge those images they find objectionable.

How Children Learn About Others

In the larger society, prejudice against racial and ethnic minority groups is decreasing gradually but is still strong. Harris and associates (1978)

I would like to thank the following individuals for their contributions to the development of this manuscript: Mako Nakagawa, Christine Sleeter, Margie Kitano, Karen Greenstreet, and Kay Sagmiller.

179

found that 60 percent of Whites sampled indicated that they would be apprehensive if their friends or relatives were to marry a Black and 79 percent would be worried if their children dated a Black. Another poll taken in 1978, replicating a 1968 poll, found improved White attitudes but growing Black disillusionment because of White refusals to make real changes. In 1968, only 60 percent of Whites had believed Blacks should be able to live wherever they want; by 1978, 90 percent of Whites believed it. But Whites saw things differently from Blacks. The percentage of Whites who believed Blacks miss out on jobs because of racial discrimination fell from 21 to 17, but the percentage of Blacks believing this rose from 39 to 47. When Blacks were asked whether most White people in their town wanted to see Blacks get a better break, the percentage of those agreeing dropped from 29 to 25; the percentage saying Whites didn't care rose from 33 to 44 (Herbers, 1978). Although there seems to be some movement away from overt discrimination, prejudice is still strong. The continued existence of prejudice is an important problem in a democracy because lack of mutual respect among citizens ultimately contributes to the low economic and political status of many minorities (Gutmann, 1987).

Children, like any other Americans, often hold misconceptions about those who are different from themselves which they have learned from their environment (Goodman, 1964). Children are aware of physical and cultural differences as early as three years of age, and by the age of four, have been found to hold attitudes about color differences (Crooks, 1970; Derman-Sparks, Higa, and Sparks, 1980; Porter, 1971). This means that before children enter school, they have learned how to group people on the basis of physical or cultural variation, and have learned societal beliefs associated with those groupings.

Children are curious about what they see, and ask questions or absorb information and ideas from a wide range of individuals, such as siblings, parents, friends, grandparents, teachers, and neighbors. For example, Derman-Sparks, Higa, and Sparks (1980) found children to ask questions about color, being puzzled by why Black people with different skin tones are all considered Black, or why Asian Americans are labeled "yellow" when their own skin color is closer to tan.

Another way children learn prejudice is through modeling. Swadener (1988) described the free play conversation of young students after a field trip to the fire station. One boy announced that he was to be the fire chief. A young girl wanted to be the "fire chief girl" but said, "I can't be the fire chief, cause girls can't be firefighters—I don't see any at the Fire Stations!" (p. 22). Although the teachers had spent a large amount of time on gender roles, the power of real-life experiences was not to be underestimated. The study also indicated that during free-play times gender roles prevailed. Modeling and personal experience are strong forces in the lives of children.

Another strong force is language, which is one of the most insidious ways in which stereotypic ideas are transmitted. Language, as the vehicle of culture, not only transfers information, but also communicates attitudes. Stereotypic language, a powerful mechanism in society, can subtly incorporate distortions. For example, using the ambiguous phrase "Don't be an Indian giver" gives children two strong messages. First, the speaker is telling children not to give something to someone and then to take it back. Second, the speaker is suggesting that Native Americans are not to be trusted. Originally the phrase described how the U.S. government made treaties with the Native Americans and then broke them. Another example of a commonly used expression which teaches bias is "She throws like a girl." Since the expression is common, it may not be questioned. But again the message is damaging. The speaker is saying girls throw differently from boys and is implying that girls cannot throw the ball as effectively as boys.

Education can help children unlearn stereotypes and negative attitudes. Swadener (1988) examined two programs in early childhood day care centers where human diversity was discussed throughout the school year. These discussions had themes of family diversity, emotions, differences in appearance, career options, roles, and anatomical differences. The activities generally did not deal directly with racial, ethnic, or cultural differences. Teachers encouraged children to respect and listen to other viewpoints. Interviews and weekly observations for a nine-month period found that the children were more accepting of others and formed friendships with a variety of peers at the end of the program. The children accepted their own diversity and modeled positive interactions among themselves.

Children learn about others from their environment. They learn about their own identity and how others are identified in society. Daily, children determine what beliefs and attitudes are acceptable to those around them. Modeled attitudes are often assimilated into the children's value systems. In order to illustrate what kinds of beliefs and stereotypes may exist in schools and in the minds of some children, I have gathered recent samples by implementing culturally sensitive activities with students from a wide range of grade levels and by observing in various elementary classrooms. These examples point to the necessity for teachers to provide many instances of positive models of women, minority groups, and elder Americans.

Examples of Stereotypes in the Curriculum

Last school year in a kindergarten class where one of the district student learning objectives was that children should learn nursery rhymes, a teacher introduced an activity which presented strong gender role messages. One of the poems the children studied was "Peter, Peter, Pumpkin Eater." Initially the teacher taught the students the poem; they then recited it from memory. Following this activity, the students cut two identical pumpkin shapes out of orange construction paper. They stapled the pumpkins together at the stem and pasted a copy of the rhyme inside the pumpkin. The teacher then told the students to cut out a magazine picture of a woman and glue it inside the pumpkin next to the poem. Though the students enjoyed this activity and learned the poem, some of them could have come away with the belief that women are dependent upon men and should be cared for by them. Though the teacher did institute a short discussion about her own independence from her husband and that she herself was not limited to life bounded by a "pumpkin," the students did not seem to hear that part of the lesson. She did not engage the children in dialogue about gender roles, and the youngsters did not initiate any exchange. Instead, they busily constructed the art portion of the activity. The teacher did not seem to understand the importance of the implicit values in the lesson.

In 1985, a student brought home a worksheet with these directions: "Color how many indians [sic] the number says." On the left-hand side there were numerals and on the right-hand side pictures of identical children who wore headbands and feathers. The student had colored the specified number of individuals. This math worksheet was offensive for several reasons. Though the illustrations did not depict this racial group accurately, the most blatant and prejudicial message was the use of Native Americans as objects to be counted. In comparison, would a teacher ask students to color in the number of French persons? Treating a group of people as things demonstrates a basic lack of respect for that group. A long-range effect may be that this depiction prepares children eventually to try to control or even eliminate that group.

The second unfortunate message of the worksheet was that Native Americans are a homogeneous population. Each of the children pictured had the same physical features and feathered headbands. This image conflicts with the fact that Native Americans are and always have been a diverse population. Some may have brown hair and eyes and others may have red hair and hazel eyes. Some have dark skin and others have light skin tones. The feather and headband in the picture also reflect a lack of knowledge about the variety of customs and ceremonial dress of many native groups. There are Native Americans, like those from the Pacific Northwest, who do not wear featured headbands; they wear other types of clothing, such as specially woven blankets and intricately carved masks. Many Americans do not realize that the images provided in books usually represent Indians who lived on the Plains, who were not like all other groups. When children are presented with these images from a variety of sources, they assimilate them into their own belief systems, accepting them as truth.

This is not an isolated example. Native Americans are often depicted in classrooms as objects of the past. A highly respected basal reading program used the following key pictures to teach vowels: *a* for apple, *e* for elephant, *o* for octopus, *u* for umbrella, and *i* for Indian. Again, this exemplifies the use of Native Americans as objects, not as respected Americans. Schools often use Native Americans as mascots for athletic teams; for example, one may see a football game in which the wildcats from one school play against the Redmen from another, their football helmets sporting "Native American" profiles.

The pumpkin project, math worksheet, and mascot examples portray stereotypes that have become part of American culture and often go unquestioned. These stereotypes have the underlying message that specific groups of people are second-class citizens and that it is acceptable to view them as such. When this message is repeated throughout the experiences of children, it can have a powerful impact on their understandings and ultimately on how they think and act in life.

These kinds of messages make what children might see or experience appear natural and correct. For example "Peter, Peter, Pumpkin Eater" makes it seem natural that men would control and restrict their wives. The Indian examples make it seem natural that Whites would enjoy some aspects of Indian culture as historic relics, but continue to abrogate treaties with Indians when they "stand in the way of progress". Stereotypes of other groups in the curriculum do the same thing: they prepare children to accept the social world as it exists and think of it as natural.

Examples of Ethnic and Cultural
Misunderstandings of Children

Often it is difficult to assess children's perceptions of others. Children may respond in a manner which they believe is expected of them. An indirect approach to understanding what young children are thinking is to gather their responses in routine class activities.

One example was found in a math lesson on story problems. The teacher asked each first grader to create a math problem. The problems they created varied; here are several:

1. There were 60 jet engines. People bought 30. How many were left?
2. One summer day I was so hot my mom went to the store and bought 85 popsicles. A couple of weeks later she bought 99 more. How many did she buy?
3. There were 2 Indians and 10 more came. How many were there altogether?

In the second example, "Mom" was the individual who customarily was perceived as the buyer. This demonstrates a gender bias. In that child's life, "Mom" was probably responsible for the grocery shopping. Students may be asked if Mother usually does the grocery shopping, and then they can discuss domestic roles of males and females, focusing upon shared responsibilities.

The student who wrote the third story problem viewed Native Americans as objects. The student's perception was similar to that of the teacher who gave out the coloring worksheet. This student had not come from the same classroom as the teacher, which illustrates the pervasive perception of Native Americans as objects.

In order to command a more comprehensive perception of student views of Native Americans, I asked a fifth-grade class to complete the following sentences:

1. Long ago Indians were . . .
2. Long ago Indians lived . . .
3. Today Indians are . . .
4. Today Indians live . . .
5. Words or phrases that I would use to describe Indians today are . . .

The children's responses demonstrated a romanticized view of Native Americans as people of the past who lived on the Plains. One child wrote, "Long ago Indians were people who never cut their hair and ate buffalo and fish, rabbits, corn, and berries and were probably smarter than todays indians [sic]." This same child described present-day Native Americans in this way: "[They are] probably not as smart and they don't hunt buffalo." Another child, writing about the contemporary status of Native Americans, indicated they were "smart, well nature users, very unusule [sic], they can do a lot more things than we can. They can dry their meat and berries and make houses out of grass." A third child wrote that Indians today are "people who dance and wear things around their heads with feathers coming out." Another student indicated that Indians today are "very unique and not at all like we are. They hunt different, they talk different and they also cook different. They don't cook their food all the way like chicken. They cook hamburger only part way and it would give us stomach aches but it doesn't [sic] to them."

The responses of these children were representative of the class. The children held inaccurate and idealistic perceptions. They saw Native Americans as a powerful group whose present-day lives are easier because of an abundance of food. All the students in this class of twenty-seven except one provided a narrow and stereotypic conception of Native Americans. One child did say that today Native Americans live "in houses in cities and in apartments, they don't live in teapee [sic] anymore." None of the students demonstrated knowledge of issues like poverty, political disenfranchisement, and mental health. Each student was asked to draw an illustration. The drawings were highly stereotypic, depicting individuals with headbands, buckskins, bows and arrows, streaks of paint on their faces, and living in teepees.

These examples show how primary-grade students already have strong misconceptions of others. Derman-Sparks, Higa, and Sparks (1980) found in interviews with children ranging from three to twelve years of age that they are not "color-blind." Students are aware of and curious about racial, physical, and cultural variabilities in people. They can be empowered to make careful decisions, but they must have accurate knowledge in order to do so. Unfortunately, much of the information that many students, both majority and minority, hold about ethnic minority groups, women, and elder Americans is inaccurate. The examples above show that students seem to have been socialized by their experiences to see Native Americans as romanticized objects of the past. There seems to be very little linkage with present reality. They often associate women with domestic chores. They are forming their conceptions of groups of people at early ages, and many of these conceptions will not lead them to act on behalf of rights, equality or justice.

Values of equality and justice form the basis for our democratic government. The impact of stereotypic images can have future ramifications. For example, in several states, the treaty rights of many Native American nations are currently being reviewed. In order to make intelligent decisions about such social issues, or to take action as the children did who helped place animals on the endangered species list, the citizens of today will need reliable information. This information should not be based upon stereotypic impressions from the past or incorrect images. Schools can provide students with an environment with a systemwide emphasis on democracy and citizenship. Education that is multicultural and reconstructionist (Sleeter and Grant, 1987) will empower students to keep our democracy strong.

Education That Is Democratic and Multicultural

Our education system is based on democratic values. Educational policymakers emphasize the importance of developing responsible citizens who participate in the democratic process (Goodlad, 1984; Gutmann, 1987; Sleeter and Grant, 1987). But often our educational ideals are not found throughout schooling. Oakes (1985) discovered a great degree of academic tracking occurring in schools where teachers had labeled students as low or high ability. She points out that it was disturbing because most low-track students were never moved into higher-track classes once they were labeled low track. In addition, the low-track status had devastating effects upon the self-image of students. The youngsters often lacked confidence in their abilities and so did not do well in school. Bennett's chapter in this book reports much the same thing. Americans believe that schools are based upon equity, but in reality, classroom content and structure vary from democratic to dictatorial systems. Goodlad (1984) showed that children have little decision-making power in many classrooms.

Our education system should reflect democratic values depicting the significance of equity and justice in three major areas: knowledge, clarification and reflection of attitudes, and skill development. These are summarized in Figure 8.1.

The first area is a strong knowledge base. This includes an understanding of what it means to be an American: our common values, our common history in the context of our values, our political system, and our responsibilities as United States citizens. The education system should reinforce the values of equality, freedom, justice, democracy, honesty, dignity, and pluralism in the daily activities of students. It is not enough simply to teach *about* these values; students gain the firmest knowledge of them by living them. Classrooms can model these values in their structure and processes.

For example, the practice of students sharing in the running of the classroom by taking on various jobs is one way students can see how their effort is important to the entire class. Teachers can also provide

FIGURE 8.1

Schools in a Multicultural and Democratic Society

Educational Goals

1. Active and Responsible Citizenry
2. Fulfilled Individuals

Educational Components

Knowledge Base	*Clarification and Reflection of Attitudes*	*Skill Development*
1. What does it mean to be an American? a. Common values b. U.S. Constitution c. Bill of Rights d. Popular sovereignty	1. Self-esteem—who am I? a. Self-identity b. Family, community, cultural identity c. American identity	1. Basic skills a. Reading b. Writing c. Computation
2. Comprehensive study of American history and literature using concepts like equality, freedom, justice, democracy, power, honesty, dignity, pluralism	2. Accept and respect different groups as part of democratic values	2. People skills a. Cross-cultural communication skills b. Cooperative skills
3. What are the rights and responsibilities of citizens?	3. Beliefs in a democracy a. How can I contribute in making this a strong nation? b. Knowing is not enough: What is my commitment to my community? Action is crucial. c. We are interdependent. d. Unity amidst diversity. e. Diversity enriches life.	3. Thinking skills a. Information processing b. Problem solving c. Critical thinking d. Decision making

Develop a Collective, Critical Consciousness Moving a Person to Act—
Making a Difference in Myself, Our Classroom, Our School, Family,
Community, Nation, and World

time for class meetings by encouraging all students to participate in decision-making activities. If the class desires a field trip and there are no district funds available, even students in first grade can, as a class, decide how money can be raised. Some students have chosen to have a baked foods sale, others have raised plants and sold them, and others have organized walkathons. When students are involved in the planning process to the implementation stage, they learn the importance of cooperative activities within the context of a democratic nation.

Within a system that relies on its own children, it is possible for students to empower themselves in the area of classroom management. Comer (1980) discussed the importance of empowering elementary students to feel that the school is their school, and of having they themselves set the tone. When new students entered the school and did not behave themselves, other students told the new pupils that no one behaved that way in this school. The students validated the system. These students made it clear that learning occurred in their school and they all were important components of the system.

Everything that is done in schools should reflect our democratic values. For example, teachers at any grade level can reinforce the importance of reading for all citizens. Students need to understand that reading skills aid citizens in gathering information that they will need in making decisions throughout life, whether in the classroom or in the voting booth. Teachers can select books and poems that teach about America's diversity and concepts related to democracy. When reading humorous poems like *Honey I Love* (Greenfield, 1977) or serious stories such as *Hawk, I'm Your Brother* (Baylor, 1976, see "Bibliography of Children's Books" for this chapter), teachers can direct their students to comprehend the commonality of their individual experiences with those of the authors. The teacher can also focus upon how personal dignity is an important value of each book. These are values which transcend ethnic, racial, or cultural boundaries. Books such as these reinforce the importance of both diversity and dignity in American society.

Student attitude is the second component of education in a multicultural and democratic society. In general, this includes student self-image and acceptance of other people. This component of education deals with the clarification and reflection of beliefs. Who am I and where do I fit within a family, local community, national, and global context? How can I contribute to making this a strong nation? As an interdependent person, what are my responsibilities in a democratic and diverse society? These are questions that can guide students in understanding themselves and their importance to their communities.

Teachers should realize that children are quite aware of their racial and gender membership, and seek positive images of these groups. When teachers try to be color-blind or when they use masculine terms to refer to everyone, they are denying some children images and information that relate specifically to themselves. For example, primary-grade African American children sometimes deny their racial membership because schools and the media give them to little positive imagery connected directly with it. Positive self-esteem and positive attitudes toward others require positive information and images that specifically reflect racial and gender-group membership.

The third and extremely important area is skill development. Not only do students need the basic skills of reading, writing, and computation, but students need to develop strong people skills. It is their people skills which will enable them to communicate effectively with a diversity of individuals. "Children are, among other things, each others' educational resources" (Gutmann, 1987, p. 160). It is important not only that they are distributed throughout schools in a balanced fashion, but that they must be able to communicate, develop common goals, and implement those goals cooperatively (see Sapon-Shevin and Schniedewind in this book). Students must also have strong decision-making, problem-solving, and critical thinking skills in order to process information and organize thoughts (Beyer, 1988). These skills, coupled with cooperative learning skills and advocacy skills, will provide the United States with strong, active citizens (Sleeter and Grant, 1987; Nakagawa and Pang, forthcoming). The last portion of this framework places a heavy emphasis on social action. Students in this system are not only receptacles of knowledge; they also exercise their skills and act.

Justice: Teaching a Social Value

One of the most powerful social values which can be reinforced throughout the schooling experience is justice. Every morning children recite "I pledge allegiance to the flag of the United States of America, and to the Republic for which it stands, one Nation under God,[1] indivisible, with liberty and justice for all." The recitation of this pledge could be followed by discussion of why it is repeated daily. The pledge provides an opportunity for teachers to incorporate multicultural education into their routine.

When beginning a discussion about justice, it may be necessary to help students brainstorm synonyms. Children may suggest the following:

fairness
being just
being equal
equality
fair play
being a good sport
playing fair and square

Preschool and older children have a keen sense of justice. Children often can be heard saying "But that's not fair." They understand the importance of dealing equitably with each other. Though justice can be discussed in terms of happenings on the playground, students also need to understand that justice is an important cornerstone of American society.

This value could provide the focus for the presentation of historical information or the present-day treatment of numerous cultural groups. For example, children can examine health care and justice, using concepts and examples that are appropriate to their developmental level. Very young children can learn what health care is by discussing health care they have experienced at home, visiting the school nurse, and so forth. At this level they can discuss justice as meaning everyone gets treated by the nurse or by someone at home when needed. In math, story problems can sensitize children to health care costs. Children can then examine which jobs in the community provide health insurance and which do not, and what kinds of people occupy which jobs. Older children can find out what provisions there are in the community for health care for poor people. Some of their own families may use such services. By examining an issue like this, drawing on their own experience and examples from the local community, students can examine the extent to which justice is actually carried out, and how they could act on behalf of it.

Examining Stereoptypes
in Children's Environment: Cartoons

Since some younger children may not have been exposed to various cultural stereotypes, I do not recommend the examination of stereotypes with children younger than seven years old, unless the issue of stereotypes has come up in class. Instruction about bias is complex, and the teacher needs to be aware of student perceptions.

In discussions of justice, children second grade and older can understand how stereotypes cloud people's perceptions and create a barrier to making just decisions. Students can be directed to examine how stereotypes found in society are untrue. An effective approach is to ask students how they would feel if someone said, "All kids are bratty." Teachers can follow up with "Do you think that is a fair statement?" in order to provide students with bridges of understanding in dealing with others. Teachers can then pose a question such as "How could stereotypes about Native Americans act as obstacles in a discussion?" This is useful in pointing out what effects misinformation can have. Students can also be asked, "How would you feel if people thought you lived in a teepee and ate buffalo?" Some children may be scared of Native Americans because of the stereotype of bows-and-arrows violence they have seen in cowboy movies. Others may respond to those they believe to be Native Americans with inappropriate behaviors. One example is for one child to go up to another, say "Ug," and raise the palm of his or her hand as in a greeting. Unsuitable actions may create impediments to the development of strong interpersonal communications.

If teachers are unsure of student impressions, then the best way to combat stereotypes is to present positive role models. Community resource people and parents who represent various cultural groups could be invited as guest speakers. A Native American engineer might expose the children to the world of structural engineering. An Asian American actor could explain how she makes television commercials. Another channel for positive modeling is the reading of children's literature. (See the "Bibliography of Children's Books," which includes books for all reading levels.) Since stereotypes provide "explanations" for many injustices in society, it is more difficult for children to accept those injustices when they have positive and accurate information about groups than when they do not.

If teachers do detect stereotypes, they can help children learn to examine and critique their own environments for the stereotypes. Figure 8.2 illustrates a set of questions that can be used in an examination of bias in cartoons. Cartoons were chosen because they are a part of the daily life of many students and are often biased. (An analysis of comic strips printed in a daily newspaper of a large suburban city indicated gender and ethnic bias (Chavez, 1985). Using two one-month samples, Chavez found men as main characters 85 percent of the time in comparison with women, who were major characters in only 15 percent of the comics. Anglo-Americans represented 98 percent of the characters.) Children watch cartoons regularly on television or read them in the comic section of the newspaper. In addition, there are many comic book readers. The questions which were developed for use with comics can be used with books too. Students need to understand that the analysis, synthesis, and evaluation skills they develop in school can be transferred to their lives outside of school.

FIGURE 8.2

Cartoons: Catching Their Messages*

1. Purpose of the Cartoon
   Why do you think the illustrator or author drew or created the cartoon?
   Is it to entertain you?
   Is it to tell you important information?
   Is it to try to sell you something?

2. Illustrations
   In the cartoons or comics, do the people or characters look like real people?
   Do they look like someone you know?
   Do all the people look alike except some faces are shaded more than others?
   Do the pictures seem to be an exaggeration of life?
   If the characters are an exaggeration of life, do you think the audience will know the cartoon is fiction and does not represent the real world?
   If the cartoon presents the heritage of a culture, is a positive and respectful image of the group shown?

3. Story Line: Relationship of the Characters
   Do all the characters have equal power in the story?
   Are some characters smarter, stronger, or kinder than the others?
   Which characters are seen to be the smartest?
   The strongest?
   The weakest?
   The kindest?
   Do you see any patterns in these relationships? If so, what are those patterns?
   Does the cartoon include a balanced number of characters representing differences of gender, class, ethnicity, age, and exceptionality?

4. Vocabulary
   Were some words used to label certain groups? If so, what were they?
   Were words used to put down certain people?
   Why would some groups be presented in a more positive way than others?

5. Tone of Dialogue
>   Do some characters speak with an accent?
>   Is that accent used to put down a character?
>   Are all characters presented as respected Americans?

6. Reflections
>   Would you make changes in this cartoon?
>   What changes would you make:
>>   in the characters?
>>   in the language?
>>   in the plot?

---

* This checklist is an adaptation of two guidelines: "Ten Quick Ways to Analyze Children's Books for Racism and Sexism," the Council on Interracial Books for Children and "Guidelines for Identifying and Counteracting Bias in Instructional Materials," State of Washington Office of the Superintendent of Public Instruction.

A review of cartoons can begin with a discussion of justice. Children can then be reminded that all people want to be presented in a fair and accurate manner. Cartoons are humorous and entertaining, but sometimes may not present people in the best light. Stephen Leacock has said, "The very essence of humor is that it must be kindly" (Lenehan, 1989, p. 15). We hope that individuals will portray others in an honest and respectful manner.

Reviewing materials such as cartoons for stereotypes is a complex process and incorporates critical reading and critical thinking skills. Students must be able to distinguish between verifiable facts and value claims. Many areas can be covered, such as illustrations, language, tone, and story line. The questions in Figure 8.2 will help to facilitate student understanding of how bias can enter into cartoons. Since there are numerous types of cartoons in comic books and on television, it is impossible to develop guidelines which will encompass all situations. The suggested questions in Figure 8.2 are to help students to begin to reflect upon the massive amount of information they encounter daily. Teachers can then use the questions that are appropriate for the experience and grade level of their students. The following is a discussion of the questions.

Purpose of the cartoon. Students should begin by identifying the purpose of the cartoon. If the cartoon is basically for entertainment, is the author poking fun at any group of people in a harmful way? This question can help children examine how humor can be used to hurt others. In order to present a balanced view of hurtful humor, the teacher can guide a discussion of how people often laugh at others to make themselves feel more important. If the author is poking fun at a group of people, ask students if they think the author is doing it intentionally, and what the author might gain by doing so.

If the goal of the cartoon is to provide accurate information, the students could examine how the characters are portrayed. Research can be done with nonfiction resources to assist students in reviewing the information presented. Critical reading skills involve students in a process of distinguishing between fact and opinion (Durkin, 1978). In reading the printed page, readers of all ages must learn that not everything found in print is a true representation of the world.

In today's society, cartoon characters often are used to sell a product. Students need to know that producers design cartoons to influence their opinion and sometimes to make a profit. The students should be asked what messages are being communicated in the cartoons. The images projected may say that whoever eats this cereal or buys that toy will be popular with others. Is this true? What does the author gain by making you think so?

Illustrations. For children, visual representation is an extremely powerful medium. Children often believe that what they see in print or on television represents reality. If they are accustomed to seeing a "Superman" male, Barbie-type female, "jiving" Black American, or "Frito Bandito" Hispanic American, they may believe that those images are truthful. They may not question them if the models are part of their media experience. Cortés, in this book, provides an example of panelists on a game show having learned to associate East L.A. with gangs because of repeated media images. Another bias is to present all characters, no matter from which ethnic or racial group, as having the same physical characteristics. The characters should have unique individual appearances; all Asian Americans should not look alike; neither should all Native Americans.

Authors sometimes use exaggerations to make their point more obvious. The illustrator may draw an Indian with buckskin and feathers because he or she may feel that the reader will immediately understand this image. The children can be asked to identify the harmful effects of always representing a group of people in this fashion.

Story line. The relationships between individual characters give hidden messages regarding abilities, worth, and status. Often women are portrayed as the weaker gender who are dependent upon their male counterparts to solve problems. Minority characters are often found in the background. They are not the powerful individuals within the story line who make decisions or initiate solutions. They are more likely to be incidental characters. Characters from a variety of groups should be shown doing dishes or leading others. Children should examine how the "good guys" differ from the "bad guys"; for example, are the "bad guys" characterized by darker coloring than the "good guys"?

Characters may be stereotyped. For example, elder Americans may be shown as forgetful and unable to care for themselves. Individuals who have limited economic stability are presented as dirty. Omission of groups should be noted. If a group is often omitted, what message does that give? For example, rarely are characters who have developmental differences included in children's stories. (Though this may not always be possible in each cartoon, students should be made aware that frequent omission of groups is also a form of bias.)

Vocabulary. Language is a powerful conduit of ideas. Biased language indirectly conveys powerful messages. Overgeneralized labels can be used as a way of name-calling. For example, characters may be shown as being all "communists" or "disadvantaged." If labels such as these are intended to evoke negative feelings, why has the author chosen these labels? Do they really mean something undesirable, or is the author drawing on popular sentiment?

Children can be directed to look for inaccurate use of language or dialects. Cartoon characters may use phrases like "ah, so" or "no way, Jose." Black English may be used to portray poor and unintelligent characters. Native Americans may be shown talking in broken English, saying something like, "You big chief. Me want to talk to you." Languages and dialects should be represented accurately and with respect. All characters, too, should be treated with respect and not as second-class citizens. For example, the term *women* should be used rather than *girls* or *career girls* when referring to an adult.

Tone of dialogue. If students are reviewing a video cartoon, they should review the voices of the characters. The accent of some characters will be used to imply that the character is devious or not as smart as others. Voices may reflect sex stereotypes. Girls, for example, may be given sweet sounding voices that suggest helplessness and not strength. Some accents are used to represent upper-class society, whereas other accents are synonymous with poverty and low status. The cartoon can be presented without sound, and children can be asked how the omission changes the message of the film.

Reflections. After analyzing the cartoon, students can be asked to review how it reinforces or devalues the concept of justice. Teachers can request that their students think of ways in which poor-quality cartoons can be changed. The students can write to the producer or illustrator of cartoons either to provide suggestions regarding misconceptions or to commend the writer on a balanced or positive presentation. In either case students can become active participants in their own society by voicing an opinion after careful analysis.

Students can create their own cartoons with new endings, incorporating their perceptions of the fallacies and inconsistencies. Their cartoons may reflect a more informed alternative. Student creations can be then displayed in the classroom or school library in a corner called "Just Cartoons."

Kidpower: Important Citizens

It is possible to facilitate the development of important knowledge, skills, and attitudes which will bring children to think, discuss, and question what they encounter. Reflection is possible at all grade levels, including primary. A first-grade teacher exposed her children to numerous minority and majority U.S. leaders. She read stories about the lives and values of these important U.S. citizens. One of them was Martin Luther King, Jr. The students discussed how people of color had been barred from public places like schools. During a handwriting lesson in which the children were to write their New Year's resolutions, one White first grader wrote: "Bet your boots 1989 will be great if we make sure that Blak [sic] people can do what we can." The underlying messages of this child's resolution are that (1) discrimination is unacceptable, and (2) it will take everyone to make a change. These are important understandings for persons of any age.

Responses from fifth graders to a unit on discrimination and stereotypes indicated that prior to this unit they had not been given the opportunity to examine these issues. The students were surprised how many stereotypic phrases such as *black listed* or *Frito Bandito* were part of American culture. One student said, "The discussion was very interesting. It got me thinking, am I prejudiced? Do I, without knowing it, have a slip of the tongue?" No matter what age group the students are, it is important to have them understand the importance of democracy and how we always work at protecting the rights of all.

As important members of society, children can be empowered to make changes. Students can practice these important skills now. It is imperative to the survival of the United States that teachers help guide students to acquire skills that will enable them to make difficult and complex decisions. In a classroom where education is seen as multicultural and social reconstructionist, students are prepared not only to understand the existence of social inequalities, but to know that they have the ability to act upon their beliefs to change those inequalities, whether based on gender, ethnicity, culture, age, or developmental ability. Multicultural education moves to empower even our youngest citizens to think about issues in their world and to challenge those arenas of life that they find unjust. The dream which Martin Luther King, Jr., gave all Americans can be kept alive through "kidpower."

Chapter 9

Classroom Use of African American Language: Educational Tool or Social Weapon?

--- *Selase W. Williams*

Introduction:
Issues Surrounding Language in Education

Language is essential to all educational endeavors. On this point, there is no disagreement. It is the primary vehicle for transmitting information from one generation to the next; it helps us to organize our reality; it shapes the way we think; and, to some degree, it limits the boundaries of what is thinkable for any given cultural group. However, whether some groups have a right to be educated, which language will constitute the medium of instruction, and which language will serve as the "standard" against which all other language forms will be evaluated are questions that have incited heated debate wherever they are raised. America has been, and continues to be, no exception to this. The fact that language is an artifact of culture contributes, in no small measure, to the intensity of the debate.

A brief historical presentation of these issues as they manifest themselves in the context of the United States allows us to consider the question of classroom use of African American Language from a broad social and political perspective. What will be observed is that most of the issues surrounding language in education have little to do with pedagogy, educational philosophy, or instructional efficiency. Rather, most of the issues are political issues with serious social, economic, and cultural consequences for large segments of American society. The fact that African American Language is not being used in American classrooms indicates more about the power relationship that exists between European Americans and African Americans than it does about the appropriateness or utility of African American Language in the educational mission. The following pages will reveal not only the source of the "language problem" for many African Americans, but will also demonstrate how the language of the African American community can be effectively used to teach new skills and empower those who speak the language.

One of the first questions to confront the British colonists in what was to become the United States was whether to educate the enslaved African population at all. During that early time period, education was almost synonymous with reading and writing, with much of the reading instruction focusing on biblical text. Some of the planters (as the slave owners were called) argued that a religious education would make the enslaved Africans more civilized and more "governable." Others objected to educating their bondsmen, knowing that the ability to read, in particular, would allow them access to printed material other than the Bible. As abolitionist groups began to gain strength in the North, publishing pamphlets that promoted the termination of slavery, this latter concern became heightened among the planters.

The enactment of a South Carolina law prohibiting the teaching of enslaved Africans in 1740, following a series of insurrections in Louisiana, New York, and South Carolina, demonstrates the relationship between the teaching of English and the threat of insurrection that was perceived by the plantation society:

> AND WHEREAS the having of Slaves taught to write, or suffering them to be employed in writing, may be attended with great Inconveniences; be it therefore enacted by the Authority aforesaid, That all and every Person or Persons whatsoever, who shall hereafter teach, or cause any Slave or Slaves to be taught to write, or shall use or employ any Slave as a Scribe in any Manner or Writing whatsoever, hereafter taught to write; every such Person and Persons shall, for every such Offense, forfeit the sum of One Hundred Pounds current Money. (*The Black American and Education*, 1972, page 10)

Laws of the type cited above continued to be enacted all the way into the 1840s. Each one had its own history, each one had its unique punishments, and each one seemed to be successively more brutal than its predecessors. Clearly, it was not intended for African people in America to be literate. The fact that approximately 95 percent of all African Americans were without the ability to read or write by the end of the

Civil War in 1865 is evidence of the effectiveness of this early policy that governed African American education.

At its founding, in the late 1700s, the United States of America was without public schools. It was made up largely of western European groups and enslaved West and West-Central Africans. Where Africans of the same linguistic groups found themselves captive on the same plantations, the oral educational traditions continued, albeit under adverse conditions, through folk tales, proverbs, naming practices, herbalism, craftsmanship training, agriculture, and family histories. On the other hand, the western European groups, primarily the English, the French, the Dutch, and the Germans, set up schools that were taught in the language of the largest group in those respective communities. Thus, there were French language schools in parts of Louisiana, German language schools in parts of Pennsylvania, and English language schools in most other parts of the colonies.

Although schools with languages other than English as the medium of instruction existed, it should not be thought that they existed without major opposition. As late as the 1880s in Missouri, the superintendent of public instruction lodged complaints against the "German element" in his state. His concern is reflected in the following statement:

> In a large number of the districts of the State, the German element of the population greatly preponderates and, as the consequence, the schools are mainly taught in the German language and sometimes entirely so. Hence, if an *American* family lives in such a district, the children must either be deprived of school privileges or else be taught in the German language. [emphasis added] (Wagner, 1981, p. 38)

It should be duly noted that the superintendent's concern was not for the most effective educational program for those who came from a German-speaking background, but rather for the rights (or privileges) of English children. His complaint was but an echo of strongly opposed voices from the previous century. Even the humanitarian statesman, Benjamin Franklin, took a strong stand against the use of the German language in the United States. In *Observations on the Increase of Mankind,* he states, "Why should the Palatine [German] boors be suffered to swarm in our settlements and, by herding together, establish their language and manners to the exclusion of ours? Why should Pennsylvania, founded by the English, become a colony of aliens, who will shortly be so numerous as to germanize us instead of our anglifying them?"

(Wagner, 1981, pp. 31-32). In Franklin's words, we find perhaps the strongest motive for opposition to the use of languages other than English in American schools, the fear of losing Anglo-Saxon cultural dominance.

Today, just like two centuries ago, if the choice of language to be used as the medium of instruction were predicated on principles of pedagogical effectiveness and instructional efficiency rather than on power relationships, the language arts curriculum would be significantly different from that which currently exists in American public educational institutions. Pedagogical effectiveness and instructional efficiency would necessarily lead to the use of the "mother tongue" in the early grades, with English and any other socially important languages being taught later as "second languages." However, what we see is the imposition of English as the only medium of instruction from kindergarten on.

Bilingual education programs in the United States have been applauded as long as they have been viewed as a strategy for phasing Spanish out and phasing English in. As soon as it was determined that bilingual education programs typically taught pride in one's own language and culture, and, in fact, helped to preserve this heritage, in addition to teaching English language skills, the support for such programs began to dwindle and the resources for such programs, at both the federal and state levels, began to dry up.

The English Only movement in the United States in the 1980s has been partially a backlash against bilingual education programs and a defense mechanism against the potential political and cultural power of the growing numbers of immigrants speaking Spanish and Southeast Asian languages in recent years. There is a real fear on the part of many European Americans that, with these growing numbers of non-English-speaking peoples, the utility of English in American education will sharply decrease. Along with this decrease in utility will come a decrease in the political, economic, and social advantage of European Americans over African Americans, Hispanic Americans, and Asian Americans.

There are lessons to be learned from other English Only-type movements. South Africa presents us with such a case. The Soweto riots that exploded in South Africa in 1976 were responses to the government imposition of Afrikaans, the language of the ruling class, in the elementary schools. This policy forced African children to give up their mother tongue as a tool for learning. So frustrated were the students and their parents by this new policy that the riots were inevitable. Although they were fully aware of the military might that the Apartheid machine could bring forth to quell the uprising, it was the students, most of whom were young children, who participated in the school boycott and the subsequent rioting. The choice of language to be used as the medium of instruction is anything but a trivial issue.

The language *policies* in American public education are not significantly different from those of South Africa. What is different about the South African and the American cases is the size of the European and non-European populations in relation to each other. In the South African context, the European population is politically and economically dominant, but numerically the minority. In the U.S. context, however, the European population is politically, economically, and numerically dominant over the collective non-European population. This numerical advantage in the United States allows the dominant population to use less repressive measures in the implementation of the language policies and to justify the policies on the grounds that English is the language of wider communication.

What the current language policies in the United States have not taken into account is the fact that language is constantly changing and that the demographics of American society are also changing. What is American English becoming? What impact will the changing demographics, especially in the classroom, have on the implementation of educational language policies if they remain essentially the same over the next twenty years? These questions will be addressed in the concluding section of this chapter.

African American Language
and Its Status in American Education

After nearly three decades of scholarship on the language of the African American community, the large majority of Americans, including those in the field of education, have only a distorted, highly stereotypical conception of African American Language. A commonly held view is that African American Language (AAL) is a disorganized set of slang expressions haphazardly thrown together to project the image of being "cool." Others believe that AAL is nothing more than "ungrammatical English" that is the result of inadequate instruction in formal English and often blamed on the parents of those who speak AAL. Still others would argue that African Americans know formal English but refuse to use it consistently as a form of rebellion against European American society. Those who hold this latter view would provide as evidence the fact that even African Americans who typically speak AAL can sometimes be heard using formal English. All of these views reveal a severe ignorance of the history and structure of AAL or, at best, a high degree of cultural arrogance on the parts of European Americans.

Although the linguistic system in question here is referred to in the literature as Nonstandard Negro English, Black Dialect, Black English Vernacular, Black Street Speech, Ebonics, and more pejorative terms, the term *African American Language* is a more accurate designation for the linguistic system that is characteristically spoken in the African American community. The term acknowledges its African cultural roots, identifies its geographical residence, and reflects the linguistic integrity of this effective communication system.

What makes African American Language unique in the English-speaking U.S. context is the fact that its phonology (sound system), its morpho-syntax (grammatical system), and its semantics (system of meanings and creativity) all derive from an African linguistic base. The linguistic contributions to AAL from English, primarily a body of vocabulary words, are much less substantive than the components mentioned above. It is accurate to say that the linguistic foundation and structural framework of AAL is African in origin and that much of the exterior is English in origin.

An elaborate presentation of the characteristic features of AAL is unnecessary here, since numerous descriptions are available to the reader (e.g., Shuy et al., 1968; Labov, 1970; Dillard, 1972; Smitherman, 1977; Baugh, 1983). What is missing from those presentations, however, is the discussion of the systematic African element alluded to above. Yet, failure to understand the nature of this systematic African element would leave one with only a very superficial understanding of AAL and would lead one to underestimate the value of using AAL as an educational tool in the classroom.

Within the sound system of AAL, there exist a number of pronunciation rules which have been shaped by the general nature of the sound systems of the African languages from which AAL developed. Just as the French-speaking person pronounces the English word *these* as "zeez" because the [z] sound is perceptually the closest French sound to the [th] sound found in this word, the Africans who were enslaved in this country pronounced a number of English sounds and sound sequences as they perceived them through their mother tongues. This phenomenon, in linguistic terms, is referred to as "linguistic interference" or "transference."

To begin, one of the most general characteristics of the sound systems of African languages is a strongly preferred CVCV (consonant-vowel-consonant-vowel) pattern for all of the words in the inventory of the language. Thus, with few exceptions, African words end in vowels, not consonants, and relatively few words contain "consonant clusters."

It is not surprising, then, to find a number of pronunciation patterns in African American speech which reduce English words to sequences of sound that are closer to the ideal African pattern than to the original English pattern. English words which end in two or more consonants (consonant clusters) are pronounced as if only the first consonant were present. Some examples are the following:

fist	>	fis
passed [past]	>	pas
sand	>	san
roped [ropt]	>	rope
lasts	>	las
blasts	>	blas

The sound represented by the letter *r* is not pronounced in African American Language if it follows a vowel, whether it is in the middle of the word or at the end of the word. Observe the examples below:

more	>	moe
for	>	foe
fir	>	fuh
fork	>	foke
mark	>	mock
mother	>	motha
father	>	fatha
preacher	>	preacha
bother	>	botha

Notice how these two pronunciation "rules" reduced the English word *master* to the ideal African form (i.e., CVCV) in early African American Language:

master	>	masa
mister	>	misa

In early versions of African American Language, before they were recorded with any degree of linguistic accuracy, many more forms of this type must have existed.

Just as the French-speaking person has difficulty pronouncing the *th*-sounds of English, the Africans also had difficulty because the *th*-

sounds were not present in the sound inventories of their languages. In fact, the *th*-sounds are rare among the world's languages. When the *th*-sound referred to as "thorn" appears in word-initial position in English, its AAL counterpart is a close approximation of the d-sound, as demonstrated below:

this	>	dis
these	>	dese
that	>	dat
those	>	dose
then	>	den

When the English *th*-sound that is referred to as "theta" appears at the end of a word, the AAL pronunciation is either *f* or *t*. Observe the following examples:

with	>	wif/wit
both	>	bof/bot
math	>	maf/mat
worth	>	worf/wort

I have argued in a paper to be published soon (Williams, forthcoming) that these variant pronunciations of word-final theta have their origins in the differing sound systems of African language groups that were enslaved in various parts of the Old South. In other words, it is the sound system of the African languages involved that has conditioned the pronunciation of English vocabulary items by African peoples in the New World. The examples presented here are but a few of the numerous examples that could be presented to demonstrate the African character of the AAL sound system.

Looking at the grammatical system, we find that the most glaring similarity between AAL and languages indigenous to West Africa can be found in the verbal system. African languages tend not to use prefixes or suffixes on verbs to indicate 'tense' or 'aspect'. Instead, such notions as 'past', 'present', 'future', and 'habitual' are indicated by tense or aspect markers that appear in front of the main verb of the sentence. For instance, the marker that indicates an action that took place in the 'remote past' is *bin*. Look at these examples:

1. Shanita *bin* pass that tes.   "Shanita passed that test a long time ago."
2. Lamonte *bin* had dat car.   "Lamonte has had that car for a long time."

The marker of 'habitual action' in AAL, which is often confused with the English verb *to be*, is the simple marker *be*. It does not change to *is*, *am*, or *are* depending upon the subject of the sentence. Notice in the sentences below that the verb form usually includes the *in'* ending:

3. Derrick *be* helpin' his momma.   "Derrick always helps his mother."

4. The teacha said, "Don't y'all *be*   "The teacher said, 'Don't playin' around wit them   bother those things.'" things."

Clearly these verbal patterns are African in character and very regular.

Although numerous other patterns could be presented here to further demonstrate the African character in the grammatical system of AAL, one more will suffice. The English verb *to be* carries a wide variety of grammatical functions in that language. It can be the main verb in sentences containing predicate nouns and predicate adjectives, as in the following:

5. Mr. Marshall *is* a pediatrician.
6. The horses *are* beautiful.

It can also be used as an auxiliary verb to indicate continuous action:

7. The girls *are* swimming in the pool.

However, the AAL equivalents of these sentences do not contain forms of the verb *to be*. The sentences numbered 5´ through 7´ are the AAL equivalents of 5 through 7, respectively.

5´. Mr. Marshall a pediatrician.
6´. The horses beautiful.
7´. The girls swimmin' in the pool.

In many African languages, noun-noun sentences, noun-adjective sentences, and noun-verb sentences are completely grammatical and acceptable. The only markers that would be inserted between them would be those which indicate a tense or aspect other than 'present'. This is true in AAL as well. If 5´-7´ were to be rendered in the 'past' tense, the following sentences would result:

5´´. Mr. Marshall *was* a pediatrician.
6´´. The horses *was* beautiful.
7´´. The girls *was* swimmin' in the pool.

Notice here that *was* is the regular 'past' marker in continuous action sentences.

This very brief description of some of the systematic patterns found in African American Language should convince even the unenlightened that AAL has a regular set of pronunciation and grammatical rules that govern the linguistic behavior of members of the African American community and that the origin of these rules is the African languages spoken by the Africans who were enslaved on this continent. However, as stated earlier, most Americans have not had the benefit of this type of presentation and consequently view AAL as little more than "ungrammatical English." This assessment has been further promoted by social scientists who have argued that African culture was eradicated through the institution of slavery.

Imagine the impact on one's self-esteem and self-concept to discover that the language that is spoken in your community and which you embrace as part of your identity is nothing more than an inferior copy of someone else's language. Imagine further that, no matter how hard you try to master the "superior" language, elements of your own language keep creeping in. This "imagined" feeling is, unfortunately, the true feeling of many African American youths in American educational institutions today.

Ignorance of the systematic, African character of African American Language on the part of schoolteachers and their unwillingness to accept it as a legitimate form of communication have turned this language variant into a weapon of social destruction. Since the curriculum presumes that those walking into American classrooms are already possessors of a variety of English that is close to the Standard Dialect, anyone speaking a variant that is significantly different is automatically disadvantaged. An incorrect answer on a language arts assignment becomes much more than that. It becomes an admission of one's inadequacy. It becomes a sign of intellectual inferiority. It makes one an outsider, a social outcast.

Test constructors, either consciously or unconsciously, include items that are acceptable in AAL, but ungrammatical in Standard American English (SAE) to test one's *language ability*. The following are typical test questions that appear in the language skills section of standardized tests:

Question #1—Fill in the blank with the correct verb form:

The fifth-grade boys _____ playing baseball on the school grounds.

Verb Forms: (a) *be*   (b) *is*   (c) *was*   (d) *are*

Question #2—Draw a circle around the sentence that is correct:

    (a) The girls was swimming in the pool.

    (b) The girls were swimming in the pool.

Whereas the sentences that result from the insertion of (a), (b), or (c) in Question #1 are grammatical sentences in AAL, only the sentence that results from the insertion of (d) is grammatical in Standard American English. Similarly, (a) in Question #2 is grammatical in AAL, but (b) is the only correct answer to the test constructor.

At best, speakers of AAL are faced with choosing between two or more forms which they know to be acceptable in AAL, each carrying a different meaning. Trying to determine which of the answers is most "correct" is virtually an impossible task. For the speaker of AAL who realizes that he or she is supposed to select the SAE form, it is clear that such a task is more difficult than being given a problem which has only one correct answer. The worst-case scenario is one in which speakers of AAL find only one answer acceptable, but that answer is the one that has purposely been placed there as an incorrect answer, thereby constituting a trap for these students. The child's language variety, then, is used as a weapon against him or her.

Most educators, especially English teachers, would deny that AAL is being intentionally used as a weapon against African American children. The majority would argue that they are simply maintaining a set of established standards and that they are evaluating students on the skills they will need to have to be productive citizens. In spite of the fact that teachers, and perhaps test constructors, are well intentioned, the consequences of current educational practices in this area are very damaging. The alienation that results from being an outcast, the frustration that comes from agonizing over confusing tests, and the inferiority complex that comes from selecting the "wrong" answers so often can be devastating to a young person who is going through a critical stage of intellectual, personal, and social development. One can only speculate on the degree to which this leads African American youths to join gangs, where they can feel accepted, where they can be rewarded for their talents, and where their language is viewed as an art form rather than as a disability.

African American Language as an Educational Tool

Why should an educator want to use incorrect or ungrammatical language forms in the classroom? Why should we teach "Black English" in the classroom—don't African American kids already know it? Wouldn't we be discriminating against African American youths if we didn't teach them the same things that we teach European American students? Isn't it racist to assume that African American children need a lower-level English course while European American children are learning the Standard variety?

These are a few of the questions that arise whenever *anyone* propos-es the use of the African American language in the classroom. These questions have to be addressed before this author makes his proposal. An understanding of how misguided these questions are will hopefully go a long way in directing us toward the real educational issues regard-ing language and the African American community.

In reference to the first question, it must be pointed out that no dialect of American English (or any other language for that matter) is "incorrect" or "ungrammatical." The fact that one systematic variety may differ from the accepted "standard" dialect, which is usually close to the variety spoken by the politically and economically dominant group, does not make the nonstandard variety either incorrect or ungrammatical. As was demonstrated in the previous section of this chapter, AAL has a distinct set of grammatical rules that must be adhered to in order to be understood in the African American commu-nity. The real question is, How do we best educate those groups whose language varieties are significantly different from the standard? Just as it would not make much sense to try to teach English to a Korean with-out using the Korean language as a tool, it does not make much sense to try to teach Standard English to speakers of AAL without using AAL as a learning tool.

Those who have equated the *use* of "Black English" in the classroom with the *teaching* of the language have clearly not understood "what's hap'nin'." Notice that the same equation is not forwarded when speak-ers of Standard American English are required to take English. No one asks, "Why should we teach Standard English to students who already know that language?" In that case it is clearly understood that certain language skills are being taught, like reading and writing. For the most part, students do not enter school with a highly developed ability in these skill areas. It is also the case that, although speakers of SAE may be fluent conversationalists in that variety of English, they probably know little about the organization, structure, and logic of the language. One does not have to be consciously aware of these dimensions of a lan-guage to speak it. Proposals for the use of African American Language in the classroom are essentially for the purpose of teaching language skills (i.e., reading and writing) and the organizational nature of language. Since speakers of African American Language are much more comfortable with AAL than with any other language variety, using it will make the learning of language skills more efficient and effective.

The question of whether the use of AAL in the classroom is a discriminatory practice also deserves a serious response. To begin, a program in which AAL is used in the classroom should not be administered to students on the basis of race. That *could* be deemed discriminatory. Such a program should be targeted to that group of students that has been evaluated as being speakers of AAL. In other words, the program is aimed at students with a particular language background. It is because their language background impacts their learning of Standard English language skills that a specialized program is proposed.

Administering specialized language instruction to those with linguistically or culturally different backgrounds is not only *not discriminatory*, but it is *required by law* for some segments of the population. Although it may be debated whether or not *Lau vs. Nichols* of 1974 should apply to speakers of African American Language, that U.S. Supreme Court decision states that *school districts receiving federal aid are required to provide special help to students unable to benefit from ordinary classes taught in English*. This law should be applicable to many African Americans, despite the fact that most of them are "receptive bilinguals," meaning that they understand most spoken Standard English but have not developed the facility to produce Standard English in spoken or written form.

In addressing the last question posed above, the answer is "yes." It would be racist to assume that all African Americans require a language skills program different from that provided to the general student body. Language is not genetic behavior; it is culturally learned behavior. It logically follows, then, that some African Americans will grow up learning AAL, and others will grow up learning something close to the standard variety of English. The reader should be cautioned, however, that a language skills development program that uses AAL should not be viewed as being on a "lower level" than the more traditional language courses. Presumably both courses would be attempting to teach the same concepts; one would simply be tailored for students with a linguistic experience different from that experienced by most children in the traditional courses.

Sound pedagogical logic dictates that teachers use the talents, skills, and abilities which students bring with them to the classroom as a foun-

dation upon which to build new skills and a higher level of self-awareness. For those students who enter the classroom with a primary facility
in African American Language, use of that communication system in
teaching other skills can provide them with a positive and enriching
educational experience for at least the following four reasons:

1. It allows them to maintain linkages with their primary culture,
thus avoiding unnecessary cultural alienation of the type typically experienced by African American students in American educational institutions.

2. It teaches students to value what they already know as tools for
future learning and later life.

3. Since language is an inextricable part of one's self-identity,
demonstrating acceptance of their language, rather than encouraging its
eradication, enhances the students' self-esteem and self-concept.

4. It improves their self-confidence and, with that, their motivation
to learn.

5. "The average gain in grade equivalent scores for the group using
the *Bridge* [*Cross-Culture Reading Program*] was 6.2 months for four
months of instruction compared to only an average gain of 1.6 months"
for students in the regular classroom. (Simpkins and Simpkins, 1981, p.
238)

Of all of the possible reasons that could be posited for using African
American Language in the classroom, it is the last one which provides
the strongest justification. The ultimate goal of such programs must be
to improve the students' ability to learn. Good reading skills are a prerequisite for success in the academic arena.

Two bidialectal programs that have been developed and successfully used are *The Psycholinguistic Reading Series* (Davis, Gladney, and
Leaverton, 1968) and *Bridge: A Cross-Culture Reading Program* (Simpkins,
Holt, and Simpkins, 1977). The former program was designed for use in
the lower grades. Initially applying oral drills to get the students accustomed to hearing the differences between what the authors refer to as
"everyday talk" and "school talk," the printed readers focus on a number of verb forms determined by the program designers to be highly
problematic for speakers of African American Language. The students
are presented with text that is written in "everyday talk" (i.e., African
American Language). Since reading is the skill of associating written
symbols (words) with spoken sounds or larger utterances, the process of
learning proceeds more efficiently and effectively if the written symbols
correspond to the reader's spoken language variety. Once the students

feel comfortable with reading their dialect, then, they are introduced to the same sentences in Standard English. In fact, the "everyday talk" version appears on the left page, and the "school talk" version appears on the right page.

Through this process, students learn not only the skill of reading more efficiently, but also how to read Standard English while maintaining pride in their own language. The key to the program's success is the systematic presentation of both language varieties, the one which the students bring into the classrooms with them and the one which teachers will expect them to perform consistently in later. Seeing one's own language variety written in the textbook necessarily reinforces a positive self-concept.

Bridge is a reading program geared for "junior and senior high school students who are underachievers in reading" (Simpkins, Holt, and Simpkins, 1977, p. 2). The program is composed of five reading booklets and five study booklets. In the first reading booklet stories are written in "Black Vernacular" (i.e., African American Language) only. Reading Booklet Two contains two stories, each one written, first, in Black Vernacular and then in a "transition" dialect. The third booklet offers two stories in three written versions, Black Vernacular, Transition, and Standard English. The stories in Booklet Four are presented in Transition and Standard English, and the final booklet contains four stories in Standard English only. Exercises, comprehension questions, and other activities that appear in the accompanying study booklets are framed in the same language varieties that appear in the stories.

The success of this program is based on the fact that the readers start with the students' language variety and build from that foundation. Students have the opportunity to systematically compare one dialect version with another dialect version of the same stories, strengthening the bidialectal skills they need to survive in the broader community. Furthermore, as indicated above, one's self-concept is greatly enhanced by seeing one's home dialect in print.

Unfortunately, neither of the programs described above is in print any longer. Why, one might ask, have effective materials of this type been allowed to go out of print? The answer, in a word, is "integration." With the increased success of desegregation efforts, English classrooms found themselves with ethnically mixed student populations. Reading programs of the type described above were thought to be inappropriate for integrated classrooms. Principals were afraid to set up special classrooms for teaching such programs on the grounds that they would be charged with resegregating the school. African American parents, most

of whom were ill-informed about the nature and logic of such programs, generally objected to anything that smacked of discrimination or
resegregation. With no appropriate setting available within which to
offer such programs and no community advocacy for them, they have
withered on the vine. And once the demand was gone, publishers
would no longer continue to print the materials. It is ironic that integration, which was intended to provide African Americans and other people of color in the United States with new opportunities for success and
advancement, has, at least in this case, prevented the continuance of the
very programs that would assist in that advancement.

The Impact of New Ethnolinguistic
Realities on American Education

The America of the 1990s is surely not the America of 1789, and the
demographic projections for the twenty-first century suggest that
America will be even more dramatically different from that earlier period than it is now. An increased immigration rate for Southeast Asians
and for Hispanics, along with proportionately higher birth rates for people of color than for European Americans, will ensure numerical dominance of Americans of non-European origins early in the coming century. Yet, the dominant value system and standards of excellence continue
to be based on Anglo-Saxon norms. Language policies and programs
have been consistent with this. There are a number of reasons for making the value system and the standards of excellence more consonant
with the new ethnolinguistic realities of America in the 1990s.

One of the new realities which America is going to have to accept is
the fact that few Americans, regardless of their ethnolinguistic background, speak a variety of English that closely resembles the written
standard. One of the answers to the question "Why can't Johnny read?"
is that Johnny speaks a variety of English that is not represented on the
written page. The English language in America has been going through
a transformation since it first arrived on these shores. It has incorporated elements of American Indian languages, African languages, Yiddish,
and many others. American English has become a hybrid.

With the integration of schools and the inclusion of more African
American programming on television has come an increased influence
of African American Language, a creolized language, on the structure,
pronunciation, and vocabulary of American English. As more European
Americans become bilingual in Spanish and English or Vietnamese and
English, which is an inevitability in spite of the English Only movement,

American English will change in other ways. In fact, with the pressure from Spanish, we may very well witness a slow but definite creolization of American English.

What are the implications of this for American education? It is safe to assume that written English will not change dramatically in the near future. Writing systems have historically been very conservative and resistant to change. However, all of the evidence suggests that a diglossic situation may very well develop in this country in the not-too-distant future. *Diglossia* is the term used to describe the situation in which two languages exist side by side in the same society, one serving a particular function, the other serving another function. One can fairly easily argue that such a situation exists for many African Americans now. What America can learn from using strategies for effectively teaching African Americans is how it will effectively teach the large majority of its young people in the decades ahead.

Language policies in America have been established largely on the basis of maintaining Anglo-Saxon political and cultural dominance, as it was pointed out in the first section of this chapter. However, America's very survival in the twenty-first century may depend on its ability to effectively educate American youths, all of whom will have acquired a language which significantly differs from the current language of the classroom. It may soon be the case that the only way to empower the few is to empower the many.

Chapter 10

The Empowerment of Language-Minority Students

——————————— *Richard Ruiz*

A central and early tenet of bilingual education advocates was that inclusion of the child's language and culture in the curriculum would lead to greater school achievement. The claims for the benefit of native language instruction were broad, including not only an increase in language proficiency, but also enhancement of more general, nonlinguistic skills such as problem solving and conceptualization (Lambert, 1978; Cummins, 1979; Kessler and Quinn, 1980). More recently, this discussion has turned from a consideration of merely cognitive and academic consequences of mother tongue instruction and bilingualism to their sociolinguistic and political consequences as well. This goes beyond suggestions that being bilingual can be of some economic or commercial advantage: it entails a general reordering of prevailing societal patterns of stratification. In other words, native language instruction in schools can be an important factor in ethnic communities shedding their minority status by sharing power with the dominant group.

The focal concept in these arguments is 'empowerment'. In the following pages, I will try to explain the general connection between language and power, the arguments concerning school language programs and empowerment, the problems and limitations of those arguments from the perspective of a critical pedagogy, and some possibilities for the role that school language programs can play in the authentic empowerment of minority students and their communities.

Language and Power

Frantz Fanon begins his book *Black Skin, White Masks* with an essay titled "The Negro and Language." He is concerned with the psychological consequences of colonialism and the role that language suppression and domination play in it: "The problem that we confront in this chapter is this: The Negro of the Antilles will be proportionately whiter—that is, he will come closer to being a real human being—in direct ratio to his mastery of the French Language" (Fanon, 1967, p. 18). By "the French Language," he means to say "the French of France, the Frenchman's French, French French" (p. 20). Fanon illustrates the relation between language and power in society: not merely social position, but ontological status, can be inferred from the language one speaks. The colonializing power of language has a long history and a large literature; the overt political effects of linguistic and cultural dominance are well documented (for a recent treatment of such questions, see, for example, *Language of Inequality*, 1985, edited by Wolfson and Manes). I am more interested in exploring aspects of this relationship that are less obvious.

A major dimension of the power of language is the power to define, to decide the nature of lived experience. In social relations, the power to define determines dominance and subordination, as Moreau (1984) says: "In social discourse, the dominated are defined (collectively) as incomplete, while the dominant are singularized and defined as the incarnation of achieved human nature" (p. 46). Put another way, subordinate minority groups are those who are named and defined by majority groups. Consider that most ethnic minority communities in the United States are known by names not of their own choosing: "Asians" and "Hispanics" are lumped into categories that deny the distinctiveness of the groups they comprise; American Indian nations usually are distinguished by names ("Papago" or "Stockbridge," for example), but those names generally are not the ones by which they refer to themselves. And, when groups do try to define themselves—when Mexican Americans become "Chicanos," when Negroes become "Blacks," or Blacks propose for themselves "African Americans"—there is resistance, not just because of the inconvenience and confusion created for the rest of us, but because of a deep-felt sense that this sort of self-definition by these groups lacks legitimacy: who has given them the right to change their name?

This concern with whether a person or group is allowed the power of self-definition is closely related to another dimension of the relation of language and power: the distinction between *language* and *voice*. The link between language and voice is put forward by Girouxi (1986): "Language represents a central force in the struggle for voice . . . language is able to shape the way various individuals and groups encode and thereby engage the world" (p. 59).

As much as language and voice are related, it is also important to distinguish between them. I have become convinced of the need for this distinction through a consideration of instances of language planning in which the "inclusion" of the language of a group has coincided with the exclusion of their voice. Guadalupe Valdes (1987) has conducted a series of important studies on the Spanish language classes designed for U.S. Hispanics. She finds that "a surprising number of Spanish-speaking students in the American Southwest are still being placed in beginning Spanish classes for non-speakers to help them 'unlearn' their 'bad' habits and begin anew as foreign speakers" (p. 7). She cites an attitude study of Texas Spanish teachers in which a common sentiment expressed was that "Spanish-speaking students should be provided with grammar explanations which show them why their way of speaking is wrong" (p.6). This is a case of a language class designed to show speakers of that language that theirs is not really that language—perhaps is not really *any* language. This is similar to my personal experiences with teachers in "maintenance" bilingual education programs, where the explicit goal is to conserve the language of the child. What I frequently find, however, is that the language of the child is rarely spoken in the classroom, much less taught in formal lessons. There are two important explanations for this. In the first place, teachers in these classrooms rarely speak the language of the child; either they have learned a textbook language that no one actually uses in everyday conversation, or they confine their speech to standard forms because of their sense of what is proper or acceptable classroom behavior. In the second place, even if they themselves speak or are familiar with the language of the child, they have appropriated the view that it is not proper language and therefore not to be encouraged in the classroom. They attain their goal of language "maintenance" to the extent that they eradicate *lonche* and replace it with *almuerzo*. One might properly ask why this is called "language maintenance."

One other case of language planning will help illustrate the distinction between language and voice. In Peru, Quechua was made an official language, "coequal" with Spanish, in 1975. This policy was hailed at the time as an enhancement of the status of the indigenous language communities to be a significant part of the nation. The problem with Quechua's officialization was the relatively minor role that the Quechua communities themselves played in the decision and its implementation. Almost fifteen years later, there is little hope that Quechua will fulfill any substantive role as an official language, or that Quechua-Spanish bilingual programs in the Highlands will have any impact on Quechua language maintenance (Hornberger, 1988).

I have offered these examples to illustrate the distinction between language and voice. *Language* is general, abstract, subject to a somewhat arbitrary normalization; *voice* is particular and concrete. *Language* has a life of its own—it exists even when it is suppressed; when *voice* is suppressed, it is not heard—it does not exist. To deny people their language, as in the colonial situations described by Fanon (1967) and Macedo (1983), is, to be sure, to deny them voice; but, to allow them "their" language (as in the bilingual education and Peruvian cases just mentioned) is not necessarily to allow them voice. Indeed, this may be the most evil form of colonialism, because everyone, even the colonizers themselves, recognize it as just the opposite. To have a voice implies not just that people can say things, but that they are heard (that is, that their words have status, influence). Giroux (1986) argues that "schools do not allow students from subordinate groups to authenticate their problems and experiences through their own individual and collective voices" (p. 65). Nichols (1984) makes a similar point regarding adult-to-child and male-to-female speech dynamics: "Children talking with adults and women talking with men are consistently and frequently interrupted by their speaking partners, as well as ignored or unsupported when they attempted to choose the topic of conversation" (p.25). The *language* of these situations is largely irrelevant; let us assume that everyone was speaking in his or her own conversational mother tongue. What is important is that some groups consistently impose their *voice* on others. When sociolinguists carry out their investigations of language use, they ask "Who says what to whom in what language?" When we investigate the issue of voice, we should ask, "Who says?"

The question of voice will be taken up again presently. We might anticipate my conclusion: voice is the central ingredient of critical pedagogy; without its consideration, there is no radical reform of curriculum. I would like now to turn to a recent proposal for curricular reform aimed directly at the language-minority student. My evaluation of it will be based on this concern for voice.

School Language and Empowerment

Jim Cummins's 1986 article in the *Harvard Educational Review*, "Empowering Minority Students: A Framework for Intervention," has become one of the most influential works in the literature on the education of minority students. He has since expanded his ideas into the book *Empowering Minority Students* (1989). His use of the term *empowerment* is already a stock item in the lexicons of various areas within the education literature, most notably bilingual education and special education.

Any treatment of the concept of empowerment in education would be incomplete without consideration of Cummins's work. Let us turn to that now.

Cummins's argument runs as follows. First, the failure of minority students is not completely, perhaps not even in major part, an academic or school matter. Instead, one should examine their subordinate status in the larger society, and the ways in which the school reinforces or reproduces that status: "Status and power relations between groups are an important part of any comprehensive account of minority students' school failure" (Cummins, 1986, p. 21). Such failure will persist so long as school reformers fail to take into account these extraschool factors. Second, school and curricular reform must involve the inclusion of the students' home cultural experiences. Here, Cummins is most concerned with four aspects of school structure: "incorporation of minority students' culture and language, inclusion of minority communities in the education of their children, pedagogical assumptions and practices operating in the classroom, and the assessment of minority students" (p. 24). To the extent that schools consistently exclude the child's home experiences from the curriculum, alienate their families and discourage their participation in the education of the children, transmit in an authoritarian way a standardized curriculum, and bias their assessment of minority children to ensure that some "problem" will be found in them, minority students will be disabled. Empowerment comes when schools are inclusionary, when their pedagogy encourages critical, independent thinking, and when they aim to find and build on a child's strengths rather than identify weaknesses. Third, and finally, in the same way that school failure is not merely a school matter, student empowerment cannot be confined to the school. There is a dynamic interrelation between home and school: real school reform and authentic student empowerment will contribute to the transformation of societal power relations as well.

This argument is significant for language-minority students because it describes deep structural reasons for school failure. The language difference of the child is no longer of primary concern; or, more precisely, particular language differences are indicators of class differences, and these are where our examination of school failure should focus. The argument is also significant because it bypasses the usual concern for cognitive or academic justifications for using the first language of these children. One might even say that Cummins's argument makes irrelevant the research on the effectiveness of various methods to use with language-minority students.

I have chosen to be critical of Cummins's work for a specific reason.

Few doubt his personal commitment to the betterment of education for language-minority students or the significance of his scholarship. I judge that Cummins is one of only a handful of academics whose work consistently determines the direction of the literature in this area. It is precisely for that reason that I offer this criticism. What I will try to demonstrate is that, even for those among us who are the most sympathetic to the concerns of minority communities and who are the most conscious of the effect of our public statements, our words sometimes betray what we intend.

Let me now take up this criticism at its most central point. It has to do with the issue of voice. Note the use of "empowerment" in the following typical passages:

> Students from "dominated" societal groups are "empowered" or "disabled" as a direct result of their interactions with educators in the schools. (p. 21)

> Minority students are disabled or disempowered by schools in very much the same way that their communities are disempowered by interactions with societal institutions. (p. 24)

What disturbs me most about such usage is the passivity of the "empowered" groups. Empowerment appears to be an action performed by others on their behalf. This is put most directly in the following passage.

> Language minority students' educational progress is strongly influenced by the extent to which individual educators become advocates for the promotion of students' linguistic talents, actively encourage participation in developing students' academic and cultural resources, and implement pedagogical approaches that succeed in liberating students from instructional dependence. (p. 35)

I do not see here any action on the part of those who are to be empowered. Instead, empowerment is portrayed as a gift to the powerless. This evokes several questions. If empowerment is a gift from those in power to those out, what kind of power would they be willing to give up? Will it be of a sort that might lead to the transformation of society? Could empowerment entail another sort of acculturation, by which we change the behavior of underachieving students to conform to that of high achievers? Are higher test scores the ultimate index of empowerment? Would empowered students become critical, or merely successful?

Beyond these important questions, we should ask, what has happened to student voice? Assuming that students' language has been included in the curriculum, whose voice is heard in it if they are not active participants? How can they be characterized as "empowered" when minority communities merely wait for schools to change in particular ways?

The radical pedagogue who treats empowerment as a gift is not yet radical. Teachers do not empower or disempower anyone, nor do schools. They merely create the conditions under which people can *empower themselves*, or not. It is certainly true that teachers impart skills—literacy, numeracy, and others; but these are not in themselves power. They are tools to be used or not, and, if used, for responsible or irresponsible ends. (If the proficiency in using a standard language to which I contributed becomes a means to denigrate the experience of nonstandard speakers, that is empowerment—but I would not boast about my connection with it.)

The idea that empowerment might be construed as a gift should be a central concern in the development or evaluation of a critical transformative pedagogy. It is one anticipated by Freire (1970), in his most famous work, *Pedagogy of the Oppressed:*

> Not even the best-intentioned leadership can bestow independence as a gift. The liberation of the oppressed is a liberation of men [and women], not things. Accordingly, while no one liberates himself [or herself] by his [or her] own efforts alone, neither is he [or she] liberated by others . . . The conviction of the oppressed that they must fight for their liberation is not a gift bestowed by the revolutionary leadership, but a result of their own *conscientizacao.* (pp. 53-54)

Freire avoids this problem, as well as the problem of voice, by eschewing an orientation of "inclusion." He does not suggest, as does Cummins, that the language and culture of the child should be "included" in the curriculum of the school; this would suggest that this curriculum is fundamentally sound but that it needs a few additions or modifications. Instead, for Freire, the language and culture of the child *constitute* the curriculum. The most dramatic example of this are the "generative words" he uses in adult literacy programs. These words are recorded in an initial period of observation in the village where the program is to take place. In the course of the training, these words are represented to the students as the basis for both decoding instruction and discussion. The discussion results in the development of more words, and these words eventually become themes for further study and discussion. In this way, student voice becomes the curriculum; furthermore, the discussion of themes with other students demonstrates how one's individual voice can be joined with other voices to effect social action on behalf of the community. This is the essence of what Freire calls *conscientizacao*, the development of critical consciousness. Although Freire's early work involved literacy training of peasant adults, he has gone on to show how his can be a more general pedagogy (Freire and Macedo, 1987).

Cummins can be criticized in his assumption that the school will contribute to its own transformation, with little active participation by the minority communities. Freire denies that this can happen, and asserts that the transformation of society will come when the oppressed empower themselves. We should now turn to a consideration of how this might happen, with special emphasis on language minority communities.

Privatization and Power

Henry Giroux (1986) chastises radical educators because they have concentrated on developing a "language of resistance" but not a "language of possibility." By this he means that we should not only understand society, its institutions, and the power relations that result in oppressed classes, but we should devise strategies by which we can take advantage of the transformative possibilities that exist even in the worst cases. In what remains of this essay, I would like to suggest a possibility for social transformation that exists in a conservative critique of bilingual education and cultural pluralism.

This critique is put forward most elegantly by John Edwards (1984). In its broadest terms, it contends that ethnic language and cultural identification are essentially private matters. To promote them in the public sector would be chaotic and fragmenting, since there is no objective measure by which to choose the ethnicities and languages to be subsidized. Besides, this is undesirable because the interest of the state is unity and coherence, and a public cultural pluralism leads to conflict. Therefore, to the extent that programs such as public school bilingual education are to be tolerated, it is only the narrowest form of transitional program that should receive public support. This would exclude "maintenance" programs designed to preserve ethnic language and culture. Presumably, this would also preclude funding any proposals such as that by Cummins, not to mention Freire.

The conservative movement of the 1980s in the United States has placed such critiques at the basis of much public policy, including bilingual education policy. Instead of cultural pluralism, we have "cultural literacy" (Hirsch, 1987) as the guiding principle of curricular reform. This entails, among other things, a national culture and history to be appropriated by everyone as a result of public schooling. From the perspective of critical pedagogy, it means a total exclusion of student voice from the school. Such a state of affairs minimizes the prospects for the empowerment of language minority communities, if we are to believe Cummins and Freire. How can a language of possibility be fashioned from such a critique?

The key lies in the distinction between public and private life. The conservative argues for what I call the "privatization of pluralism," and makes a distinction between private pluralism and public unity. Some advocates of bilingual education see such arguments (rightly, I think) as a way to limit funding for and eventually suppress these programs. Their reaction is to increase the pressure in favor of public funding. Although I do not disagree with the effort to conserve such public school programs, I believe another strategy is advisable if language maintenance and authentic empowerment are the aims. This strategy is to be more conservative than the conservatives by developing the power of privatization.

My study of two contrasting cases has brought me to this point; I refer to them often in my classes and when I write, but it is only now that I articulate the essential lesson in them. These are the German communities of the Midwest in the latter half of the nineteenth century and the Mexican communities of the Southwest at precisely the same time. The Germans were afforded the most extensive programs of public school bilingual education in the history of the country. The public school districts in cities within the so-called German Triangle, Cincinnati, St. Louis, Milwaukee, Chicago, Indianapolis, and others, also developed formal offices of German instruction to supervise the programs. Seminaries and institutes established in part to train German teachers for both public and private schools flourished in Milwaukee and Chicago. In some school districts, as much as 70 percent of the school population took some of their instruction in German as late as 1916. This situation persisted until the beginning of World War I, when anti-German sentiment made German study unpopular. By 1920, the programs that had been so pervasive in the public schools virtually disappeared (Ruiz, 1988). This case is easily contrasted with that of the Mexicans. Not only did they not receive instruction in their own language, but their language was actively suppressed. In some districts, Mexicans were prohibited from attending public schools; when they were allowed, they were prohibited from speaking Spanish, even outside class. This situation persisted into the 1960s, when federally funded Spanish-English bilingual programs were allowed for the first time in the schools of the Southwest.

There is another important contrast to be made in these cases. Today, German communities have effectively lost their language: they are culturally but not linguistically German communities. On the other hand, in spite of much individual language loss, Spanish-speaking Mexican communities still flourish in the Southwest. How is that explained? How is it that publicly supported school programs have led to language loss, whereas linguistic discrimination has resulted in language maintenance? In large part, the explanation lies in the dynamics of privatization. The German communities had strong cultural maintenance institutions of their own—schools, churches, civic organizations—which were neglected in the period of public subsidy. When public support was suddenly withdrawn, those institutions weakened considerably. Along with that, the reversal of public sentiment toward Germans made those communities less willing to engage in activities of cultural and linguistic loyalty which would only intensify social conflict for them. The Mexicans, on the other hand, had no reason to believe that their cultural institutions would be supported outside their communities; they turned inward for support, thereby strengthening those very institutions—the church, the family, and neighborhoods—which would allow for long-term language maintenance. The difference in these two cases demonstrates the potential power of privatization.

I am not the first to suggest such a strategy for language-minority communities. Geneva Smitherman (1984) describes how traditional White education has pulled Black people away from Black language and community. She explores the possibilities for self-empowerment through the reclaiming of Black language within the Black community. Similarly, Shirley Heath (1985) makes a distinction between *maintenance* of language, or the efforts of those outside the community to preserve the language, and the *retention* of language, whereby the community itself acts out its language loyalty. This is put most forcefully by Kjolseth (1982), an advocate of bilingual education and cultural pluralism:

> Chicano families who desire the maintenance of their ethnic language *must* exercise their control over that single domain of language use where they do have effective and continuing con-

trol: the family. Parental insistence upon the use of Spanish by themselves and their children within the private family domain is the *only* realistic hope. (p. 25)

Privatization implies two things: developing the resources readily available to minority communities to increase what the critical theorist calls their own "cultural capital," and minorities taking control of their own lives in such a way that their communities can act positively in their own interests. Such action may include pressure on the public sector for subvention of their activities, but it need not be dependent on such support. School programs that aim at these goals might very well resemble Mr. Hardcastle's English class, of which one student reported the following: "If the type of English work we have been discussing continues, then the possibility of taking control of our own lives, our own education, and becoming our own experts, is extremely exciting" (McLeod, 1986, p. 49). Privatization and "taking control" is another way of saying that the student's voice is developed and heard in the educational experience.

Let me conclude by suggesting two modifications to the lexicon of critical pedagogy. First, we should understand that when we say "language," we often mean "voice." I hope I have shown how we delude ourselves into thinking that because we include the first we include the second. And second, *empowerment* may not be desirable in English because of our tendency to use it as a transitive verb; this denies both voice and agency to students and communities. A convenient one-word substitute does not come readily to mind; *appropriation* is not exactly synonymous with *taking control*. Perhaps this discussion will provoke someone to think of something suitable. The point to be made is that voice and agency are central to critical pedagogy; without them there is no such thing as "empowerment."

Chapter 11

Changing Our Ideas About Ourselves: Group Consciousness Raising with Elementary School Girls as a Means to Empowerment

———————————————————— *Lee Anne Bell*

"You made me change my whole entire idea about myself."
— Amy, grade 5

This chapter describes a process for challenging barriers to female achievement that emerged from an ethnographic research project in one urban elementary school.[1] The project was designed to explore the perceptions and experiences of elementary school girls through listening to them talk about their lives in school. We met weekly with two groups of girls, a third- and fourth-grade group and a fifth- and sixth-grade group, to explore achievement-related issues described in the educational and psychological literature as problematic for females. The process that evolved through our discussions with these two groups of girls can best be described as "consciousness raising."

The evolution of this process and the learnings about potential interventions to empower girls in school are described below and illustrated by examples from the project.[2] Also described is the process by which we, the researchers, and other teachers in the school raised our own consciousness of the dilemmas females face in our culture and ways we might change our practice to challenge these dilemmas more effectively.

Consciousness Raising: Metaphor and Method

The meaning of *consciousness raising* as it is used in this chapter derives from two sources. One source is the feminist consciousness-raising process of the early 1970s, a process by which individual women explored their experiences in a supportive group and through naming their problems and concerns collectively were able to see the ways in which what appear as an individual's problems are faced by all women in a patriarchal system. Through such insights, consciousness of the oppressive socialization and institutional power relations in the culture was heightened, thus opening new possibilities for collective action.

A second source is Freire's notion of 'conscientization', by which people who are oppressed work collectively to name, analyze, and change the conditions of their lives (1971). In this theory, the act of naming reality collectively is a means of taking power over it and claiming the right to challenge oppressive conditions. This meaning of consciousness raising also informs the project described here.

The consciousness-raising nature of our work as a research team and in our group interviews with the girls evolved as we grappled with ways to explore how and why female achievement in school is restricted. The process of searching for a way to proceed affected our interactions as a research team, how we connected and worked with teachers in the school, and the process by which we engaged the girls in our research. *Consciousness raising* emerges as a descriptive metaphor for the process we created.

The Research Team: Inviting Multiple Perspectives

The core staff consisted of a multiracial team of four women with diverse professional backgrounds and orientations. Two were university professors—Myra Armstead, historian who is African American, and Lee Bell, an educational researcher who is Anglo/White. Two were practitioners—Laura Shapiro, a staff development person who is White/Jewish, and Evy Morales, a Latina who is a counselor for Talent Search, a program that identifies and encourages minority high school students to plan for college. We saw our racial, ethnic, and work experience diversity as assets that would help us be more conscious of the dynamics of race, class, and gender as we observed in classrooms and interacted with the girls.

Part of our ongoing process as a team was to examine continually how we were going about the project, the questions we were posing, and how these were informed by our diverse backgrounds and experiences. This meant building in as much flexibility as we could so that the group sessions and observations could build on our evolving knowledge. It also meant being willing to question each other and challenge taken-for-granted notions in ourselves and in the literature we were reviewing, and mining our own memories and experiences as sources of data.

Reclaiming Our Own Girlhoods

For the first four months we gathered literature on female achievement in schools, with particular emphasis on finding literature that looked at race and class. We then met once a week to discuss the readings and to focus self-consciously on our own girlhoods and on how our racial, ethnic, and class identities affected our development as females. We used these discussions to shape the questions for the study and to examine the methods we proposed to use.

These discussions raised our own consciousness. They helped us recall what it was like to be in elementary school, how we felt about ourselves as learners, what we remembered our parents and teachers saying to us about ourselves as learners, and how we related to other students in our classes. Through our discussions we recalled childhood experiences with classmates and teachers and examined their impact on our development as women, in particular our inner sense of competence, achievement, and power. We told each other stories about our best and worst experiences in school and then analyzed how these stories reflected gender, class, and racial oppression. We analyzed how we resisted, conformed, and survived. We became sensitized to the issues raised in the literature and critical of research that violated or ignored aspects of our respective realities. We challenged research that purported to be inclusive and discussed how we might avoid ethnocentrism in our own work.

We also became conscious of the power of research to distort and oversimplify complex realities. We became more critical of what we read and less tentative about voicing our own analyses and theories. We became angry at the picture research paints of females, one that presents us as deficient. We began to ask, What are female strengths and how are these ignored or downplayed?

This reflective practice became a core part of our team process. We began observing in the school, comparing our observations with what we found in the literature and with our own experiences as students. At our weekly meetings we continued to share our personal reactions to what we observed. We reflected upon our differing reactions to different teaching styles and teacher behaviors, the students to whom our attention was drawn, whom we ignored, and how these selective perceptions might be shaped by our own class or race lenses. These discussions made us more open, more sharply observant, and less likely to overlook interactions in the classroom that reveal race and class dynamics.

School-Team Partnership:
The Struggle to Bridge an Unequal Relationship

We were joined in this reflective process by two teachers from the district who we hired as teacher-researchers. Ruth Goins is an African American woman who has been teaching for twenty-eight years and is currently a curriculum specialist in the district office. Roberta Kerman is a White/Jewish woman, a K-6 teacher who has taught for twelve years.

Our goal was to build in expertise from the school level, people who would teach us about their system and who would become the in-house experts on what we learned from the project. The realities of their schedules and limitations on how we could pay them meant, however, that they were less central to the project than we had hoped. We were able to meet as a whole group only once a month, and Ruth and Roberta were constantly catching up with what the rest of us had been reading, discussing, and doing. In hindsight, there is much to learn about the limitations on school-university partnerships in the process we experienced.[3]

Nonetheless, Ruth and Roberta also shared their experiences in school as learners and as teachers and engaged in a process of self-reflection that added significantly to our conceptualization of the issues. They too became more conscious of the race, class, and gender dynamics in the environment around them. They also kept us conscious of the frustrations and constraints teachers experience on a daily basis and kept us grounded in the realities of daily school life and the dilemmas of how to effect change in schools.

We met with the entire staff of the school at the beginning of the year to describe our project and request permission to observe in classrooms. We also conducted in-depth interviews with nine teachers and the principal. At the end of the year, four teachers from the school met with us to go over our tentative findings and to discuss possible next steps. This session followed the same consciousness-raising format: we began with sharing our own personal experiences as girls in school and using this grounding to discuss what the girls in the study had told us. We examined themes common to these experiences and compared them with themes raised by the girls. We talked about how we as adults could challenge these barriers in our classrooms and discussed how schools could be restructured to be more supportive of female achievement.

This meeting with teachers reaffirmed for me the importance of challenging my own misconceptions about teachers and diverse teaching styles. It helped me to appreciate the ways in which female and minority teachers themselves are restricted by the racism and sexism inherent in the school culture and the value of taking time to explore these issues in a supportive group as a vehicle for change.

For example, one African American teacher we observed spoke very loudly and (to us) harshly to students, exhibiting a very different style from the nurturing, supportive style I have come to regard as the most student centered. In getting to know this teacher through sharing our personal experiences, I realized that her own history of being ignored by teachers because of her race and gender made her extremely concerned about her students, especially female students. Her style reflected her desire to challenge students to be assertive and stick up for themselves. Furthermore, we learned that the students themselves understood the intentions behind her behavior. They were describing to us their favorite teachers one day, and several girls named this teacher because "we know she loves us."

Forming a Multiracial, All-Girl Group

We decided to interview girls in groups so that we could learn from their interactions with one another and because we felt it was more likely that they would find it interesting and be willing to talk with us if they could be with other girls. From the first session and often throughout the time we met, the girls remarked on how unusual it was to have an all-girl group and how much they liked being together without boys around. The following excerpts reveal the similarity of concerns that arose in both groups.

Third and fourth graders:

Carmen (third grade, Hispanic): I think it's real fun because sometimes if boys were here and you tell them things that are embarrassing and they always laugh in your face and they don't take it serious.

Susan (third grade, Black): If boys were here, everything we said they would go tell their other friends.

Keisha (third grade, Black): They try to get us aggravated and if you say something wrong, they'll tell everybody in the whole school.

Beth (fourth grade, white): That's because they think they're much better than us, than girls.

Fifth and sixth graders:

Julie (fifth grade, White): I like the group of girls because every time a boy is around you or anything they laugh at you and make fun of you and you feel weird and I don't like that.

Natasha (sixth grade, Black): They start to argue.

Katherine (sixth grade, White): After you say what you have to say they'll go off and tell someone else what you said.

Betsey (sixth grade, White): Well, I don't think it's bad for a group to have boys but it's just that it's harder to open up to them or to say what you want to say. I think maybe it's easier to do that with girls because the same things are happening to them.

The individual stories they told shared a common theme of frustration and conflict with boys' behavior. According to the girls, an all-female group provided safety, trust, common experiences, confidentiality, and equality. These are similar to the conditions affirmed in feminist consciousness-raising groups. When we asked what the disadvantages of an all-girl group might be, there was a resounding "None!" When pushed, one girl, Betsy, suggested that talking to boys might also be useful "so then maybe it'll be easier to talk to them like if you know a little bit more about them." But this was clearly not the predominant view.

The significance of the group for the girls was also evidenced by their attendance and comments from their teachers. The group was voluntary; there was no penalty for not attending. We had to meet at a different time each week so they wouldn't miss the same part of their classes, and thus ended up with a fairly complicated rotation that they had to remember themselves. Despite that, only three girls missed a session in the entire fourteen weeks. One teacher commented: "I know that the girls who go [to Project REACH] are very enthusiastic. We have many programs in the school. And that is the one the girls absolutely want to go to. Wanika for example has dropped out of [a special program]. It's boring and she doesn't want to be in it. When it's time for Project REACH, they are right there ready and happy."

A second aspect of the group that was important to the girls was the opportunity to share experiences, learn from each other, and discover that they were not alone in feeling or perceiving as they did. They were able to verbalize together previously taboo or unexplored subjects such as the implicit rules of the school, popularity and social relations, and how they felt about success, failure, and achievement. They had the opportunity for a kind of cross-race interaction and dialogue that was not prevalent in the regular school environment.

Also significant was the opportunity to observe, ask questions, and interact with five adult women. One very important member of the team from the girls' perspective was Alexis Mariette, our video person. A young African American woman and college student, she served as a important role model for the girls, someone closer to them in age and with whom they could more easily identify. They looked forward to seeing her and were interested in her knowledge of video production, her college experiences, personal life, and future plans. Different girls were also drawn to each of the four of us and became quite interested in different aspects of our lives—Myra's pregnancy and college teaching, Laura's art, Evy's running, Lee's writing.

Empowerment Activities

The activities we found most powerful for the girls and for our own learning about what happens to females in school are described below. These activities emerged through our interactions with these particular girls. Although the issues they raised are reflective of a broader female experience in school, the power of these particular activities came from their immediacy and connection to the felt concerns of this group. The specific activities described here could be replicated by others and are described in enough detail that this would be possible. More important for replication, however, is the process by which girls can be engaged in expressing their concerns in a supportive group and helped to reflect on the broader issues that unite these concerns so that greater options for individual and collective action become visible. The process itself is empowering. Any number of unique activities might be developed through this process and tailored to the specific needs and concerns of a particular group.

Forming the Group to Reflect
the Diversity of the Community

I believe our random selection and deliberate plan to reflect the racial and class diversity of the district was important to the learnings in the group. Most of the girls were not friends before they met with us, though many shared the same classes. We deliberately structured activities so that the girls could get to know each other better, so that every girl had the opportunity to speak in every session, and so that cross-race interaction and dialogue occurred regularly. Establishing this structure at the outset was important in developing norms for participation.

We were struck in our observations by very obvious race and gender segregation in almost every classroom in this school. When we asked teachers about this in the interviews, most attributed the segregation to student choice based on common neighborhoods and friendships outside of school. Many teachers did not see it as their job to intervene or foster corss-race and cross-gender interaction within their classrooms. Those few who did intervene were notable.

In the initial sessions we played name games that allowed each girl to get to know everyone else in the group and to signal that this would be different from "regular school." We wanted to establish an atmosphere in which the girls could express themselves without fear of judgment and in which diverse opinions would be encouraged. We paired girls cross-racially to interview and get to know one another. We asked them to talk about likes and dislikes, favorite music, activities, and ways to spend private time. Many different connections among diverse girls began to develop.

Generative Themes: Identifying Key Problems

The literature talks about success and failure as problematic for females (Dweck et al., 1978; Frieze, 1980; Horner, 1972; Maehr and Nicholls, 1980; Stein and Bailey, 1973). In order to explore these issues we paired girls cross-racially and asked them to interview one another. First they told each other about a time they were very successful and what that felt like. Then one member of each pair summarized the discussion for the whole group. Next we asked the pairs to discuss a time they failed or did poorly at something, and this time the person who had not reported the first time to the whole group was asked to do so.

When we reviewed the videotape of this session, we noticed that, in all but one case, the White member of the pair had spoken first. This signaled us to be constantly alert to patterns of dominance and to intervene carefully to ensure that the Black and Hispanic girls were heard as loudly and as often as the White girls.

We discussed this issue in our team meetings and explored what type of group structure, process, and content appeared to privilege one racial group over another. For example, the Black girls preferred not to talk a great deal about their homes and families, whereas the White girls appeared to be more comfortable talking about family topics. The process of discussing issues in pairs rather than as a whole group seemed more comfortable for the shyer girls, in particular one Black girl and one Hispanic girl. We tried to structure our questions to accommodate these preferences.

The previously described activity was intended to elicit from the girls the kinds of situations that signified success and failure for them. The success situations they described were athletic or interpersonal, such as learning to dive off the high dive or learning to take care of a younger sibling. The failure situations were either athletic or academic, such as striking out in a baseball game or doing poorly on a test.

We took the situations the girls provided and developed role plays that explored these situations in more depth in succeeding sessions. The girls divided into small groups and prepared to act out the role play. A sample role play instruction was as follows: "You are waiting in line to have your turn to shoot a basket during gym. A boy comes over and says, 'Give me that ball, I'll shoot it. You can't do it.' You give him the ball." The whole group next discussed the role play in terms of how they thought the girl felt and how she might respond differently in order to get what she wanted and feel good about herself. In this case, the group decided that the girl had a right to learn how to play basketball and would never be able to learn if she didn't get the chance to play. The interventions they suggested were to say no and take your turn, to invite the boy to help you improve instead of taking the ball away, and to ask other girls to intervene and support the girl's right to have a turn and not be harassed.

A second role play that proved powerful was one in which one girl won a science prize but dismissed her achievement in front of a friend who was envious. The situation illustrated a core dilemma girls experience arising from the perception that achievement and affiliation are mutually exclusive. We asked the girls to examine the situation and think of alternatives that would enable both girls to feel good about themselves and get what they want, to feel good about achieving and get the friendship and support they value. The group eagerly engaged in a discussion which yielded such options as "tear the trophy in half," "give it to the teacher," "leave it in school," "give half to the other girl," and "give the trophy away, it's just a piece of metal." All of the suggested options sacrificed achievement in order to preserve the relationship. However, when the girls explored these options in more depth, they decided that all still left one or both girls feeling bad. The "winner" couldn't enjoy her success and the "loser" was left with unacknowledged, negative feelings.

We reiterated our challenge to the group to find a solution that would affirm both girls. They struggled and seemed stuck until Hadley, a fourth grader, offered the following: "When they [the judges] pick, probably a lot of people could have gotten first place, but they can only pick one. She wasn't there [to hear the judging process], she could have won too." The sense of breakthrough was palpable. Immediately several new solutions emerged. All aimed at restructuring the situation to allow everyone to do creative, high quality projects by working together cooperatively. The problem was externalized onto the system of judging rather than internalized as defects in individual girls.

The girls were completely engrossed in this process of analyzing situations that reflected actual problems they faced in school and generating alternative ways to understand and address common problems. By expanding their analysis to a larger context, in this case the competitive structure of the situation, the girls broke through dilemmas and generated new options for confronting competitive situations. This process exemplified consciousness raising in that a situation that had previously seemed self-evident expanded to a whole new vision of possibility; a situation that seemed one of personal failure was expanded tone that challenged the system itself.[4]

Exposing Contradictions:
Be Successful But Don't Let Anybody Know

Exposing the contradictory messages females receive and analyzing how these messages affect behavior raises our consciousness of the societal constraints that restrict us. The girls in Project REACH were quite articulate in describing the contradictions they experienced with regard to achievement and success.

One such discussion focused on norms governing success in school. Success is a loaded experience for females in this culture and embodies a myriad of conflicting feelings, values, and cultural messages about gender, race, and class. Girls receive contradictory messages about success from a competitively oriented society that on the one hand claims that females can be and do anything, but on the other promotes the belief that females should be "feminine," passive, and protected from risk (Chodorow, 1974). Females are often said to avoid success because it conflicts with the feminine role (Horner, 1972).

This issue is complicated by other cultural messages about race and class that focus on individual achievement rather than on societal discrimination. To the extent that people of color, women, and working-class people internalize this ideology, they learn to blame themselves for failure to achieve without questioning a win-lose system that builds in failure for certain groups. On the other hand, members of marginal groups also are in a better position to examine the conflicts with success they experience and to have insight into the unspoken norms governing social situations, norms that are often invisible to those who benefit and thus have no reason to question the status quo (Miller, 1976).

Our girls expressed pride in success but did not want to achieve it at the expense of others. Their responses showed that they don't fear success itself so much as the isolation with which they associate success (Sassen, 1980).

> Judith: One time we had to take a math test in second grade and I was the only one who passed it.
>
> Lee: How did that make you feel?
>
> Judith: Proud.
>
> Lee: How did the others in the class react?
>
> Judith: I didn't tell them.
>
> Lee: Why not?
>
> Judith: I would feel like I was bragging.

This theme of hiding success for fear of seeming to put oneself above others was prevalent among all the girls in our sample regardless of grade. One sixth grader grappled with the dilemma in the following way:

> Jane (after receiving a compliment on a science prize): Well, I don't feel that great when you say that to me because I feel like everybody's equal and everybody should have gotten a prize no matter what they did. I think Chris should have gotten it.
>
> Myra: OK Jane, tell the group why you didn't say, "I feel good about winning this prize."
>
> Jane: Well I feel like um, like everybody's looking at me and um saying, "Oh, she shouldn't have won that prize, I should have won," and everybody's gonna be mad at me because um, I won and they didn't.
>
> Myra: Is there any situation that you could think of where you won an honor that you were deserving of and felt good about it?
>
> Jane: If other people won also.

Although Jane felt uncomfortable about acknowledging her success publicly, she did feel good about her accomplishment.

Myra: When you said that you didn't want to accept a compliment and thought other people should win, did you also really think you deserved it deep down? Just within yourself, not worrying about other people?

Jane: Yeah, I thought I deserved it but I didn't want to say it because then other people might think I was bragging.

The literature on achievement motivation depicts girls as more likely to attribute success to external causes such as luck, timing, or the help of others, whereas boys are more likely to take credit for success by attributing their achievements to ability or effort (Dweck et al., 1978; Maehr and Nicholls, 1980). Our research found that girls learn to muffle acknowledgement of their successes in order to avoid the appearance of bragging.

The term *bragging* was brought up so repeatedly by girls in both groups that it symbolized a core issue. This issue has at least two aspects. First, girls do not like to place themselves above others, partly because they fear ostracism but also because they value social solidarity (Maehr, 1983). Second, girls, particularly minority girls, may see more clearly the actual conditions that govern success in a competitive system. As members of subordinate groups, as Fordham's chapter in this volume shows, they experience a value conflict that the dominant group does not. Part of the difficulty they have in taking credit for success may be the result of perceptive insight into a competitive system that mystifies the conditions for success: that is, although the system purports that individual effort alone is necessary, in fact social class, race, status, and opportunity have a great deal to do with actual achievement.

To the extent that girls do not become conscious of the conflicting values embedded in their reaction to success, they internalize the problem. Their ambivalence about success can lead to failure to own their achievements, an unwillingness to take appropriate risks in order to achieve, and ultimately an avoidance of success situations. Helping girls to affirm their achievements publicly and at the same time take seriously their aversion to competitive structures by helping them analyze and explore alternatives allows them to consider more than an either/or option to this dilemma.

Making the Implicit Explicit

Consciousness raising makes the implicit explicit so that taken-for-granted common wisdom is opened to scrutiny and challenge. Several of the activities we designed focused on naming unspoken norms so that the girls could analyze the effects of these norms on their feelings and behavior in school.

An example of this process came up in a discussion about what it means to be smart in school. The unspoken norm that was verbalized was "You should be smart, but not too smart." We asked how one could effectively follow such an injunction and received the following advice:

> Wanika: Just raise your hand and like if she [the teacher] looks your way, just put it back down. When she's not looking put it back up.

> Lee: No, be serious.

> Wanika: No, I'm serious because then she would pick on you.

> Lee: The teacher?

> Wanika: So then she wouldn't call on you. Like, OK, say you kept on raising your hand and she keeps on calling on you. Then people are going to say, "Oh man, I have the answer too and I had the same answer that's right" and everything. So [giggles] what I do is when the teacher's not looking at me, I raise my hand and then when she's looking, I go like this [lowers hand] raise my hand a little bit. And then I keep on going like this when she's not looking [raises hand high and waves it].

This behavior functions to distribute the teacher's attention equally so that no one person stands out, a creative solution to the injunction to be smart but not too smart. However, it also serves to disempower girls by preventing their full participation. This led to a discussion of how such an injunction could be harmful, what the effects might be on learning and achievement, and how the injunction might be challenged. We asked the girls how they would change classrooms so that it was OK to be smart and participate fully. Again, their suggestions demonstrated a preference for a cooperative system where being smart would not be at the expense of others.

Rehearsing Alternative Behaviors

Once girls became aware of the disadvantages of responding to situations in certain ways, they were eager to experiment with new ways of responding that would get them what they want and help them feel good about themselves. We began to role-play alternative responses to oppressive situations.

For example, we discussed how girls typically respond when they fail or do poorly at something and what the advantages and disadvantages to responding this way might be. If success is problematic, girls receive even more conflicting messages about failure. Research says they are more likely to internalize failure, whereas boys are more likely to externalize it (Frieze, 1980). Boys' ability to accept and learn from failure more easily is attributed to their wider experience with competitive team sports and the greater amount of critical academic feedback they receive from teachers (Sadker and Sadker, 1982). The failure dilemma is further compounded by race since many teachers give less attention to and hold lower expectations for Black children, reward nonacademic, custodial behaviors in Black girls, and give them fewer opportunities to respond in the classroom than they do boys and White girls (Grant, 1984; Irvine, 1986; Scott-Jones and Clark, 1986).

We asked each of our girls to tell about a time when she did poorly or failed. Many described athletic or academic situations. One fourth grader related this representative example:

> Alexis: I was at baseball and we were losing the game. I was the last person to bat and I had to not get out. And I got out and they all said "You're no good."
>
> Evy: How did that make you feel?
>
> Alexis: Like a basket case.

The result of doing poorly or failing was embarrassment and humiliation. We asked, "When you make a mistake or fail like everyone does, what do you do to make yourself feel better?" Their responses were to withdraw from the situation and to focus on feelings. None focused on how to improve their performance, persist, or challenge the dynamics of the situation itself.

> Anika: I lie to myself and say I don't care.
>
> Judith: I turn my head away from everyone til everyone stops laughing. When they try to act nice, I'll be cheered up by them.
>
> Rosa: I call my friend up and talk for two or three hours.
>
> Celeste: I write something on notes then I hide them away in my treasure box.

We asked them to consider how they might respond differently. The discussion was a struggle until they moved beyond the all-or-nothing dilemma of performing with perfection or withdrawing. No other alternatives emerged until we suggested the possibility of asserting their

feelings about what was going on and ideas for change within the situation itself. They practiced responding assertively within the situation rather than withdrawing:

> Kamillah: I feel angry when you say I can't act because I study a lot and I learn my lines.

> Amy: I feel insulted when you say I should give up on math because it's not fair. I could just work harder and I could try to do it.

Spontaneously, we started challenging, really pushing the girls to stick up for themselves. At first, they had great difficulty finding words to say and acted like they wanted to flee, but eventually they became more assertive and eager to be challenged so they could practice answering back.

> Laura: OK, Carmen, let's say I come up to you and you just said you like sports. OK, and I say "Oh come on, I know you're good now but it's really gonna get harder. You can't, you can't do that. Oh, give up!"

> Carmen: No I'm not.

> Laura: So what are you gonna say to me?

> Carmen: Well, I don't know [how good I'll be] until I try.

> Laura: So you say, "I'd really like a chance. I deserve a chance."

> Carmen: You don't know what will come for me.

> Laura: OK, who else would like to try with something that they like?

> Voices: Me! Me! Me!

> Sandy: I like music.

> Laura: Oh, but music that's really hard, you really have to work hard, read all that music and practice all the time. You wouldn't want to do that.

> Sandy: Well um maybe that's just your opinion.

> Laura: And what's your opinion?

> Sandy: Maybe you don't like music but I do.

> Laura: You mean you really think its worth practicing all that time? Do you?

Sandy: I like a lot of music.

Myra: What if I told you the harder music gets the more like math it is?

Sandy: I'm gonna say um, I'm gonna ask someone to help me.

Laura: All right! Atta way.

Hadley: Um, I like science.

Laura: Science! Ugh, that's gross. That's all for men and you won't be able to handle all that stuff. You'll get all messed up, you'll get all confused so forget it. What are you gonna say to me?

Hadley: I don't know . . . I won't!

Laura: What makes you think you won't?

Hadley: I can do it. I've enjoyed it for a long time now and I've never messed up yet.

Laura: Yeah, well that's now, but wait until later. It gets really hard. Are you sure you can put up with that?

Hadley: Well, I know how hard it is . . . but I still like it. I can do it!

Celeste: I have two. One's math and one's baseball.

Laura: Math! Oh, math, math is fun now in elementary school but boy, you know it's really not for girls. It's really not for you. You have to work really hard and you have to read lots of books, what are you gonna say to me?

Celeste: Well I'm good at math and if I can keep working on it, I'll get better. And when I go to college I'll be as good as the others.

Myra: But there are hardly any girls who do math.

Celeste: Well, I like it.

The option of proactively responding to such situations rather than withdrawing passively and internalizing the response was perceived as liberating. Each time a girl was challenged and responded assertively, the others cheered enthusiastically and the respondents became more confident and eager to try.

An interesting outcome of this discussion was observed in one fourth-grade classroom following this session. The teacher was working with a small reading group, and, as we had noticed repeatedly in our observations, boys dominated the group by raising their hands more, calling out for the teacher's attention, and misbehaving. One of our girls, small for her age and usually quiet, turned to the boy next to her who was pounding the table to get the teacher's attention and said, "When you do that it annoys me. Please control yourself. I want a chance to answer the question." The boy looked shocked and then acceded to her request and stopped pounding the table.

Analyzing Cultural Messages:
Media Beauty Versus Marginality

Another highly engrossing consciousness-raising activity was examining media messages about beauty. Physical appearance is important to girls even at this early age. A recent newspaper article reported that a large percentage of fourth-grade girls are on diets and consider themselves too fat. The importance of appearance and its effect on girls' behavior was vividly expressed by one fifth grader:

> Wanika: So um all you gotta do is, like the people you wanna be in with, watch the way they act and act like that . . . like you wanna act like yourself, be yourself, you wanna wear your own clothes, your own hairstyle. But you, you wanna be in the cool group too, you wanna do both at the same time, but you can't do both . . . Can't get everything you want.

We explored the role physical appearance plays in girls' attitudes toward success by asking them to list the media messages females receive about how we should look in order to be successful. The following is a composite list from both groups:

tall	blonde	blue-eyed
thin	rich	long hair
beautiful	skinny	good looking
pretty	popular	famous
long, wavy hair	fur coats	wear makeup
dainty personality	nice figure	nice smile
matching clothes	accessories	clothes and dress
look neat and in	(extra stuff)	for every
place even with		occasion
babies		

Even the most superficial examination of this list reveals messages about gender, race, and class that limit and restrict girls' images of how they might be successful.

We then displayed a collection of pictures we had assembled on three walls of the room. These pictures included girls and women of all sizes, shapes, races, ages, and social classes doing a variety of interesting things. We asked the girls to examine these pictures and make a list of ways in which they contradicted the media messages. Their conclusions were listed on the board as follows. "You can be successful and look . . ."

fat	skinny	young
old	Black	White
poor	rich	sloppy
dressy	Spanish	in the middle
handicapped	not rich	tough
wrinkly	beautiful or	boyish or feminine
many different	not beautiful	old, young and
ways	doing different	in-between
lots of different	things	
shades and colors		

The girls discussed the differences between the two lists and why there might be such a discrepancy between media images and reality. During this discussion the following interchange occurred:

Laura: What race is she? [one of the pictures on the wall].

Susan: Puerto Rican.

Keisha: Nuh uh!

Susan: Pork chop.

Keisha: Wait, I never saw a, a Puerto Rica . . . I never saw a successful Puerto Rican.

Susan: Oh? La Bamba is successful.

Keisha: He ain't no Puerto Rican.

Lee: I'd like to stop a minute. What were you saying about Puerto Ricans?

Keisha: I said, I said Puerto Ricans, I never knew a Puerto um Puerto Rican successful guy or woman and and . . .

Lee: Well, we have a successful Puerto Rican woman in our group.

Keisha: Who? [looks at Evy].

Evy: Did you think that Puerto Ricans eat pork chops? Is that what you meant?

Carmen: Sometimes I don't eat pork chops and I'm Puerto Rican and Dominican.

The discussion continued about stereotypes and how we learn them. We talked about what the media says about different cultural groups and how it feels to be defined in such ways.

Then we asked the girls to work together on a definition of beauty that would include all the females in the pictures. Their responses included the following:

"Beauty is . . . doing your own thing.
            having lots of interests.
            believing in yourself.
            looking how you want to."

Through this activity the girls challenged the "success = beauty" dilemma and created new awareness. This session had a lasting impact and was referred to often by the girls. At the beginning of this session one third-grade Black girl whispered to me, "I really want to be White. I told my parents and that's what I want." At the end of the session we asked each girl to write an essay entitled "Ways in which I am beautiful." This girl then wrote, "I am beautiful because I am proud of my race, I'm smart and I have pretty brown eyes." Another girl who had initially stated that she wanted to look like Vanna White, a stereotypic blonde, blue-eyed TV game show hostess, later wrote, "I am beautiful because I'm good in school, I'm Puerto Rican and Dominican, and I'm good at sports."

Women Using Tools:
The Power to Shape the Environment

We examined media messages again in a session on tools. For this session we invited a local educational consultant who has built her own house and uses tools all the time. We introduced her and then asked the girls, "What kind of messages do we get as females about using tools?"

Jane: We're not strong enough.

Melissa: Some commercials say um women are supposed to like work in the house and not jobs. If we use tools we might hurt ourselves.

The speaker then talked about her own experiences as a young girl, preferring to work with her hands and frustrated by her alienation from school activities that relied solely on paper-and-pencil learning. The rapt attention of the girls suggested that many of them identified strongly with the speaker's story. Next, she laid out a large assortment of tools and invited the girls to share their knowledge about the functions of these tools. A great deal of collective knowledge as well as misinformation was gathered and discussed.

A particularly captivating activity for many of the girls was the opportunity to learn to use large power tools. These included a table saw and a jigsaw. The speaker talked about safety and how best to use these tools and also related a story about being cautioned that as a woman she shouldn't use heavy power equipment. To conclude the session the girls worked in teams of four to design a dog house, window box, playhouse, or tree house and to decide which tools they would need to complete the project. In so doing they challenged taken-for-granted notions about women's abilities to work with tools and examined whom such messages serve. As one girl said, "If girls don't think they can do it, the boys get to have all the fun!"

Conclusion

Project REACH concluded with an end-of-the-year gathering on campus hosted by the staff for the girls and their parents. After some introductory remarks we asked the girls to gather in small groups and develop skits that would illustrate for the parents and teachers what Project REACH had been about and what they had learned from participating. These skits were creatively designed and enthusiastically presented. We marveled at the self-confidence, critical awareness, and assertiveness they exemplified when contrasted with our first meetings with the girls. Ruth Goins was particularly impressed by the change in Maria, an excruciatingly shy fifth-grade Hispanic girl, who stood in front of an audience of twenty-five peers and fifteen or so adults and acted out her role in the skit with aplomb. Additional comments from parents and other teachers reflected surprise and pleasure at the change in confidence and self-assurance they noticed in their daughters and students.

In late fall of the following year, we hosted another campus event for the girls and their parents during which we engaged them in a science lesson and a women's history lesson. Their enthusiastic participation in these lessons demonstrated continuing confidence and ability to engage in critical analysis of issues in their lives. The women's history lesson included creation of a time line listing significant dates in women's history that extended around the four walls of the room and ended with the current date and the names of all of the girls in Project

REACH followed by an open-ended space for inclusion of their own yet-to-be-created contributions to women's history. After the group left campus, I found a note addressed "to Lee, Evy, Myra and Laura from the girls of Project REACH—women shall rool the world!"

It remains to be seen how the girls who participated in Project REACH will fare as they enter middle and high school and confront the increased pressures to conform to a restrictive female role. If their participation in Project REACH helps them to be conscious and critical of norms that oppose their own interests and to believe in their right to assert their own preferences, perhaps they will find creative ways to survive these pressures and maintain a belief in themselves as capable.

For those of us who are educators, the girls in Project REACH taught us how we might change schools to be more affirming of girls. Among these approaches are creating a participatory and cooperative learning environment where social solidarity is an asset to learning; fostering connections and dialogue among students from diverse racial and social groups; and helping students name, analyze and challenge classroom, school, and social norms that are oppressive. In addition, groups of teachers can use this consciousness-raising process with themselves to build a support group and find ways to expose and analyze the contradictions they face as teachers and as females. In so doing, we can recognize that the problems that plague us are not individual and that collectively we can empower ourselves to take action and in effect "rool" our own lives.

Chapter 12

Who Is Empowering Whom?
The Social Construction of Empowerment

———————————————————— *Susan R. Takata*

Introduction

In recent years, there has been an attempt to "democratize" higher education which has resulted in some dramatic changes in today's student population. As a result, undergraduate students bring with them a highly individualized cultural baggage which reflects their diversity of lifestyles and experiences. Inevitably such changes have an impact on the quality of university life. It is important for the university to understand the context and contents of such baggage brought with the "atypical" university student. The word *atypical* is used to refer to the first-generation college student, the working- or lower-class student, the nontraditional older student, the non-White student, or any combination thereof. Such students begin their university experience at a clear disadvantage, which may be reflective of years of oppression (Freire, 1972; Blauner, 1968; Carnoy, 1974; Clark, 1965). A combination of oppressions results in numerous educational deficiencies in atypical students. They do not typically attend the university; therefore fitting in may be a problem. Because they are few in number, they wonder about their own sense of belonging. As a "norm breaker," these students receive little, if any, support and encouragement and have few role models to turn to. Mixed messages are sent to the student which fre-

Special thanks are extended to the twenty-four students involved in undergraduate sociological research at the University of Wisconsin, Parkside. I am also grateful to Jeanne Curran and Hans Mauksch for their gentle guidance and constant support.

quently lower expectations while squelching hopes, and ultimately result in a self-fulfilling prophecy of failure.

Education is one avenue which offers opportunities for success. Drucker (1968) states, "Education has become too powerful to go unchallenged for schooling increasingly controls access to careers, opportunities, and advancement" (p. 313). Clark (1965) notes, "In American life, where education is considered the first prerequisite for adult success, the issue is especially sensitive" (p. 117). The focus of this chapter is on the atypical student who attempts to resolve the initial contradictions presented by two very different worlds—home and neighborhood life versus university life—which may or may not lead to eventual success.

The purpose of this chapter is to discuss one teaching approach that demonstrates the social construction of empowerment for students and future teachers. All too often the creative imaginations of atypical students as well as teachers are stifled by a system of policies, traditions, norms, rules, and regulations. How does one survive? In other words, how does one manage to overcome those aspects which constantly stifle creativity? If teachers are not empowered as a group to release the creativity and imagination within their students, then what becomes of the teacher, not to mention the students? Therefore, the critical question is, How are teachers empowered?

Unfortunately, undergraduate students are rarely afforded the opportunity to test out their knowledge and skills in the real world prior to commencement. Even student-teaching is an extremely structured, short-term exercise providing the student with few opportunities to be creative. In other words, students spend much of their undergraduate energies as passive receivers of information rather than active learners applying their knowledge.

This chapter describes *learning by doing*, a nontraditional approach integrating teaching, research, and community service at the undergraduate level. Students are asked to grapple with such real-world issues as the politics of research, the power games in the community, ethical dilemmas in the workplace, and so forth. In the process, students develop skills to survive and become successful. The construction of this approach is based on the theoretical works of Bruner (1966, 1977, 1979), Holt (1964), and Freire (1972). Recognized in this chapter are theoretical linkages with similar models such as the moot court program at the California State University, Dominguez Hills.[1] A learning-by-doing model is not confined to the undergraduate level, but is very much in agreement with Bruner's philosophy of "any subject at any age." In other words, such a model is extremely adaptable to other disciplines as well as to a variety of age groups. What will be presented here are the major elements for constructing an environment conducive to empowering students.

Empowerment Through Divergent Thinking

Today's traditional undergraduate experience lacks imagination, creativity, and enthusiasm. All too often such an experience is typified by the professor lecturing while the students busily take notes; later the facts and figures are to be regurgitated in the form of an "objective" multiple-choice exam. Little *real* learning takes place. Unfortunately, such an approach is commonly accepted. According to J.P. Guilford (1967), this practice reflects "convergent thinking," which forces the student to converge on the right answer. In contrast, learning by doing encourages divergent production in which students are required "to produce their own answer, not to choose from alternatives given to them" (Guilford, 1967, p. 138).

Many recent reports have criticized the university for the passive acceptance of the lecture format and have advocated more involved learning (*Involvement*, 1984). For example, Chickering and Gamson (1987) state the following:

> Good practice encourages active learning. Learning is not a spectator sport. Students do not learn much just sitting in classes listening to teachers, memorizing pre-packaged assignments, and spitting out answers. They must talk about what they are learning, write about it, relate it to past experiences, and apply it to their daily lives. They must make what they learn a part of themselves. (p. 1)

But the entire blame should not be placed on the university. Many, many years of educational socialization have taught our students to "converge" on the "right" answer. Holt (1964) distinguishes between the producer and the thinker: "Schools give every encouragement to producers, the kids whose idea is to get the 'right answers' by any and all means. In a system that runs on 'right answers,' they can hardly help it. And these schools are often very discouraging places for thinkers" (p. 48). And Freire (1972) states the following: "A careful analysis of the teacher-student relationship at any level, inside or outside of the school, reveals its fundamental narrative character. This relationship involves a narrative subject (the teacher) and patient, listening objects (the students) . . . Education is suffering from narration sickness" (p. 57).[2]

Whether it is called "narration sickness," "banking education," or "convergent thinking," one possible solution to this myopic approach to teaching and learning can be found in an attempt to close the gap between the university and the real world. One concept which is associated with the closing of this gap is Guilford's (1967) "divergent production," and Holt (1964) describes this approach as simply that of "the good thinker." Freire (1972) uses the term *problem-posing education*: "In problem-posing education, men develop their power to perceive critically the way they exist in the world with which and in which they find themselves; they come to see the world not as a static reality, but as a reality in process, in transformation" (p. 70).

In a recent one-woman show, Lily Tomlin humorously declares: "I refuse to be intimidated by reality anymore. After all, what is reality anyway? NOTHIN' BUT A COLLECTIVE HUNCH. My space chums think reality was once a primitive method of crowd control that got out of hand" (cited by Wagner, 1985, p. 18). Similarly, W.I. Thomas is often quoted: "If men define a situation as real, they are real in their consequences" (1928, p. 584). In addition, Edward Teller states, "It isn't technology, it's politics. It isn't facts, it's perceptions" (1982, p. 185). Other more sociological explanations of the social construction of reality are discussed by McHugh (1968), Berger and Luckmann (1966), and Goffman (1959). For example, in Goffman's dramaturgy, he (1959) notes, "At one extreme, one finds the performer can be fully taken in by his own act; he can be sincerely convinced that the impression of reality which he stages is the real reality" (p. 17). Berger and Luckmann (1966) state, "Reality is socially defined. But the definitions are always embodied, that is, concrete individuals and groups of individuals serve as definers of reality" (p. 116).

Rarely does undergraduate education afford the opportunity for students to test out their ability to "make it" in the real world. Instead, students graduate with naive and idealistic world views with no reality testing. Some administrators and faculty members believe that the undergraduate is not prepared for such rigorous reality testing until *after* commencement, when the young graduate is "plunged" into the real world. The learning-by-doing approach challenges that belief.

In an attempt to provide a more meaningful and involved learning environment at the university level, learning by doing attempts to undo years of educational socialization based on "the right answer," or convergent production. Again, it is important to note that such a teaching and learning model is one of several currently in operation. The next section will discuss the social construction of such an environment con-ducive to the discussion of Guilford's "divergent production" and Freire's "problem-posing education."

The Social Construction of Empowerment

The ultimate goal of empowerment is the institutionalization of innova-tions resulting in social changes for the better. Thus, it is important to recognize that empowerment is all about *attitude and persuasion*.[3] Through a learning-by-doing approach, students who have typically struggled through more traditional courses learn that they can do it, and begin to realize that they can "make it" too. Students' self-confidence and self-esteem improve as their academic skills and abilities are strengthened. Over time, such an approach often helps students to over-come the self-fulfilling prophecies of failure by altering their expecta-tions. Individually, these students become empowered to choose from a variety of alternatives knowing that they now have choices. Collectively, empowered students develop a powerfully creative and imaginative source from which innovations are developed and social changes are directed.

Prior to providing a detailed description of the social construction of empowerment, it is important to present a brief overview of the learning-by-doing approach. Such an approach provides students with the rare opportunity to become active, imaginative learners regarding a real-world problem or issue. From spring 1986 to summer 1988 at the University of Wisconsin, Parkside (UWP), a series of undergraduate sociological research projects were presented to students. All of these projects focused on research of the local youth gang problem as well as the evaluation of youth services and programs. Such research projects empowered students to take on a very real challenge in their own com-munities.

Briefly, the learning-by-doing approach presents a *controlled crisis*.[4] Students are provided with a setting in which they are challenged by a real-world issue. With community and school support, the professor's role is to understand each student's strengths and weaknesses and to channel the student's energies. In learning by doing, Freire (1972) states, "The teacher is no longer merely the-one-who-teaches, but one who is himself taught in dialogue with the students, who in turn while being taught also teach. They become jointly responsible for a process in which all grow" (p. 67). It is somewhere at this point that the answer to who is empowering whom becomes unclear. The learning-by-doing approach is so intense because it is the *real* thing with real consequences. Students find it easier to grasp onto what is most real to them. Therefore, what is real is relevant.

The required elements in the social construction of an environment of student empowerment are (1) the community, (2) the school (administration), (3) the professor, and (4) the student. The major focus of this chapter will be on the student.

The Community

Networking within the community and understanding the local political climate is an important element to the success of the learning-by-doing approach. Students learn who is who in the power games—who supports them, and who their opposition is. Students who have lived in the community much of their lives are surprised at how extensive their established networks are.

The undergraduate research took place in Racine, which is located in southeastern Wisconsin on the shores of Lake Michigan between Milwaukee and Chicago. Its population of 88,349 is about 80 percent White, 14 percent Black, and 6 percent Chicano. Racine manufactures tractors and farm equipment, wax products, automobile equipment, metal casting, and lithographed materials. Because the local economy is closely linked to industry, the city has been susceptible to high unemployment rates of about 10 percent and a high school dropout rate of 6.6 percent. During the early 1980s, there was much activity in Racine. A shopping mall opened. Factories were failing or moving out. Community agencies were experiencing budget cuts, and unemployment was at another high.

On February 22, 1984, Resolution 9376 called for the establishment of the Mayor's Task Force on Gangs and Juvenile Delinquency. After much debate of the gang situation, in November 1985, the task force asked me to conduct an exploratory study of the gang situation—the Racine Gang Project (RGP). It was the community reaching out to the university for assistance. The important first step in constructing an environment of student empowerment is the identification of local community needs, issues, and problems. The gang situation became the focal point of a series of undergraduate sociological research projects at the university.[5]

During the summer of 1986, the results of the RGP were documented in a 137-page report and presented at a press conference in city hall. Since this first project, three other undergraduate sociological research projects have been funded. Two of the projects were direct follow-ups to the RGP. On the basis of the recommendations from the RGP report, the Racine Community Collaboration Project was proposed. Together the city's parks, recreation, and cultural services department with the technical assistance of UWP drafted the grant proposal to examine the local coordination of youth services. The Racine Youth Needs Assessment became the third step in responding to the local gang problem. Through the support and funding of a local private foundation, current youth programs and services were evaluated in an attempt to identify the unaddressed needs of Racine's youths.

In addition, as a result of successes in Racine, the students from Kenosha took the initiative to obtain funds for a study of the gang situation in their local community; hence the Kenosha Gang Project. Kenosha is located just north of the Illinois border and south of Racine.[6] Until December 1988, the auto industry was the focal point of Kenosha's economy. In December 1986, the Task Force on Gangs commissioned the UWP to conduct a study analyzing existing data within the Kenosha Police Department, the Kenosha County Department of Social Services, and the Kenosha Unified School District.

It is important to note that the projects following RGP were developed on the basis of community needs. As MacKay (1988) notes in *Swim with the Sharks*, "In order to supply something, you must create first a demand" (p. 35). Research and evaluation are valuable tools that the university has to offer its surrounding communities.

The economic argument is one of the strongest and most convincing selling points of the learning-by-doing approach. The total cost of RGP was $2,000. Undergraduate researchers who are obtaining college credits for the experience are rarely paid.[7] One of the best compliments that the RGP students received was from the grants officers from the Wisconsin Council on Criminal Justice, who said the report reflected $20,000 worth of research effort and documentation. Initially, little funding is required in trying to construct this teaching and learning model which empowers students. In later projects, funding came from local and state agencies, private foundations, and the university. Therefore, as a track record is established, funding becomes much easier to obtain.

Such compliments and rewards were not without local politicking and power games. Of course, there are always the avid supporters who are daringly venturesome. But there are also the perennial pessimists who have little faith in the students' abilities to do the job. For example, there was some discussion that the students were not professional enough to conduct such a research project. It was probably this skeptical opposition that motivated the students the most. The students wanted to dispel the myths and stereotypes.

Because undergraduate students doing research was such a novel idea on campus as well as in the community, there was much to be proven. The students understood early on what was at stake. Students countered early stereotypes by dressing like professionals and conducting business in a very professional manner. They did role playing in order to anticipate the variety of scenarios with which they might be confronted. Such exercises gave students practice thinking on their feet. Their professionalism was put to the test time and time again. By the end of the first project, some skeptics were converted. They had underestimated the students' capabilities. In fact, by the third project in Racine, the UWP students were perceived as having too much power by certain factions. The research projects became increasingly politicized. But despite such opposition, and because of the overall community support and the encouragement of key leaders, the students were able to overcome local political obstacles.

The School (Administration)

University support from the administrative and departmental levels is another important element in the learning-by-doing model. Without such support, the professor is forced to stay within the very traditional and typically unimaginative practices of university teaching. Such support also provides an important endorsement of the work done by the professor and his or her students, which students find a most encouraging gesture.

The University of Wisconsin, Parkside (UWP), which is located between Racine and Kenosha, presently has five thousand undergraduates and three hundred graduates. UWP faculty adhere to a *teacher-scholar* philosophy, which is characterized by the general accessibility of faculty to students and small-sized classes. Applying learning by doing to a series of undergraduate sociological research projects is an ideal example of the teacher-scholar philosophy.

The key to obtaining administrative support derives from collegial support campuswide. Initially, collegial support is much more valuable than funding. The university's faculty and staff constitute a vast source of expertise that involved learning-by-doing students and professors utilize. For example, students did not rely on the professor of the course as the sole expert. They began to utilize all available resources on campus: the computer center assistants, other professors, statisticians, and librarians. Nonmonetary administrative support, such as space, loaned equipment, "release" time, postage, office supplies, telephone usage, and so forth, is also initially important. It is easier to get the administrative endorsement for an activity which has no expenses or risks attached. Economic support for something as novel as learning by doing may not be quickly obtained until a proven track record is established. Eventually, the administration may be willing to buy into the concept. Other groups on campus, such as the alumni association and the committee on research and creative activities, will follow suit.

In exchange for administrative support, learning-by-doing professors and students provide a positive link between the university and the community. The university is always interested in improving and expanding its relations within the community. Learning by doing provides a valuable resource to the community in exchange for improved community relations with the university. The students become ambassadors representing the university during their research work in the community. For example, when a student is interviewed by a local radio station, the university is credited for its community efforts.

Support at the departmental level is especially vital. At this level, it may be perceived as a luxury to test out a new, innovative course at the expense of one of the more traditional required courses. It is important to start by working within the existing structure, the main objective being to establish a good track record. It is much more difficult to obtain acceptance for adding something radically different into the curriculum. For example, I identified an existing research seminar as the course most appropriate for the activities planned for the Racine Gang Project. Special topics, independent studies, practica, field experiences, or other similar course titles are general enough to test out a new teaching and learning model.

In addition, the department serves as an advocate for the professor and his and her students as well as an important liaison to the administration. Departmental colleagues provide the first-line support and advice to the professor and his and her students. For example, it is at the departmental level that limited supplies and equipment are offered initially. There was much departmental acceptance for the first project. Such encouragement leads to administrative support.

The Professor

The learning-by-doing model combines the multiple duties of today's university professor—teaching, research, and community service. When I was first approached to study gangs in Racine, I was relatively new to the campus and the community. But I knew that most of my students were very familiar with their own neighborhood, and they had well-established networks throughout the community. Perhaps I could have designed this research project in the traditional manner of principal investigator with research assistants as "go for's" to collect and code the data. Instead, this project presented an ideal opportunity for undergraduates to become involved in sociological research. Such a model was not new to me because, as an undergraduate at the California State University, Dominguez Hills, I was involved with research. Curran and Telesky (1975) state the following: "The faculty assume three major teaching responsibilities which are (1) The faculty help students identify their strengths and learn to make realistic self-assessments of their skills. (2) The faculty provide a supportive environment in which student strengths can most effectively grow. (3) Faculty teach specific skills and provide a constant challenge to students to increase the scope and level of their research skills" (p. 10). Thus, I have attempted to replicate the Dominguez model at UWP.

In constructing an environment which is conducive to empowering students, it is important for the professor to recognize his or her role and relationship with his or her students. Freire (1972) states, "Education must begin with the solution of the teacher-student contradiction, by reconciling the poles of the contradiction so that both are simultaneously teachers *and* students" (p. 59). My role as the professor was to provide gentle guidance and to teach as well as to learn alongside by students. My most important task was an accurate assessment of each student so that energies could be properly channeled.

The Students

How does a professor deal with atypical and disadvantaged undergraduate students? Because such students do not fit into the normal scheme of things, some professors are frequently baffled. C. Wright Mills's (1959) concept of "the sociological imagination" helps us to understand our students by examining the intersections between "personal troubles" and "public issues." In other words, the professor should be conscious of each student's biographical situation within the larger historical context. The sociological imagination is a useful tool in understanding today's atypical student.

A report, *Involvement in Learning* (1984), states that "administrators and faculty must also recognize the extent to which instructional practices affect student involvement. Traditional classroom teaching in higher education favors the assertive student. But our analysis indicates that the instructor should give greater attention to the passive or reticent student" (p. 23). Most atypical students are passive and reticent. Empowerment is important for these students, especially those who are first-generation college. Such students lack the know-how and the confidence to enter the foreign world of university life. An uncomfortable presence combined with an unfamiliarity with university life creates an unknown that greatly affects a student's desire and ability to succeed. In turn, the university must recognize and value the skills and knowledge that such students bring with them.

Since 1986, twenty-four students have been involved with the undergraduate sociological research. Most were first-generation college. In addition, some of them were older, nontraditional students and/or were from working- or lower-class backgrounds. As Table 12.1 shows, the ratio of males to females was about equal, and nearly 21 percent of

TABLE 12.1

Sex and Race of Participating Students
Undergraduate Research

	White	*Non-White*
Male	11	2
Female	8	3

the students involved were from minority groups. This percentage is much higher than the overall percentage of minorities at UWP. Of the five minority students, there were four Blacks and one Asian.

Table 12.2 compares traditional with nontraditional students regarding the number of semesters in which they participated in under-

TABLE 12.2

Number of Semesters Participating, by Type of Student
Undergraduate Research

	One	*Two to Three*	*Four Plus*
Traditional	12	5	2
Nontraditional	1	0	4

graduate sociological research. It is particularly significant to note that nontraditional students participated in four or more semesters, whereas the traditional students participated in only one semester. A learning-by-doing approach attracts the nontraditional student for the long term.

For the nontraditional students, taking several semesters of research is a confidence builder, and over time they realize their ability to succeed. Thus, such an experience provides the necessary support required of this special student population.

Table 12.3 shows a high graduation rate for students involved in undergraduate sociological research. Today, many are working in the local community. Three graduates have gone on to graduate school in sociology. This is a testimony to the kind of professional socialization that occurred while students were involved with research at UWP, especially in light of the fact that these students were first-generation college. Two students obtained their M.A. in 1989, and one student will continue on into a Ph.D. program in the fall.

TABLE 12.3

Present Status, by Race
Undergraduate Research

	White	Non-White
Still at UWP	4	2
Graduated UWP	13	1
Left UWP	0	2

The two individuals who left UWP were minority males. They left UWP in order to join the armed forces. One joined for financial reasons in order to obtain support to further his college education. It is uncertain what role financial status played in the other's situation.

After the second project in Racine, four high school students were employed to assist in clerical work and research-related tasks, which benefitted them. Of the four, three were Black. They were not only exposed to university life and the undergraduate students as role models, but they learned marketable skills such as word processing, various aspects of sociological research, mainframe and personal computing, and so forth. One student has gone on to graduate from high school and now works full-time for a local law firm as a word processor, and another student is now attending UWP.

In considering students for these projects, I was mainly looking for those who were committed, responsible, and interested, and who had something to offer the projects. Student motivation and interest varied. Some were interested in doing research in order to obtain specific skills, and others wanted to do something to help their community. It is important to note that there were no restrictions, such as "freshmen need not apply." Students ranged from second-semester freshmen to last-semester seniors. Some students had taken research methods and statistics; others had not. All majors were welcomed. Although most students were sociology or political science majors, a variety of other fields were represented, such as psychology and computer science.

The first few weeks of each semester of research became the period of testing and sorting students to identify their interest, abilities, strengths, and weaknesses. Knowing your students is one of the keys to the learning-by-doing approach. The *controlled crisis* which is constructed for the students, if done properly, can ensure success and guard against failure.[8] The initial weeding-out process helps to ensure the proper social construction of a controlled crisis. Much intensive training also takes place during the first few weeks because of the variety of skills levels. It is important to note that this approach is not for every student. Some students who did not demonstrate responsibility and commitment dropped out of the course.

Students were presented with a list of research tasks to be accomplished during the semester. Then, they discussed the tasks with me, and, in consultation, contracts were drafted. Those students who "earned their stripes"[9] took on leadership and supervisory responsibilities, while others were learning new skills, such as administering surveys or conducting interviews. In addition to the contracted research tasks, field notes reflecting activities and experiences were expected weekly of each student. The purpose of the field notes was to teach students the practice of writing as well as the discipline and importance of documenting one's activities.

Once the training was complete, students were busily involved in a variety of "contracted" research tasks. Each of the projects had a multi-methodological research design. Students were involved in such activities as designing a survey, conducting interviews, attending task force meetings, preparing for presentations, and so forth. Through a learning-by-doing approach, they were confronted with many real-world dilemmas: for example, selecting the strategy which would most likely optimize the community survey response rates. Students had to make decisions which they would have to defend later. And some of these decisions were not simple.

In much of the work, students were divided into subgroups or teams. Teamwork is another real-world concept students must understand. Much of traditional undergraduate education is based on individual competition rather than teamwork, but the working world adheres more to the teamwork approach. In a learning-by-doing environment, students help each other out. For example, these students shared their interview experiences and helped each other to obtain data-rich interviews. Eventually, group cohesion solidified each research team. Thus, students became totally consumed by the variety of project tasks. There was much sharing and exchanging of information. During spring breaks, there would always be a few students willing to spend their entire break working on the projects.

Students took responsibility for every phase of the research process—from the development of the research design to the presentation of the final report. They saw how their efforts were affecting their communities. They felt a part of what was going on beyond the four walls of the university lecture hall. Their excitement and enthusiasm permeated the entire group. It was highly contagious.

Learning by Doing: An Analysis

Learning by doing is very different from the traditional classroom simulations, and laboratory experiments, and even different from the traditional research setup at the university, where research assistants (usually graduate students) have little creative input into the research design or the writing of the final report, but whose main task is to serve as the "go for" (as trained collectors and coders of data).

Particularly for the atypical student, the professor signifies a power and authority which is rarely challenged or questioned. Such stereotypes and perceptions as the professor is "all-knowing and never makes mistakes" demonstrate the powerful results of many years of educational socialization. The student, as Freire describes, becomes merely a passive receptacle.

Learning-by-doing students readily recognize early on that the professor plays a unique role, one that is much different than what they have grown accustomed to. It is necessary for the professor to redefine his or her role to the students so that they will better understand how learning by doing works. For example, as one core group of students progressed from semester to semester, they were not completely comfortable calling me "Susan," but they also did not want to be so formal as to address me as "Dr." or "Professor" (although they did understand that during community meetings and in the public eye such formality was necessary. But while they were in the research laboratory, the students came up with their own name for me—"Doc"—which provided a happy medium with which everyone seemed comfortable. This example demonstrates how the unique role of the professor became understood by the students as time progressed.

It is true that "nothing beats the real thing." For students, doing something "real" is truly motivating and exciting. A real situation also has real consequences. Students are confronted with numerous dilemmas from which they can choose several alternatives. For example, the time pressures and deadlines are very real. If the final report was not completed as scheduled, the consequences were much more severe than receiving an "F" on an objective final exam. There was much more at stake than the individual student paying the price. The entire research team was affected. When the consequences are real and students are given the opportunity to make responsible decisions, real learning is taking place. Students agonize as they carefully weigh the pros and cons of every step they take, knowing they will have to answer to or defend their decisions later. The key here is giving students the responsibility to determine how an issue will impact their future as well as the lives of others. All too often, administrators and professors are afraid to put such "power" in the hands of students.

After years of being socialized to "converge" on the right answer, students eventually take on the belief that the world is two-dimensional—there is a right and wrong; things are black and white. Learning-by-doing students realize some of their naive assumptions and world-views. When students are first exposed to the learning-by-doing approach, they quickly learn how gray and fuzzy the real world is. For example, during the construction of a community survey, students had argued for a few days on the wording of questions. Realizing the eventuality of their deadline to complete the survey, they soon became tired of arguing among themselves and seemingly getting nowhere. They became increasingly frustrated as they waited for me, the professor, to intervene at any moment. Instead, I sat back and observed. Finally, one completely exasperated student approached me by asking, "What's the right answer?" I quietly responded that there were no absolute right or wrong answers. They must come up with their own answer and be satisfied to defend it later. It was at this moment that the students knew that this was truly their project. They could not defer to me as the professor. They would be given all the glory if successful and all the "hell" if not. "Welcome to the real world!" I told them.

For the students, learning by doing became a sometimes painful process of trial and error. Some students learned the hard way. For example, when one student failed to do his part for a presentation, the wrath of the rest of the research team was more than enough punishment. And it is certainly something no one ever forgets. Learning from one's mistakes is another important part of learning by doing.

It soon became apparent, as the various research teams began to come together, that these projects touched dimensions of the students that normally do not get touched. As Hans Mauksch once explained to my students, who had reached a point of struggling through some frustrating moments, "Traditional classes don't get the student 'too wet.' Nontraditional classes such as this one get you totally immersed." After all, real learning is total immersion. Students realized this as they began to stay on campus longer and took work home, even other classes began to suffer as they became totally immersed in their research. Maslow (1971) uses the term *self-actualization* to describe this experience.

Other than from the limited lessons learned from a mentor, where else does a student learn what survival and success in the real world is all about? Learning by doing empowers students to take responsibility and control over their future. Other lessons learned are professional socialization (what it means to be a professional, how professionals act), understanding social organizations and institutions (becoming familiar with bureaucracies and how to deal with them), the political realities (the power games everywhere they go—in the community, on campus, etc.), and their own interpersonal growth (learning about themselves, their abilities, their weaknesses as well as strengths). The empowerment of students provides them with just such a confidence builder—knowing "I can do it!" Many of the students involved with the undergraduate sociological research truly surprised themselves. Few had ever stuck to it before. They learned what persistence and commitment were all about. They also learned the meaning of success.

"Can Do" and "Breaking Out": Self-Empowerment

Everybody involved with the learning-by-doing environment wins. The students provide a much-needed service to the community in their efforts to address the local gang situation. The community, in turn, utilizes an economical and yet underutilized resource—the young people. For the university, such projects provide excellent university-community relations. The university is able to offer the local community its resources and expertise. The gap between the ivory tower and the local neighborhood is closed—the students provide the important linkage. The professor gains by incorporating teaching, research, and community service into the classroom. The professor's rewards are numerous, but the most gratifying is observing the changes and growth in the students.

Most importantly, the students gain the most from learning by doing. Self-empowerment is the positive result of the learning-by-doing approach, which provides the student with the "can do" attitude for "breaking out."[10] Holt (1964) states the following: "My own feeling is that success should not be quick or easy, and should not come all the time. Success implies overcoming an obstacle, including, perhaps, the thought in our minds that we might not succeed. *It is turning, "I can't" into "I can, and I did"* (p. 61). Empowerment is all about *attitude and persuasion.* According to Berger and Luckmann (1966), "Identity is, of course, a key element of subjective reality, and like all subjective reality, stands in a dialectical relationship with society. Identity is formed by social processes" (p. 173).

Involvement

An active learner is an involved learner. A learning-by-doing approach certainly involves the learner to the point of total immersion. It was incredible to observe the students' enthusiasm when they were involved in even the most frustrating moments. Students were totally consumed in *their* research. For example, some students were eager to become involved in all aspects of the research project. But sometimes they were not altogether realistic about the kind of time commitment that meant. Their eagerness was tempered with a realistic assessment of their abilities and time constraints. Learning by doing is an excellent solution to the problems of student retention because these students are involved in more satisfying and successful learning experiences while at the university.

Discovery

Students experienced many discoveries, surprises, and "aha's." Students always amazed themselves. For example, one student might remark, "I surprise myself. I didn't think I'd ever get that interview done." As another example, a group of students developed shortcut methods to input coded data more efficiently into the mainframe. Students began to transform "You can't do that" to "Yes, I can!"

Through a learning-by-doing approach, the student makes many discoveries along the way. According to Bruner (1979), "one encounters repeatedly an expression of faith in the powerful effects that come from permitting the student to put things together for himself, to be his own discoverer" (p. 82). One vivid example of discovery were those students who initially had computer fears and anxieties. After some time and careful coaxing, they emerged as confident computer users. They were surprised to see themselves computer literate, and some of them even became very dependent on the computer. They felt like welcomed members into the twenty-first century.

Persistence

According to Bruner (1979), "persistence is another feature of strategy, a characteristic compounded of what appears to be two factors: sheer doggedness and a persistence that stems from the sequential organization that a child brings to the task" (p. 86). For example, after spending several hours laboriously inputting coded data into the university's mainframe, one student called her output "Tired." During another semester, when major chunks of inputted data were accidentally "dumped," one student stayed on campus until 3:30 a.m. trying to re-input the data so that precious time would not be lost. Now, that is persistence.

Divergent and Creative Production

In *Alice in Wonderland*, there are several passages which reflect creative production—for example: "For you see, so many out-of-the-way things had happened lately that Alice had begun to think that very few things indeed were really impossible" (Carroll, 1986, p. 6). Similarly, students involved with learning by doing began to realize that there was no limit to what they could do. They began to understand that it never hurt to try anything once just to see what would happen. Students also began to experiment and become more creative and imaginative in their thinking. A fuzziness as to who is empowering whom becomes even more problematic. But it is nonetheless a wonderful feeling for students and professor.

In Takata and Leiting (1987), the value of dreaming, envisioning, or engaging in anticipatory socialization is discussed. Such dreaming opens new perspectives and alters expectations and goals. For example, students were excited about making presentations during professional sociological and criminological meetings. They would excitedly "daydream" and anticipate their presentations.

Creativity and divergent production are also tempered by realistic self-assessments and worldviews. Students gain a more realistic understanding of the social, economic, cultural, and political conditions within a given situation or issue.

Self-Confidence Builders

A "can do" attitude reflects growing self-sufficiency, which in turn empowers students. The practice of learning by doing led to the growing self-confidence and self-sufficiency of these students. Having accomplished a series of very rigorous and challenging research projects gave them a "can do" attitude. Much interpersonal growth and development resulted from the learning-by-doing experience. Students discovered their major strengths and learned how to cope with major weaknesses. For example, a few students were mystified by the language of SPSSx and forced themselves to become more knowledgeable of this computer language, because they knew that if they could conquer SPSSx, they could do "anything."

Role models are of particular importance. Community leaders and other prominent figures serve as role models for students so that they learn to believe that they, too, "can do." In fact, the public exposure students received from their communities gave them much visibility and prominence. After the city hall presentation and press conference presenting the results of RGP, two students became involved in a series of local radio interviews.

Breaking Out and Redefining Reality

Our most creative students are being bored, scared, and confused by their schooling. They are discouraged and frustrated by a school system which oppresses them. As chapters in this book by Bennett, Fordham, Sleeter and Grant, and Weis illustrate, the atypical student described in this chapter has experienced many years of various kinds of oppression, and thus begins university life at a great disadvantage. As a result of learning by doing, students learn to break out of stereotyped roles, labels, and expectations, and thus redefine reality. This strategy of empowerment shows students that they do not have to be stifled by the norms, traditions, policies, and practices set forth. Students are allowed to let their creativity and imagination "go wild." They learn many lessons in surviving and succeeding in he real world: how to survive, how to work the system, how to circumvent, the importance of regrouping and redefining, how to innovate, and so forth. Bruner (1979) notes, "The result in increased awareness represents a powerful form over reality" (p. 137). In the process of self-empowerment, students are encouraged to "stretch the corners of their mind."[11] While students are encouraged to self-actualize, to discover their own potentials, the professor must learn to "let go." This is, of course, a very innovative approach in that the student manages to take over by taking responsibility for his or her actions and decisions, while the professor takes a back seat. This exciting process begins to take on a life of its own. This is the ultimate "can do." In fact, the answer to the question of who is empowering whom becomes lost.

This approach is of particular importance to oppressed individuals and groups, who learn how to overcome oppression by understanding power, and perhaps effecting social change. For example, these students witnessed some of their recommendations become reality, and they continue to see the impact of their research on their community.

Conclusion

Curran notes: "If you believe in your students, they can learn."[12] Similarly, Bruner (1979) states, "Any subject can be taught to anybody at any age in some form that is honest" (p. 108). Part of the problem in our schools is a limited perception of what our students can and cannot do. This stifles much too much creativity, imagination, and "can do."

Because of the disadvantaged status that atypical students bring to their university experience, one of the initial obstacles that they must overcome is their sense of hopelessness and fear of failure. Fromm (1968) states, "Hope is a decisive element in any attempt to bring about social change in the direction of greater aliveness, awareness, and reason" (p. 6). By providing them with a controlled crisis, learning by doing teaches students, particularly atypical students, who need this approach the most, that they can perform despite the obstacles. As a result of their successes, the students' expectations are altered into "Yes, I can do it!" Eventually, these students realize that they can transfer their knowledge and apply their skills to a variety of settings and situations.

Curran once said to me, "The more I teach students, especially new students, the better the chance for our survival in a democracy. If we don't give them the means, there will be trouble. There already is trouble." She was referring to the real need to democratize education. Drucker (1968) feared the "diploma curtain": "If we do not eliminate the diploma curtain, it will turn the opportunity of knowledge into a nightmare. It will make the diploma a symbol of discrimination—which is what it has already become to the poor Negro in the ghetto. It will impoverish our society and economy, and deprive us of a great reservoir of human energies" (p. 333). And Weber (1946) states the following: "Democracy fears that a merit system and educational certificates will result in a privileged 'caste'. Hence, democracy fights the special-examination system" (p. 240). Learning by doing attempts to counter this diploma curtain. There is a continued need to democratize education, for, as Curran states, it increases our chances for survival.

Empowerment through multicultural education also addresses this need. Learning by doing is a powerful strategy for the empowerment of students as well as future teachers. Empowerment is all about attitude and persuasion.

PART III

Empowerment and Teacher Education

Chapter 13
The Rationale for Training Adults as Teachers

Martin Haberman

From 1800 until the present there has been a continuing shortage of teachers to work with poor children and in rural and urban schools serving racial and language minorities. An interruption of this trend occurred in the 1930s during the Great Depression. There have also been brief periods when selected urban school districts have instituted reductions in force (RIFs) such as the one that occurred between 1971 and 1973 in New York City. Essentially, teachers have been produced in adequate supply for all other constituencies.

The schools and colleges of education in the universities of this country expand and contract in their production of teachers in response to the overall national demand for teachers, with about a three-year time lag. The national data usually compare total positions with total graduates and conclude that there are sufficient teachers without revealing that there are great (even desperate) needs for teachers in schools serving the poor or racial and language minorities. For example, national data currently show an oversupply, but the state of Texas may be short by as many as 9,000 teachers by 1990. This gap between the numbers being prepared to teach and those willing to teach the poor and minorities is continuous. A few years ago the state of Washington had an oversupply of teachers numbering approximately 2,200; the Houston public schools were short 2,200 teachers and instituted an alternative certification program to train them in the public schools.

In a very real sense, teacher education is a self-selected profession. Almost all who want to become teachers can do so if they persist or if they are willing to move to another institution or another state. The overwhelming majority of trainees also select the grade or content they wish to teach. Finally, the graduates apply to the schools in which they would like to work, generally trying to avoid the urban schools and other schools serving the poor, where the need for teachers is greatest and the most demanding. Teachers seek to work within one hundred miles of home in "amenable" conditions.

The schools and colleges respond to their clients, predominantly late adolescents and young adults, by offering them programs that will attract and generate more student credit hours (the basis of university budgets) rather than by training the types of teachers schools need most in the ways that are most relevant and practical. One notable example of this unresponsiveness on the part of schools and colleges of education is the lack of special programs for training middle-school teachers. It is painfully clear that public schools (particularly urban schools) have needed specially trained middle-school teachers for more than forty years, but the youngsters (customers) being trained in schools and colleges of education do not self-select to become middle school teachers. These trainees want broad certification in grades one through eight, or in both middle and secondary school, in order to enhance their subsequent search for jobs. Colleges of education are most willing to oblige this clientele. In my own institution, the first faculty motion to allot even a part of one faculty member's load to the preparation of middle school teachers was not passed until 1989, and even now there is some question of whether this will be a specifically focused program.

It is important to note that the students preparing to teach on this self-selected basis who opt to not work in schools serving the poor or racial and language minorities in urban schools may actually be demonstrating sound judgment. They are well aware of the fact that they are the wrong people to prepare for teaching in these situations. Further, the faculty in schools and colleges of education have neither the expertise nor the experience to train teachers for teaching in low-income or multicultural situations. Less than 5 percent of education faculty have ever taught in urban schools. The content of typical education courses is largely irrelevant to practice in these schools. Finally, student teaching and other direct experiences are, in effect, simply more sophisticated selection criteria and not real training for teaching the children of the poor and language minorities. These experiences do not change students' views of low-income and minority pupils. On the contrary, by selective perception, student-teachers tend to merely reinforce whatever they were predisposed to believe at the outset. The few who are predisposed to perceive strengths in minority children and families do so, while the vast majority who see only the negatives use their student-teaching to confirm and enhance their stereotypes.

Before teachers can be prepared for teaching the poor and racial and language minorities, they must first have a vision of what multiculturalism in America means for all citizens and its specific implications for the work of the teacher. Second, they must be trained by knowledgeable classroom teachers (mentors) in real schools and not by faculty in schools and colleges of education who have never taught in such schools. Third, those learning to teach must be adults, not late adolescents or young adults with little life or work experience. It is this last contention that will be the focus of the analysis which follows.

Varied theoretical approaches will be examined. Each supports the general contention that the overwhelming majority of those being trained to teach are, essentially, an inappropriate constituency. Although it is true that the typical age of college graduates has risen from twenty-two to twenty-six, it is still generally true that most of those preparing to teach are college-age youth, that is, late adolescents and young adults. The analysis which follows does not advocate preventing all such individuals from becoming teachers but aims to shift the balance. Whereas now the emphasis is on teacher training for college-age youth, with approximately 20 percent of the students being "older" adults (usually called special certification students or denigrated as "retreads"), I propose that the emphasis be reversed so that the majority of trainees would be adults and the exceptions (up to 20 percent) might be those young people who really have achieved the personal identity and level of experience needed to prepare for teaching. Finally, although more space is devoted to discussing psychological theories of human development, this should not be taken to mean that the social-psychological or sociological theories are less persuasive. It is merely that my search of the literature has generated more research and theory supporting the various subdivisions within the psychological approaches. All approaches, in my judgment, support my overall contention, and the situational theories are as persuasive as the personality theories.

Developmental Models

Erikson has proposed a theory of human development in eight stages (Erikson, 1963). These stages cover trust versus mistrust (first year); autonomy versus doubt (second and third years); initiative versus guilt (fourth and fifth years); industry versus inferiority (ages six to eleven); identity versus role confusion (ages twelve through eighteen); intimacy versus isolation (eighteen through young adulthood); generativity versus self-absorption (middle age); and integrity versus despair (old age).

For teacher educators it is critical to determine what occurs to individuals in stage 6 (intimacy versus isolation), which spans the ages of late adolescence and young adulthood. For Erikson this stage gives rise to an interpersonal dimension of intimacy at one extreme and isolation at the other. When Erikson speaks of intimacy, he means more than lovemaking; he refers to the ability to share with and care about another person without losing oneself in the process. If a sense of intimacy is not established with friends or a marriage partner, the result, in Erikson's view, is a sense of isolation—of being alone without anyone to share with or care for.

It is important to emphasize that a fundamental assumption of development theories is that individuals must pass through all stages in sequence and that each stage is a prerequisite for the next. With this in mind, consider Erikson's seventh stage (middle age), which brings either generativity or self-absorption. "Generativity" refers to a person beginning to be concerned with others beyond his or her immediate family, with future generations, and with the nature of the society and world in which future generations will live. This quality of generativity is most common in young parents but is not limited to them; it can be found in any individual who is actively concerned with the welfare of young people and with making the world a better place in which they can live and work. Those who fail to establish a sense of generativity fall into a state of self-absorption in which their personal needs and comforts become their predominant concern.

It is quite clear in Erikson's formulation that it is normal, indeed desirable, for young adults to be concerned with achieving some form of intimacy—a relationship or relationships—and that it is only in the seventh stage, the stage attributed to middle age, that the need for generativity or service to others becomes a normal expectation. The implication for the appropriate ages to train teachers is obvious.

Researchers building on Erikson's model have studied college students to determine at what point they develop a sense of their own identity (Marcia, 1976). Using open-ended interviews, Marcia found that only 22 percent of college youth achieved identity. The status of the others was identified as identity moratorium, foreclosure, or diffusion. These statuses have been defined and sequenced in the following manner. "Moratorium" refers to the need to test oneself in a variety of experiences to increase one's knowledge of oneself. It is a searching of oneself prior to making a life commitment. Twenty-eight percent of college youth were in this stage. "Foreclosure" refers to an identity stage in which the individual accepts whatever role authority figures and influential others prescribe. Twenty-six percent of college youth were in this stage. "Diffusion" refers to an identity stage in which there is no commitment to anyone and no commitment to any philosophy or set of beliefs. There is an emphasis on relativity, living for the moment, and not delaying gratification. All things are considered possible. Twenty-four percent of college youth were in this stage (Waterman, 1985).

This type of study clearly supports the contention that only a minority (approximately 22 percent) of college youth have developed the identity status Erikson regarded as prerequisite to the life stage of generativity. My own experience is that this percentage is an overestimate.

The classical developmental and organismic model of cognition is Piaget's theory of cognitive development (Inhelder and Piaget, 1958). In this model, which describes the development of the formal and logical aspects of thinking, the fourth stage, formal operations, is most relevant to this analysis. *Formal operational thinking* is (1) abstract thinking, the ability to think about possibilities, and thinking that is not constrained by concrete reality; (2) propositional thinking, the ability to think about logical relationships among ideas, concepts, and propositions; (3) combinatorial thinking, the ability to generate all combinations of ideas as well as cognitive operations; (4) hypothetical-deductive thinking, the ability to think scientifically about the definition and control of variables and about the generation, testing, and revision of hypotheses; (5) the ability to think ahead, to solve problems by defining, planning, selecting strategies, and revising; (6) the ability of metacognition, including the thinking about cognitive processes, memory, learning, and language; and (7) the ability to be self-reflective about cognitive processes, identity, existence, morality, and personal relationships (Keating, 1980).

Formal operations are theoretically achieved in adolescence. Typically, studies of these operations assess students by interview regarding their approach to solving some Piagetian-type problem. The percentages of individuals who actually display thinking that is representative of formal operations varies from 0 to 100 percent, with most estimates in the 40 percent to 70 percent range; this percentage rises as the ages of those in the samples increase (King, 1986).

Kohlberg's cognitive-developmental theory of moral reasoning includes six stages (Kohlberg, 1976). The final level of development involves relativistic reasoning about individual rights and the social system, as well as universal ethical principles such as equality and human rights. Kohlberg suggests that individuals progress from a focus on power and authority and individual interest to reasoning that takes into account the relationship of rules to the maintenance of the social system.

Teacher educators, bombarded by preservice students' fears and apprehensions regarding classroom discipline, are well aware of the early, even childlike stage in which many about to be certified find themselves. There is seldom little, if any, concern with the higher levels of moral development regarding issues such as equity, justice, and the relationship of rules to the values of society. Indeed, there is quite the reverse: a narrowing down of student interests as they move toward program completion which inevitably defines "the problem" as "Will I be in control of the class?" This is a moral stage which, in some very real ways, precedes even late adolescence and characterizes the need for power and control characteristic of early adolescence.

In studying the content of college students' reasoning, some researchers have followed them through four years of college (Perry, 1981). In the early stages, students are moral and intellectual absolutists: there are correct solutions for every problem and authorities are assumed to know what these are. (This is also still the stage of many teacher education graduates. They simply shift their definition of authority figures from school of education professors to master classroom teachers.) In Perry's middle stages, student thinking is relativistic: one opinion is as good or as useless as another. In the final stages of this model, students become committed to a search for and an expression of their own identity.

Loevinger's model of ego development is an eclectic rather than an original theory (1976). She conceives of ego development as encompassing moral, personality, cognitive, and interpersonal development. The stages include (1) impulsive, (2) self-protective, (3) conformist, (4) conscientious, (5) individualistic, and (6) autonomous. It is not until level 5 is reached that the individual cherishes individual differences and tolerates ambiguity. Cummings and Murray (1989) state the following:

> At the self protective level, knowledge is viewed as a means to concrete ends while at the conformist level it is seen as being useful to meet the standards of others. In contrast, at the conscientious level, knowledge is thought to be needed to achieve competence and meet internal standards. Finally, at the autonomous level, knowledge is perceived as being for self development and self knowledge. (p. 22)

Others have found that empathetic ability is found only in postconformist individuals (Carlozzi, Gaa, and Lieberman, 1983). Still others have found that teachers who remain in the profession tend to be at least at the self-awareness level, while those who leave the profession are at the conformist level (Glickman and Tamashiro, 1982). There is much rhetoric about the "best and the brightest" not choosing to become teachers because they perceive little opportunity for initiative, creativity, and self-realization, there is also some evidence that those who actually begin teaching but quit are conformists and concrete thinkers who perceive too few rules and too high a level of complexity and ambiguity. It may very well be that both conditions are to some degree true of schools and that the nature of the teachers' perceptions rather than objective reality is the critical determinant of what the school situation is "really" like.

The issue argued here is not the value of merely getting older but that serious reflection upon one's life experiences is likely to result in an individual reaching a higher level of development. Similarly, having employment of a sustained nature provides individuals with the requisite experiential material to integrate into their cognitive and affective system, thereby enabling them to make sense of and come to terms with their subsequent teaching experiences.

Other models of adolescent and adult development focus on the development of the individual's beliefs and assumptions regarding the nature of knowledge itself (Kitchener, 1986). This model relates very closely to several of the dimensions on the selection interview I have developed to predict who will be successful as a teacher in urban schools: it deals with college students' beliefs about what can and cannot be known and how such knowledge develops (e.g., through research, theory, personal experience, expert opinion, or authority). Such student beliefs influence how they define problems and goals and what they would regard as a teaching method or educational treatment. Briefly, Kitchener's model moves through stages of knowing that are in some ways similar to Perry's. Beginning with direct experience as the support for an absolutist view, it moves through stages of weighing conflicting perceptions (relativism) and ends with a mature view of reality that combines personal experience with expert opinion, research, and multiple ways of knowing. It is indeed ironic that young trainees and beginning teachers, who are almost totally focused on their own experiences as their basic learning mode, do not extend their ideological commitments to the children and youth they teach. The great emphasis in schools is on texts and vicarious learning, particularly in elementary schools, and is in direct contradiction to what trainees say they believe and how they behave regarding their own learning behavior.

Contextual and Knowledge-Based Models

In contrast to the preceding models, it is important to note that other approaches beside the psychological have been successful at explaining and predicting human development. The lifespan approach is a contextual model of human development which assumes many different causes of development: biological, social, psychological, physical, and historic. Development is not assumed to be a function of different or specific life events encountered by individuals, but an interactive process between multiple situational factors and how the individual interprets them. If carried to an extreme, contextual models can be problematic bases upon which to generalize, since all life situations can only be understood, ultimately, in terms of the individual's perception of them. On the other hand, some have argued that education courses should be the means for changing students' views of themselves, the nature of knowledge, teaching, and learning. If students begin with an approach that values only personal experience and intuition, it is the responsibility of the education faculty to help them perceive other paradigms for knowing. To do so, the education faculty would have to (1) be fully aware of their students' perceptions, (2) have powerful activities and experiences to offer students, and (3) be willing and able to dialogue with students on an in-depth level over a sustained period in an effort to affect their perceptions. Some theorists have suggested that knowledge of self, just like knowledge of disciplines or knowledge of thinking, can be organized to help explain individual development.

Through experience, but even more, through reflection upon one's experience, different concepts of self can be evoked by different situations (Markus and Wurf, 1987). Individuals develop different representations of self: achieving self, nurturing self, competitive self, anxious self. This model proposes multiple selves, all of which are autobiographic as well as reality based. The potential for teacher growth—through reflection—is great. So too, are the dangers for those individuals who have difficulty reflecting accurately upon their strengths and weaknesses. Clearly, individuals who have had more life and work experiences have had greater and more varied opportunities to build up their perceptual repertoire. Reflection itself may be a process more characteristic of advanced life stages and less characteristic of youth.

It is important to note that there are information processing theories that seek to deal with how people acquire knowledge and expertise. Metacognition theories refer to the individual's awareness of knowledge about cognition and his or her control and regulation of it. Many now contend that teachers' metacognitive knowledge about their own learning and how their pupils learn is a critical component of their knowledge base. Theories of intelligence have also advanced from assumptions of a static factor which stops developing at eighteen years of age and accounts for individual differences to dynamic aspects of thinking and problem solving which develop on a lifelong basis. Similarly, there are theoretic formulations related to value development, creativity, and affective development, all of which are affected by life experiences and which continue to develop throughout life.

Teacher Educators' Experiential Knowledge Regarding Teacher Trainees

The collective wisdom of experienced teacher educators is that, with exceptions, the more mature students do better as trainees and as practicing teachers. With no allegiance to any particular theory of human development, with no single vision of what constitutes good teaching, with no general agreement about how to best prepare teachers, the collective wisdom of most teacher educators is that there is a positive correlation between age and the demonstrated abilities of trainees. Again, this is not to argue that every older preservice student is more able than every young one, but rather to call attention to the need to pay attention to teacher educators' cumulated craft wisdom. Just as we must recognize that experienced classroom teachers know much that education professors do not, so too must we recognize the experiential knowledge which leads most teacher educators to recognize and appreciate the greater learning aptitudes of most older trainees. Life experiences and work experiences both increase the likelihood that trainees will learn more and become more competent practitioners.

Discussion

The implications of an analysis of these or any other schema for explaining adult development should be clear to teacher educators, all of whom can cite their career-long struggles with students preparing to teach who are absolutists, or at best relativists, and who do not reach the more difficult, higher levels of cognition while in training. Teacher educators can also document similar experiences with schema of moral development. The typical view of the nature of knowledge, that it is essentially a matter of personal experience and intuition, is also characteristic of teacher education students, and indeed of most other college youth. The teacher education students I have interviewed over a period of twenty-seven years typically define *generalization* as synonymous with *stereotyping*. "You can't generalize about people!" is what they believe, not only upon admission but *at the time of graduation and certification*. If this is their sincere belief (and I am convinced it is), what can such teachers really know or teach about political science, history, economics, geography, literature, sociology, anthropology, and psychology, all of which are collections of generalizations grouped into principles and theories? The notion that social science generalizations can explain and predict critical aspects of human behavior, without having to be totally true, strains their credulity to the point of disbelief. They believe that things cannot be true if there are exceptions, and therefore that generalizing about people is inherently wrong. The stage of knowledge development which characterizes the overwhelming number of late adolescents and young adults in teacher education seems to be an ongoing, deep-seated confusion between their ideology regarding the worth of the individual and the fact that social science deals in generalizations about individuals and groups. It seems to many of them that individuals lose their value or are somehow demeaned if there is any systematic attempt to explain or predict their behavior. This conflict between student ideology and the nature of social .science theory and research is further sharpened by the process of knowing; personal experience is the premier knowledge source to those fixated at the level of ideology, whereas all ways of knowing are available to the mature thinker. What I have argued may very well support the contention that all university-level education is wasted on most people before the age of twenty-five or thirty, but that is an argument beyond the scope of this analysis. The critical point is that

> we need to specify which kinds of behaviors can be predicted
> by developmental stage and which behaviors are irrelevant. If,
> for example, we wanted persons to perform some kinds of
> mindless, jejune task, their level of cognitive stage would prob-
> ably demonstrate little correlation to successful performance.
> On the other hand, if the task required higher-order abilities
> such as understanding and applying abstract concepts in a
> humane mode, then indeed the level of psychological maturity,
> the assessed level of cognitive development, may be an impor-
> tant predictor. And it probably comes as no great surprise to
> say that such outcomes are supported by multiple research

studies. The most general study was done by Douglas Heath (1977) in his studies of adult success in four countries. He used a multiple index of success and quality of life, and he used a broad variety of predictors (over 200). He found that there were four general developmental characteristics which were highly relevant to success: a) symbolization of experience, b) allocentrism-empathy, c) autonomy, and d) a commitment to democratic values. It is also interesting to note that the common or standardized predictors, such as academic grade point average and scores on the Scholastic Aptitude Test, were meaningless with one exception: In his American sample there was an inverse correlation between success in adulthood and SAT score. (Thies-Sprinthall and Sprinthall, 1987).

A very few distinguished teacher educators have tried to compensate for this situation by matching student teachers and cooperating teachers on the basis of their developmental level and by engaging in long-term, individualized training which seems to move mentors (aged thirty to fifty-five) to new levels of thinking (Thies-Sprinthall, 1980, 1984).

My recommendation is that teacher education can be most readily improved by making teacher training more available to more experienced, older constituencies. This is a most vital need as we consider the needs of urban schools and the competencies required of teachers to work with low-income children and children who represent racial and language minorities. It takes somebodys to make somebodys; nobodys don't make somebodys. Those still engaged in the struggle to develop their own identities are the last people we should seek to place as teachers with children and youth who need confident, competent role models. It is no accident that 50 percent of beginning teachers quit in less than five years; in some urban districts this level of turnover occurs in three years.

In higher education the *golden age* is the term used to refer to the decade after World War II, when millions of older, more experienced veterans filled our universities and matured the student cohort. Similarly, the decade of the National Teacher Corps, which began in 1964, is regarded by many as the "golden age" of teacher training. More mature, more experienced students changed the character of our teacher education programs.

A final caveat is in order. The arguments presented here have not dealt with the likelihood of different maturation rates or different life developmental stages on the basis of sex. I have avoided this issue for lack of a theoretic base to build an argument. My experiential base, however, clearly leads me to believe that males, particularly young college-age males, are the least likely cohort to prepare for teaching and the most likely to need longer periods of life and work experience to reach the developmental stages appropriate for teacher training.

Chapter 14

The Power to Empower:
Multicultural Education for Student-Teachers

—————————————— *Renée Jeanne Martin*

Recently a student approached me at a workshop for student teachers. He asked if we might speak privately regarding an incident which had occurred in the classroom in which he was doing his student-teaching field experience. He explained that not long before, as he had been correcting a homework assignment in an eighth-grade science class, he noticed that a student had drawn a Nazi swastika with the words *death to the Jews* on the back of a page of homework. Prior to returning the homework, the student-teacher showed the anti-Semitic drawing and remark to the cooperating teacher and asked for advice as to what to do regarding it. The cooperating teacher's initial comment was that the student-teacher was justified in issuing a reprimand because students in the class were permitted to write on only one side of a sheet of homework paper. This student had violated the classroom rules. When the student-teacher mentioned his specific concern regarding the drawing and the racist remark, the cooperating teacher said that it was probably just doodling and that there was no real reason to make an issue of that aspect of the behavior. Recognizing that he was not in his own classroom and therefore not in a position to institute any substantive change in this particular instance, the student-teacher chose to let the issue subside.

However, the student-teacher remained frustrated by the incident. As we discussed possible alternatives for dealing with similar problems in the future, several factors became apparent to me. The student-teacher had approached me with an air of uncertainty. He was ambivalent about discussing the incident in other than hushed tones and expressed the fear that the revelation of our conversation might lead to negative repercussions regarding his student-teaching performance. Concerned that he had raised an unpopular issue, he sought reassurance that dealing with such topics would not cause him to be viewed as a troublemaker or as unprofessional. When I inquired as to whether he had consulted the university supervisor to whom he had been assigned, he said that he did not perceive the supervisor to be particularly supportive or knowledgeable about such matters. Further, he felt that little within his own academic background offered him any substantive approaches for determining a solution to the problem.

At another school, a student-teacher working in a third-grade classroom was told to create a bulletin board representative of important historical events during the month of February. She worked diligently throughout a weekend designing a display highlighting the accomplishments of Black Americans. On Monday morning, however, her efforts were rewarded with a disdainful response from the cooperating teacher, who expressed doubt as to their relevance. The cooperating teacher's discomfort was underscored by her remark to the student-teacher that children in the third grade "are a little young for this sort of thing." The student-teacher refrained from asking at what age children are old enough to recognize the existence and accomplishments of Black Americans, and dutifully created a more traditional bulletin board.

In a third incident, a student-teacher reported a conflict between her nonsexist linguistic style and that of the classroom teacher. After having been taught to use nonsexist language, the student-teacher found herself the object of ridicule in a sixth-grade language arts classroom. When she attempted to substitute nonsexist terms such as *firefighter* and *police officer* for the more traditional terms *fireman* and *policeman*, the cooperating teacher reprimanded her in front of the class for use of "feminist language." The student-teacher related that this and similar incidents had a negative impact upon her ability to interact with the boys in the class, who subsequently made denigrating remarks to her such as "Oh, what do you know? You're only a girl."

Scenarios in which student-teachers experience dissonance between the goals of preservice programs and the implementation of those goals in the field setting are not atypical. What is unique is that each of these students recognized an opportunity to confront issues of race, class, and gender and attempted to infuse multicultural strategies. These situations afford us valuable insights into the influence of the cooperating teacher and the power struggles which can occur for the student-teacher who tries to implement multicultural instruction in the public school setting. The student-teachers in these examples experienced a sense of powerlessness and frustration which ultimately rendered them ineffective as multicultural agents. Each was aware of the power differential between themselves and the cooperating teacher, but none was able to successfully negotiate the power struggle in her or his favor without compromising his or her multicultural goals.

This work will assess the roles which the teacher education institution and the cooperating teacher play in the creation of a multicultural environment for empowerment in the student-teaching experience. It will also underscore the importance of providing student-teachers with a knowledge base for multicultural education that includes the historical and philosophical foundations of the discipline. Finally, it will discuss the need for creating an awareness of the dynamics of power which inherently influence the effectiveness of multicultural strategies in the school setting.

It is important to note that, although some students may lack knowledge regarding multicultural education and others may not be convinced of the efficacy of multicultural approaches, this chapter assumes that student-teachers have been acquainted with basic strategies associated with multicultural teaching. It does not address the issue of student-teachers who lack multicultural preparation or who perpetuate bigotry in the form of racist, sexist, or classist behaviors. In addition, it is assumed that student-teachers who may be committed to multicultural reconstructionism recognize the limitations of the student-teaching field experience. Among the obvious constraints is that student-teachers will be allowed to practice limited infusion but will be obliged to acknowledge that total restructuring to create a consistently significant multicultural experience is reliant upon their ultimate authority as an independent classroom teacher.

Before student-teachers can create meaningful multicultural experiences for their own students, they must become competent in the articulation of the philosophical constructs of multicultural education. It is imperative that these future educators be encouraged to critically examine their multicultural philosophy, to survey the perspectives and assumptions surrounding it, and to discern the educational conditions under which they will attempt to institutionalize that philosophy.

A Multicultural Environment:
"You Gotta Know the Territory"

Although comprehension of the theoretical foundations of multicultural education is paramount to implementing multicultural strategies, of equal importance is an understanding of the setting in which the student teacher will attempt to employ those strategies. Too frequently student-teachers, as well as experienced educators, have been catapulted into environments which are not conducive to multicultural education. They are often underprepared and overwhelmed by the magnitude of the task confronting them. Lending to the confusion within the educational arena is an array of government mandates and social justice movements which have had a major impact upon curricula but whose purposes have not always been made apparent. Howsam and others (1976) have noted the following:

> Often with cataclysmic suddenness the courts give schools mandates to drastically alter programs, administrative arrangements, teacher assignments, and resource allocation. These mandates dramatically change the lives of teachers. Teachers are not prepared either personally or professionally for such service. Most have been reared in middle or lower class homes and communities ensconced safely away from minority and lower socioeconomic groups. Many possess conventional wisdom biases toward minorities. Probably few could look forward with anticipation to assignment to inner city schools; fewer still know how to go about instructionally and socially redressing the injustices that have been done to minorities. All teachers need professional preparation for this role. (p. 23)

Advocates of multicultural education are not unlike parachutists who in wartime have been used to landing in terrain that is sparsely populated and difficult to traverse. The success of the venture is dependent not only upon the skill of the parachutist but also upon the climactic conditions into which one jumps. The word *parachute* is a derivative of French words meaning "to prevent falling." The multicultural education parachute has the capability to prevent us from falling into the conventional behaviors which have traditionally plagued many educational settings. However, the successful multicultural educator, like the successful parachutist, must be equipped with the skill and a climate conducive to emerge victorious.

As part of their training, preservice educators must be given multicultural equipment for empowerment. Their parachute is a knowledge of the historical and legislative context of multicultural education and an understanding of the power governing the settings in which they will attempt to use those strategies. It is important for future educators to comprehend that, although the terrain may be sparsely populated, there are multicultural advocates and an existing framework of support for their strategies.

The Historical and Legislative Context

Within the past thirty years a plethora of legislation has emerged to mediate some of the perceived social inequities in American institutions. Nowhere has the responsibility for redressing the imbalances been more pronounced than in American education. Numerous accreditation agencies and educational associations have provided guidelines for the infusion of multicultural components in teacher education and in the public school sector. The National Council for the Accreditation of Teacher Education (N.C.A.T.E.) and the American Association for Colleges of Teacher Education (A.A.C.T.E.), the Civil Rights Acts (1964), the Elementary and Secondary Education Act (1965), the Bilingual Education Act (1968), Public Law 94-142, the Education for All Handicapped Children Act (1975), and Title IX of the Educational Amendments (1972) are among the numerous agencies and mandates that have attempted to strengthen the quality of schooling of those considered to be educationally disadvantaged. In addition, twenty-seven states have implemented some sort of human relations or multicultural component within their teacher preparation curriculum (Martin, 1986).

A cursory glance at the proliferation of legislative and social mandates would lead the casual observer to conclude that multicultural education has a strong foothold and that the social inequities highlighted by such legislative reforms must be rapidly disappearing. However, multicultural education has frequently been misinterpreted and misunderstood. Preparing skilled multicultural educators has historically been difficult partially because of the variety of programs in existence and the fragmentary nature of those programs.

Recently there has been an attempt to organize the characteristics of multicultural or human relations programs into a definitive framework. Reviews by Grant and Sleeter (1985), as well as studies by Banks (1984) and Baker (1983), have sought to clarify the confusion over terminologies and programmatic elements. However, as author Geneva Gay (1977) has noted, multicultural education is "fraught with ambiguities" (p. 103). Knowledge of the disparate nature of multicultural education and an awareness of the legislation which precipitated its infusion can alert prospective educators to carefully choose the programs which they will employ in their classrooms. That awareness creates a philosophical rationale for the student-teacher's use of multicultural strategies. This in turn allows the student-teacher to negotiate some of the traditional impediments to the success of multicultural education.

Historical and philosophical knowledge can empower student-teachers. For example, the student-teacher can assess what kind of multicultural strategies have been implemented by the school in which he or she will be teaching. Student-teachers should determine the philosophical goals of the district and discern how multicultural education has historically been interpreted within that framework. Informal discussions with the cooperating teacher and the university supervisor could help students determine the extent to which multicultural education has been a prevalent strategy at the school in which they will teach, thus enabling them to identify how they will best be able to infuse multicultural concepts. Students should be encouraged to visit their prospective classrooms prior to the student-teaching experience. The cultural milieu of the public school which the student-teacher enters will play a significant role in her or his professional assimilation. Factors such as the population of the school, the experiences of the cooperating teacher and the pupils, and the existing relationship among all of these directly affect the potential of the student-teacher to establish congruence between the strategies which the university has advocated regarding multicultural infusion and the implementation of those strategies in the field experience setting. Additionally, student teachers should become conversant with the policies and practices of the school and of the particular teachers with whom they will be teaching.

Once student-teachers have determined the extent to which multicultural education has been a prevalent strategy at the school in which they will teach, it is important that they identify how they will best be able to infuse multicultural concepts. It is critical that student-teachers gain an awareness of the audience with whom they will be working. An initial visit prior to student-teaching allows the student-teacher to get a profile of students' attitudes regarding issues of race, class, and gender, and gives them important insights regarding the power struggles among student peer groups. Analysis of the power and oppression among student groups is a valuable tool in the negotiation of struggles which will occur in classrooms. These initial inquiries not only resolve unanswered questions for the student-teacher, but they also underscore the university's multicultural programmatic goals and offer the cooperating teacher the opportunity to become part of a multicultural ensemble.

Setting the Stage for Empowerment

The student-teaching experience might be compared to a theatrical production in which numerous components must be integrated in order to achieve a successful performance. The classroom setting, climate, and tone, as determined by the administration and the classroom teacher, are of paramount importance. Setting the stage and creating an appropriate atmosphere influence the ability of a student-teacher to become a talented and effective multicultural educator.

Although many teacher education institutions are aware of the need for student-teachers to work in multiracial, multiethnic, or urban field experiences, there is usually little recognition of the factors within those settings which may make it difficult for student teachers to function as effective multicultural educators. Doyle and Ponder (1975) note that there appears to be a relationship between what they have identified as "classroom ecology" and the teaching behaviors of student-teachers. They have theorized that if a student-teacher perceives that a skill which she or he is trying to integrate is in harmony with the environment of the classroom, the student will be more likely to employ that skill. According to the results of a series of research projects conducted by Copeland (1988), "student teachers' ability to use many skills they learn during their university training depends not only on the quality of the initial training they receive, but on the environment in which they must practice use of those skills, the student teaching classroom" (p. 194).

Copeland (1988) suggests that teacher educators should not only be concerned with the ways in which they train their students in the use of technical skills, but they must also develop a clearer and more integrated understanding of the realities present in classrooms. As the producer of the program, the university can set the stage for multicultural teaching to occur via its requirements and expectations for the cooperating teacher.

Rewriting the Script

Critical to the success of the student-teacher's implementation of multicultural approaches is the degree to which the cooperating teacher has been acquainted with and consequently is willing to encourage the practice of multicultural strategies in her or his classroom. Some cooperating teachers may feel threatened or resentful of students who advocate multicultural strategies. Others may remain unfamiliar with multicultural education and reluctant to become involved in what they perceive to be controversial or irrelevant issues. Consequently, some cooperating teachers may unwittingly undermine or thwart the efforts of student-teachers who engage in multicultural education.

Nickolai-Mays and Davis (1986) have suggested that "schools are often populated by veteran teachers who are expected to work effectively in environments they were not prepared to encounter at the time they received their teacher training" (p. 169). Veteran teachers, like veteran actors, must be acquainted with the multicultural classroom script. Use of multicultural materials can be a welcome addition to the cooperating teacher who may have been struggling with the absence of such materials. However, student-teachers may also be viewed as rewriting the script with which the cooperating teacher has become familiar. Caution must be exercised to ensure that student-teachers do not appear to be viewed as stealing the spotlight from the veteran teacher or threatening the existing order unjustifiably. Student-teachers who present material in a way which is different from what has traditionally been taught may experience some negative interaction from a teacher who is less skilled or not well acquainted with multicultural approaches.

All materials and curricular ideas should be relevant, and their infusion ought to be rehearsed with the cooperating teacher well in advance of their use. Numerous suggestions for infusion of multicultural concepts can be found in texts by authors such as Andrzejewski (1985), Banks (1984), Gollnick and Chinn (1983), Grant and Sleeter (1989), and others. Familiarity with such materials provides the student-teacher and the cooperating teacher with valuable references and acts as a foundation for implementation.

In addition, students should be required to enter the student-teaching experience armed with multicultural strategies which they have authored in an original unit of instruction in a major content area. As an incentive, the university could assemble the work of students who author particularly creative multicultural units and publish them in a handbook which would be made available to other students in the program. Cooperating teachers might also become interested in authoring materials for similar publications, thereby creating a valuable instructional resource. Creating a videotape library of the multicultural teaching episodes of student-teachers offers another possible resource which university faculty might then use in their classes. Tapes could serve as a method of determining which concepts within multicultural components may need additional attention and which have been effective.

Teacher education institutions can empower student-teachers by encouraging ensemble performances from cooperating teachers and student-teachers and by expecting cooperating teachers to model multicultural behaviors. In this way the veteran or cooperating teacher plays a supporting role in the cast of an educator who can encourage the student-teacher in the performance of multicultural behaviors. In what is frequently an improvisational atmosphere, the student-teacher should be able to rely upon the cooperating teacher to give the consummate performance of multicultural teaching, enabling the student-teacher to expand her or his own repertoire. This is important because there is research to suggest that student-teachers tend to imitate the behaviors of their cooperating teachers. Copeland (1988) has attempted to determine what prompts student teachers to employ in the field experience a skill which had been taught prior to the field experience. That research indicates that student-teachers who employ skills in their student-teacher experiences reflect the tendency of the cooperating teacher to employ the same skill (p. 195).

Casting the Characters

Historically, the process of screening cooperating teachers has been fairly haphazard. Although some states may stipulate specific supervision standards such as a minimal number of years of experience in the classroom, there is no evidence to suggest that cooperating teachers who supervise are required to be proficient in formal multicultural training. Several approaches might be employed in the selection of cooperating teachers which would result in an atmosphere more conducive to multicultural education. Cooperating teachers could become part of an in-service program that would acquaint them with multicultural strategies for use with student-teachers in their own classrooms. As part of the in-service, cooperating teachers would be required to teach and critique sample units of instruction utilizing multicultural approaches which would, upon completion of the in-service program, become theirs to return with to their schools. The sample units would enhance their curricula, and the university could then develop a resource pool of educators conversant in such strategies from which they would eventually be able to draw student-teaching placement sites. Stipends or graduate credits could be used to attract cooperating teachers to model programs. Teacher education programs could provide additional incentives with monetary allowances for multiple enrollments from one school or district. This would assure teachers a built-in support network within the school or their district as they began the development of multicultural programs. It would also establish a buddy system model into which student-teachers could be inducted, thus developing collaborative strategies among veteran and entry-level professionals. Additionally, universities might consider offering annual awards for outstanding teaching or stellar multicultural performances by educators in public schools.

To promote networking, student-teachers should be encouraged to plan lessons which are interdisciplinary and which aid them in developing alliances with educators in other departments. For example, a student-teacher in the English department might consider planning trips to the museum with an art instructor's class, designing panel discussions with the science classes about prominent women and minorities, or collaborating in planning to read a novel pertinent to a period of history being studied by a social studies class in order to raise issues of race, class, and gender. This affords the student-teacher the opportunity to infuse multicultural issues with the support of experienced teachers. Other teachers might be enthusiastic about capitalizing on the student-teacher's multicultural knowledge and would probably welcome her or him as an additional resource. If more than one student-teacher has been placed at a school site, they might work as a company of actors to combine their talents and insights to reinforce multicultural approaches across the curriculum. Acquainting student-teachers with strategies which encourage ensemble performances gives them concrete insights into cooperative strategies among professional educators. Further, it teaches them to learn to mediate the power within their environment by building a supportive network composed of experienced educators and peers.

Members of the community can also be cast in the roles of those who support the multicultural strategies which the student-teacher is attempting to infuse. Identifying community groups concerned with multicultural issues, asking women and minority persons to be guest lecturers, or employing the talents of parents who are active in the perpetuation of issues of equity can provide additional support and contact with the community in which the student-teacher may one day seek a permanent teaching position.

Capturing Critical Acclaim

Terry (1974) has noted that "institutional practices and policies set structure, define roles, and allocate rewards and punishment . . . If the club (in this case represented by the university) were committed to becoming such an organization, it would require that those not firmly committed to anti-racist postures either be refused employment or be required to get additional training which is how other employment standards are handled" (p. 17). Teacher education institutions must begin to require that cooperating teachers and school settings be conversant in and conducive to the goals of multicultural education. Further, they must provide student-teachers with mechanisms for the achievement of multicultural goals. In light of recent reform movements, teacher education institutions must consider promoting only those students who are fully capable of demonstrating excellence in all facets of their chosen profession. It is only then that the institutions and their graduates will receive the rave reviews and critical acclaim which they seek.

> It is no longer defensible to send beginning teachers into schools with the same naivete to make the same mistakes that generations of teachers before them have made . . . The total institution must be staffed by persons aware of how differences are valued, how those differences have been internalized by the individual student, and how the school can reinforce creative differences without demeaning any. The task is one for every teacher, and for every person the institution employs. Reeducation of teachers can and should be shared by the school system and the college or university and planned with individual teachers to meet their needs. (Banks and Grambs, 1972, p. 209)

If multicultural education is to become a viable mechanism for empowerment, teacher education components which socialize prospective teachers into the profession must be founded upon realistic assessments of the expectations and norms of the existing power structure and of those factors which can represent success for the aspiring teacher. Teacher education institutions must clearly and firmly articulate multicultural goals to their students, faculty, supervisory staff, the public school educators with whom they work, and the communities in which they exist. There must be a proliferation of forces at all levels which support multicultural education.

Banks (1983) has suggested that "the position of the United States as a world leader demands that we deal more imaginatively and constructively with the enormous cultural differences within and outside our borders" (p. 559). Multicultural education is the first step toward empowering all students in a global society. Teacher education institutions can perpetuate a cycle of empowerment which begins with their advocacy of a model of teaching that presents professional candidates who are competent in representing the needs and aspirations of an increasingly diverse school population.

NOTES AND REFERENCES

Introduction:
Multicultural Education and Empowerment

Notes

1. Grant and I have used the term *multicultural education* to refer to this approach since it is the most common approach that appears in the literature on multicultural education, but Carlos Cortes has suggested that this renders terminology rather confusing. He has suggested that the term *cultural democracy* fits this approach quite accurately; I agree.

References

Ashcroft, L. (1987). Defusing "empowering": The what and the why. *Language Arts, 64*, 142-156.

Banks, J.A. (1981). *Multiethnic education: Theory and practice.* Boston: Allyn and Bacon.

———— (1989). Integrating the curriculum with ethnic content: Approaches and guidelines. In J.A. Banks and C.A.M. Banks (Eds.), *Multicultural education: Issues and perspectives* (pp. 189-207). Boston: Allyn and Bacon.

Banks, J.A., and Banks, C.A.M., (Eds.). (1989). *Multicultural education: Issues and perspectives.* Boston: Allyn and Bacon.

Baptiste, H.P., and Baptiste, M.L. (1979). *Developing the multicutural process in classroom instruction.* Washington, D.C.: University Press of America.

Bennett, C.I. (1986). *Comprehensive multicultural education.* Boston: Allyn and Bacon.

Brickman, P., Rabinowitz, V., Kazura, J., Coates, D., Cohn, E., and Kidder, L. (1982). Models of helping and coping. *American Psychologist, 37*, 368-384.

Butler, J.E. (1989). Transforming the curriculum: Teaching about women of color. In J.A. Banks and C.A.M. Banks (Eds.), *Multicultural education: Issues and perspectives* (pp. 145-164). Boston: Allyn and Bacon.

Chan, A., Brophy, M.C., and Fisher, J.C. (1981). Advocate counseling and institutional racism. In O.A. Barbarin, P.R. Good, O.M. Pharr, and J. A. Siskind (Eds.), *Institutional racism and community competence* (pp. 194-205). Rockville, Md.: National Institute for Mental Health.

Charnofsky, S. (1971). *Educating the powerless.* Belmont, Calif.: Wadsworth Pub. Co.

Checkoway, B., and Norsman, A. (1986). Empowering citizens with disabilities. *Community Development Journal, 21,* 270-277.

Colangelo, N., Foxley, C.H., and Dustin, D. (Eds.). (1979). *Multicultural nonsexist education: A human relations approach.* Dubuque, Iowa: Kendall Hunt.

Cummins, J. (1986). Empowering minority students: A framework for intervention. *Harvard Educational Review, 56,* 18-36.

Dunst, C.J., and Trivette, C.M. (1987). Enabling and empowering families: Conceptual and intervention issues. *School Psychological Review, 16,* 443-456.

Ellsworth, E. (1989). Why doesn't this feel empowering? Working through the repressive myths of critical pedagogy. *Harvard Educational Review, 59,* 297-324.

Fordham, S. (1988). Racelessness as a factor in Black students' school success: Pragmatic strategy or Pyrrhic victory? *Harvard Educational Review, 58,* 54-84.

French, J.R.P., Jr., and Raven, B. (1959). The bases of social power. In D. Cartwright (Ed.), *Studies in social power* (pp. 150-167). Ann Arbor: University of Michigan, Institute for Social Research.

Gay, G. (1983). Multiethnic education: Historical developments and future prospects. *Phi Delta Kappan, 64,* 560-563.

Giroux, H.A. (1983). *Theory and resistance in education.* South Hadley, Mass.: Bergin and Garvey.

———— (1988). Literacy and the pedagogy of voice and political empowerment. *Educational Theory, 38,* 61-75.

Gollnick, D.M., and Chinn, P. (1986). *Multicultural education* (2nd ed.). Columbus, Ohio: Charles E. Merrill.

Grant, C.A. (1977) *Multicultural education: Commitments, issues, and applications.* Washington, D.C.: Association for Supervision and Curriculum Development (ASCD).

Grant, C.A., and Sleeter, C.E. (1986). Race, class and gender: An argument for integrative analysis. *Review of Educational Research, 56,* 195-211.

Hernandez, H. (1989). *Multicultural education*. Columbus, Ohio: Charles E. Merrill.

Hicks, E. (1981). Cultural Marxism: Non-synchrony and feminist practice. In L. Sargeant (Ed.), *Women and revolution* (pp. 219-238). Boston: South End Press.

Hughes, R., Jr. (1987). Empowering rural families and communities. *Family Relations, 36,* 396-401.

Kipnis, D. (1976). *The powerholders*. Chicago: University of Chicago Press.

Kramer, J.M. (1989, May). *The American health deficit: Hazards of being minority and poor*. Paper presented at the Green Bay Colloquium on Ethnicity and Public Policy, Green Bay, Wisconsin.

Lewis, M., and Simon, R.I. (1986). A discourse not intended for her: Learning and teaching within patriarchy. *Harvard Educational Review, 56,* 457-472.

Maher, F.A. (1987). Toward a richer theory of feminist pedagogy: A comparison of "liberation" and "gender" models for teaching and learning. *Journal of. Education, 169,* 91-100.

McCarthy, C. (1988). Rethinking liberal and radical perspectives on racial inequality in schooling: Making the case for nonsynchrony. *Harvard Educational Review, 58,* 265-279.

McLaren, P. (1989). *Life in schools*. New York: Longman.

―――― (1988). Language, social structure and the production of subjectivity. *Critical Pedagogy Networker, 1,* 1-10.

Schniedewind, N., and Davidson, E. (1983). *Open minds to equality*. Englewood Cliffs, N.J.: Prentice-Hall.

Scotch, R.K. (1988). Disability as the basis for a social movement: Advocacy and the politics of definition. *Journal of Social Issues, 44,* 159-172.

Shor, I., and Freire, P. (1987). What is the "dialogical method" of teaching? *Journal of Education, 169,* 11-31.

Simon, R.I. (1987). Empowerment as a pedagogy of possibility. *Language Arts, 64,* 370-382.

Simon, R.I., and Dippo, D. (1987). What schools can do: Designing programs for work education that challenge the wisdom of experience. *Journal of Education, 169,* 101-116.

Sleeter, C.E., and Grant, C.A. (1987). An analysis of multicultural education in the United States. *Harvard Educational Review, 57,* 421-444.

—— (1988). *Making choices for multicultural education.* Columbus, Ohio: Charles E. Merrill.

Suzuki, B.H. (1984). Curriculum transformation for multicultural education. *Education and Urban Society, 16,* 294-322.

Takaki, R. (1989, May). *The fourth iron cage: Race and political economy in the 1990's.* Paper presented at the Green Bay Colloquium on Ethnicity and Public Policy. Green Bay, Wisconsin.

Tetreault, M.K.T. (1989). Integrating content about women and gender into the curriculum. In J.A. Banks and C.A.M. Banks (Eds.). (1989). *Multicultural education: Issues and perspectives* (pp. 124-143). Boston: Allyn and Bacon.

Tiedt, P., and Teidt, I. (1986). *Multicultural teaching: A handbook of activities, information and resources.* Boston: Allyn and Bacon.

Trueba, H. (1988). Culturally based explanations of minority students' academic achievement. *Anthropology and Education Quarterly, 19,* 270-281.

Wilkerson, M.B. (1983). Lifting as we climb: Networks for minority women. *New Directions for Higher Education, 12,* 59-68.

Wrong, D.H. (1979). *Power: Its forms, bases and uses.* South Hampton, England: Basil Blackwell.

Youkin, L. (1989). Protest: What's the most effective way to change things? *Disability Rag, 10*(3), 1-7.

Chapter 1.
Doing School in an Urban Appalachian First Grade

References

Allington, R. (1977). If they don't get to read much, how they ever gonna get good? *Journal of Reading, 21*(1), 57-61.

—— (1980a). Teacher interruption behaviors during primary grade oral reading. *Journal of Educational Psychology, 72,* 371-377.

—— (1980b). Poor readers don't get to read much in reading groups. *Language Arts, 57,* 872-877.

—— (1983). The reading provided readers of differing abilities. *Elementary School Journal, 83*(5), 548-559.

—— (1984). Content coverage and contextual reading in reading groups. *Journal of Reading Behavior, 16*(2), 85-96.

Barr, R. (1974). Instructional pace differences and their effect on reading acquisition. *Reading Research Quarterly, 9*(4), 526-554.

——— (1975). How children are taught to read: Grouping and pacing. *School Review, 83*(3), 479-498.

——— (1982). Classroom reading instruction from a sociological perspective. *Journal of Reading Behavior, 14*(4), 375-389.

Borman, K., and Mueninghoff, E. (1982). *Work roles and social roles in three elementary school settings.* Paper presented at the meeting of the American Educational Research Association, New York.

——— (1983). Lower Price Hill's children: Family, school and neighborhood. In A. Batteau (Ed.), *Appalachia and America.* Lexington: University Press of Kentucky.

DeFord, D. (1985). Validating the construct of theoretical orientation in reading instruction. *Reading Research Quarterly, 20*(3), 351-367.

Dreeben, R. (1984). First grade reading groups: Their formation and change. In P. Peterson et al. (Eds.), *The social context of instruction: Group organization and group process.* New York: Academic Press.

Featherstone, H. (Ed.). (1987). Organizing classes by ability. *Harvard Education Letter, 3*(4), 1-9.

Gambrell, L., Wilson, R., and Gantt, W. (1981). Classroom observations of task attending behaviors of good and poor readers. *Journal of Educational Research, 74,* 400-404.

Giroux, H. (1983a). Theories of reproduction and resistance in the new sociology of education: A critical analysis. *Harvard Educational Review, 53*(30), 257-293.

——— (1983b). *Theory and resistance in education.* South Hadley, Mass.: Bergin and Garvey.

Giroux, H., and McLaren, P. (1986). Teacher education and the politics of engagement: The case for democratic schooling. *Harvard Educational Review, 56*(3), 213-238.

Goetz, J., and LeCompte, M. (1984). *Ethnography and qualitative design in educational research.* New York: Academic Press.

Jones, L. (1975). Appalachian values. In R.J. Higgs and A.N. Manning (Eds.), *Voices from the hills: Selected readings of southern Appalachia* (pp. 507-517). New York: Ungar.

McDermott, R. (1977). Social relations as contexts for learning in school. *Harvard Educational Review, 47*(2), 198-213.

Oakes, J. (1985). *Keeping track*. New Haven, Conn.: Yale University Press.

Shavelson, R., and Stern, P. (1981). Research on teachers' pedagogical thoughts, judgments, decisions and behavior. *Review of Educational Research, 52*(40), 455-498.

Tickamyer, A.R., and Tickamyer, C. (March, 1987). *Poverty in Appalachia*. Appalachian Data Bank Report #5. Lexington, Ky.: Appalachian Center, University of Kentucky.

Urban Appalachian Council fact sheet. (1985). Cincinnati, Ohio: Urban Appalachian Council.

Weinstein, R. (1976). Reading group membership in first grade: Teacher behaviors and pupil experience over time. *Journal of Educational Psychology, 68*(1), 103-116.

Chapter 2. Mapping Terrains of Power: Student Cultural Knowledge Versus classroom Knowledge

References

Ashcroft, L. (1987). Defusing "empowering": The what and the why. *Language Arts, 64,* 142-156.

Cummins, J. (1986). Empowering minority students: A framework for intervention. *Harvard Educational Review, 56,* 18-36.

Cusick, P.A. (1973). *Inside high school*. New York: Holt, Rinehart and Winston.

Dewey, J. (1944). *Democracy and education*. New York: The Free Press.

Everhart, R.B. (1983). *Reading, writing, and resistance*. Boston: Routledge and Kegan Paul.

Fine, M. (1987). Silencing in public schools. *Language Arts, 64,* 157-174.

Frake, C.O. (1980). *Language and cultural description*. Stanford, Calif.: Stanford University Press.

Goodenough, W.H. (1956). Componential analysis and the study of meaning. *Language, 32,* 195-216.

Grant, C.A., and Sleeter, C.E. (1986). *After the school bell rings*. Lewes, England: Falmer Press.

Greene, M. (1986). Reflection and passion in teaching. *Journal of Curriculum and Supervision, 2,* 68-71.

Gup, T. (1989, April 3). Foul! *Time*, pp. 54-60.

Hoover, K.H. (1982). *The professional teacher's handbook* (3rd ed.). Boston: Allyn and Bacon.

Levi-Strauss, C. (1963). *Structural anthropology*. New York: Basic Books.

McLaren, P. (1986). *Schooling as a ritual performance*. Boston: Routledge and Kegan Paul.

Pickles, J. (1985). The role of place and commonplaces in democratic empowerment. *Issues in Education, 3,* 232-241.

Reitman, S.W. (1981). *Education, society, and change*. Boston: Allyn and Bacon.

Saxe, G.B. (1988). Candy selling and math learning. *Educational Researcher, 17,* 14-21.

Shor, I., and Freire, P. (1987). What is the "dialogical method" of teaching? *Journal of Education, 169,* 11-31.

Simon, R.I. (1987). Empowerment as a pedagogy of possibility. *Language Arts, 64,* 370-382.

Spradley, J.P., and McCurdy, D.W. (1972). *The cultural experience*. Chicago: Science Research Associates.

Walsh, C. (1987). Language, meaning, and voice: Puerto Rican students' struggle for a speaking consciousness. *Language Arts, 64,* 196-206.

Chapter 3. Peer-Proofing Academic Competition Among Black Adolescents: "Acting White" Black American Style

Notes

1. I have developed this idea elsewhere (see Fordham, 1989). As I view it, reinventing racial identity among Black and other non-dominate-group students is a systematic attempt to transform their racial and cultural identity in ways which minimize their connectedness to the Black community. Essentially, as schools are currently structured, the core curriculum and other institutionalized practices in the school context are designed to make Black students Black in skin color only. All other aspects of the school curriculum are intended to separate them from those persons who resemble them racially and or culturally.

2. Capital High and all other proper names are pseudonyms used to protect the identity of the school and its officials as well as those members of the community who voluntarily and involuntarily participated in this ethnographic study.

3. Elsewhere (Fordham, 1989) I have postulated the existence of a three-tier historical time frame in the life of people of African descent in America. I have noted that the first 350 years of Black people's history in this country can be accurately described as the period when they were forbidden to "act White." I have labeled the second stage of this time period—the time focus of my study of Black adolescents' school success—as a transition period or the period when Black Americans are compelled to "act White" in order to be successful. This historical period began about 1966 and ended about 1986. It is also the period immediately following the culmination of the civil rights movement. This is important, in my view, because the civil rights movement wrought changes in the internal organizational structures of both the Black and White communities (see Blassingame, 1982; Sitkoff, 1981). Inarguably, although some social barriers were dismantled during this historical period (e.g., legalized segregation), others emerged—maintaining many of the practices which were abhorrent during the pre-civil rights era. I am postulating that the existence of these socially unacceptable barriers, cloaked in the guise of equal opportunity for all, undermines Black adolescents' school achievement efforts. I have labeled the third and final period of Black people's history in this country as a period of cultural diversity or what some people are beginning to describe as "neo-segregation." The true shape and texture of this historical period is not clear, and hence I simply identify and label it. We must await its clear shape and configuration.

4. By "repetition," I do not mean the mindless drill and practice usually associated with the curriculum offered lower-track students. What I am suggesting instead is recognition of a cultural propensity among Black people to value richness and detail over parsimony and breadth in their interactions (see B. Williams, 1988). Hence, in the development of a core curriculum, greater attention will be given to how to present information so that the vividness and richness of phenomena under study are not sacrificed in favor of breadth and blandness.

5. Bailey's (1977) claims are not specifically addressed to the members of the Black community. Much of his work was done in India. Nonetheless, his theoretical position appears to be applicable to the Black community in America.

6. I am not claiming that Black Americans have a monopoly on this phenomenon. I am simply trying to point out how what I learned about Black Americans' preferred interactional style might be used to enhance the school performance of a larger number of them. Also, I am trying to show how their preferred style of interacting with individuals might be used in helping them to better handle the school's greater emphasis on nonhuman subject matter. The fact that students at Capital value richness, vividness, and striking details in their human interactions is important in the development and implementation of core curricula.

7. I am not an educator. In the tradition of social and cultural anthropolo-

gy, my fieldwork at Capital High School was descriptive rather than prescriptive. It is against this background that I offer these "peer-proofing" suggestions. As an anthropologist, I know that what is culturally significant for different human populations is implicated in their reaction(s) to it. Hence, if the school curriculum recognizes and incorporates into the seams of its structure that which is familiar and culturally meaningful to the population(s) it serves, students' involvement and cooperation are likely to rise. Conversely, if that which is culturally meaningful to a particular school population is either denigrated or ignored in the school curriculum, the affected students' effort and willingness to participate are seriously undermined. Unfortunately, for far too long, the American system of public schooling has either denigrated or ignored that which is culturally meaningful to people of African descent (see Fordham, in process).

References

Abrahams, R., and Gay, G. (1972). Talking black in the classroom. In R.D. Abrahams and R.C. Troike (Eds.), *Language and cultural diversity in American education*. Englewood Cliffs, N.J.: Prentice-Hall.

Bailey, F.G. (1977). *Morality and expediency: The folklore of academic politics*. Chicago: Aldine Publishing Company.

Bishop, M. (1986). Updates. *Sports Illustrated, 58*(7), 43-44.

Blassingame, John. (1982). The revolution that never was. *The Civil Rights Quarterly Perspective, 14*(2), 3-15.

Castile, G.P., and Kushner, G. (1981). *Persistent peoples: Cultural enclaves in perspective*. Tucson: University of Arizona Press.

Fordham, S. (1981). *Black student school success as related to fictive kinship: A study in the Washington, D.C. Public School System*. Dissertation proposal submitted to the Department of Anthropology, The American University.

———— (1982, December 3-7). *Cultural inversion and Black children's school performance*. Paper presented at the eighty-first annual meeting of the American Anthropological Association, Washington, D.C.

———— (1985, December 5). *Black students' school success: Coping with the burden of 'acting white'*. Paper presented at the eighty-third annual meeting of the American Anthropological Association, Washington, D.C.

———— (1986). *Black students' school success: An ethnographic study in a large urban school system*. A Preliminary Report. Submitted to the Spencer Foundation, Chicago, Illinois.

———— (1987). *Black student school success as related to fictive kinship: An ethno-*

graphic study in the District of Columbia Public School System. Unpublished dissertation, The American University, Washington, D.C.

——— (1988a). Racelessness as a factor in Black students' school success: Pragmatic strategy or pyrrhic victory? *Harvard Educational Review, 58*(1), 58-88.

——— (1988b). Correspondence, racelessness, collectivity, and individuality in the Black community: A reply to Hawkins. *Harvard Educational Review, 58*(2), 422-425.

——— (1989, May 3). *Black students' school success: 'Acting White' while remaining Black.* Paper presented at the National Academy of Education meeting, Princeton, New Jersey, Educational Testing Service.

——— (in process). *Acting White and book-black Blacks: An ethnology of school success at Capital High.* Unpublished book manuscript.

Fordham, S., and Ogbu, J.U. (1986). Black students' school success: Coping with the "burden of 'acting white'." *The Urban Review, 18*(3), 176-206.

Gray, J. (1985, March 14). A Black American princess: New game, new rules. *The Washington Post,* pp. E1, E5.

Hanna, J. (1982). Public social policy and the children's world: Implications of ethnographic research for desegregated schooling. In G. Spindler (Ed.), *Doing the ethnography of schooling: Education anthropology in action* (pp. 316-355). New York: Holt, Rinehart and Winston.

Haskins, K. (1975). You have no right to put a kid out of school. In Arthur Tobier, Four conversations: The intersection of public and private. *The Urban Review, 8*(4), 273-287.

Holt, G. (1972). "Inversion" in Black communication. In T. Kochman (Ed.), *Rappin' and stylin' out.* Urbana: University of Illinois Press.

Lauter, P., and Howe, F. (1970). *The conspiracy of the young.* New York: World Publishing Company.

MacLeod, J. (1987). *Ain't no makin' it: Leveled aspirations in a low-income neighborhood.* Boulder, Colo.: Westview Press.

Monroe, S. (1987). Brothers: A vivid portrait of Black men in America. *Newsweek. 109*(12), 53-86.

Monroe, S., and Goldman, P. (1988). *Brothers: Black and poor—A true story of courage and survival.* New York: William Morrow.

Neira, C. (1988). Building 860. *Harvard Educational Review, 58*(2), 337-342.

Oakes, J. (1985). *Keeping track: How schools structure inequality.* New Haven, Conn.: Yale University Press.

Ogbu, J. (1974). *The next generation: An ethnography of education in an urban neighborhood.* New York: Academic Press.

——— (1978). *Minority education and caste: The American system in cross-cultural perspective.* New York: Academic Press.

——— (1980). *Cultural differences vs. alternative cultures: A critique of 'cultural discontinuity' hypothesis in classroom ethnographies.* Paper presented at the seventy-ninth annual meeting of the American Anthropological Association, Washington, D.C.

——— (1981). On origins of human competence: A cultural ecological perspective. *Child Development, 52,* 413-429.

——— (1984). *Understanding community forces affecting minority students' academic effort.* Paper prepared for the Achievement Council, Oakland, California.

Rosenbaum, J.E. (1976). *Making inequality: The hidden curriculum of high school tracking.* New York: John Wiley.

Rosenfeld, G. (1971). *"Shut those thick lips!": A study of slum school failure.* New York: Holt, Rinehart and Winston.

Sargent, E. (1984, July 4). Freeing myself: Discoveries that unshackle the mind. *The Washington Post,* pp. D6-7.

Silverstein, B., and Krate, R. (1975). *Children of the dark ghetto: A developmental psychology.* New York: Praeger Publishers.

Sitkoff, H. (1981). *The struggle for Black equality: 1954-1980.* New York: Hill and Wang.

Spicer, E. (1980). *The Yaqui: A cultural history.* Tucson: University of Arizona Press.

Spicer, H. (1971). Persistent cultural systems: A comparative study of identity systems that can adapt to contrasting environments, *Science, 174,* 795-800.

Treisman, U. (1985). *A study of the mathematics performance of Black students at the University of California, Berkeley.* Unpublished manuscript.

Weis, L. (1985). *Between two worlds: Black students in an urban community college.* Boston: Routledge and Kegan Paul.

Williams, B. (1988). *Upscaling downtown: Stalled gentrification in Washington, D.C.* Ithaca, N.Y.: Cornell University Press.

Williams, M. (1981a). *On the street where I lived.* New York: Holt, Rinehart and Winston.

——— (1981b) Observations in Pittsburgh ghetto schools. *Anthropology and Education Quarterly, 12*(3), 211-220.

Chapter 4.
Disempowering White Working-Class Females:
The Role of the High School

Notes

1. Ellen Israel Rosen makes this point clearly when she suggests that women factory workers "choose" such jobs in order to earn more money to help fulfill their traditional responsibilities of caring for a family. See Rosen, 1987.

2. This is not to deny the very important role of the state itself in the perpetuation of certain forms of gender relations. Change in gender relations is not *simply* a matter of changed consciousness, of course. See Connell (1989).

3. Grant and Sleeter (1986) come to a similar conclusion based on their ethnography, as do Steinitz and Solomon (1986).

4. Twenty-five students are in the "advanced class." This refers to a college preparatory sequence of courses.

5. I am not suggesting here that female teachers have nothing to say. I am simply suggesting that they do not have an articulated and coherent voice (or voices) within this working-class school. In so arguing, I do not mean to imply that there is anything innate in the notion of "female voice."

6. This occurred in other ways as well. Applicants pointed out that they "lived in Freeway all their lives," that they "currently own property there," that they "worked in Freeway in summer recreation," and so forth.

7. I have argued this point at length in Chapter 5 of *Working Class Without Work* (1990).

References

Apple, Michael. (1983). Curricular form and the logic of technical control. In M. Apple and L. Weis (Eds.), *Ideology and practice in schooling.* Philadelphia: Temple University Press.

Carlson, Dennis. (1985). Curriculum and the school work culture. In P. Altbach, G. Kelly, and L. Weis (Eds.), *Excellence in education: Perspectives on policy and practice.* Buffalo: Prometheus Press.

Connell, R.W. (1989). *The state in sexual politics: Theory and appraisal.* Mimeo.

Eisenstein, Zillah (1984). *Feminism and sexual equality.* New York: Monthly Review Press.

Elder, Glen (1974). *Children of the Great Depression.* Chicago: University of Chicago Press.

Grant, Carl, and Christine Sleeter. (1986). *After the school bell rings.* Philadelphia: The Falmer Press.

May, Marthy. (1987). The historical problem of the family wage: The Ford Motor Company and the five dollar day. In Naomi Gerstel and Harriet Engel Gross (Eds.), *Families and work.* Philadelphia: Temple University Press.

McRobbie, Angela. (1978). Working class girls and the culture of feminitity. In Women's Studies Group (Ed.), Women take issue. London: Hutchinson.

Rosen, Ellen I. (1987). *Bitter choices.* Chicago: University of Chicago Press.

Rubin, Lillian. (1976). *Worlds of pain.* New York: Basic Books.

Smith, Dorothy. (1987). Women's inequality and the family. In Mary F. Katzenstein and Carol M. Mueller (Eds.), *The women's movements of the United States and Europe.* Philadelphia: Temple University Press.

Steinitz, Victoria, and Solomon, Ellen. (1986). *Starting out: Class and community in the lives of working class youth.* Philadelphia: Temple University Press.

Tentler, Leslie, W. (1979). *Wage earning women: Industrial work and family life in the United States, 1900-1930.* New York: Oxford University Press.

Valli, Linda. (1986). *Becoming clerical workers.* New York: Routledge and Kegan Paul.

Weis, Lois (1988). High school girls in a de-industrializing economy. In Lois Weis (Ed.), *Class, race and gender in American education.* pp. 183-208. Albany, N.Y.: State University of New York Press.

——— (1990). *Working class without work: High school students in a de-industrializing economy.* New York: Routledge and Kegan Paul.

Wolpe, Ann Marie. (1978). Education and the sexual division of labor. In Annette Kuhn and Ann Marie Wolpe (Eds.), *Feminism and materialism: Woman and modes of production.* London: Routledge and Kegan Paul.

Chapter 5.
A Curriculum for Empowerment, Action, and Change

References

Baldwin, J. (1985). *The price of the ticket: Collected nonfiction, 1948-1985.* New York: St. Martin's Press.

Banks, J.A., and Sebesta, S.L. (1982). *We Americans: Our history and people* (Vols. 1 and 2). Boston: Allyn and Bacon.

Banks, J.A. (1988). *Multiethnic education: Theory and practice* (2nd ed). Boston: Allyn and Bacon.

———— (1989, Fall). The battle over the canon: Cultural diversity and curriculum reform. *Allyn and Bacon Educators' Forum, 1*, 11-13.

Banks, J.A., and Clegg, A.A., Jr. (1990). *Teaching strategies for the social studies: Inquiry, valuing and decision-making* (4th ed.). White Plains, N.Y.: Longman.

Bates, D. (1987). *The long shadow of Little Rock.* Fayetteville: University of Arkansas Press.

Berger, P.L., and Luckman, T. (1966). *The social construction of reality.* New York: Doubleday.

Bloom, A. (1987). *The closing of the American mind.* New York: Simon and Schuster.

Coleman, J.S., et al. (1966). *Equality of educational opportunity.* Washington, D.C.: U.S. Government Printing Office.

Fleming, J. (1984). *Blacks in college: A comparative study of students' success in black and white institutions.* San Francisco: Jossey-Bass Publishers.

Garrow, D.J. (1986). *Bearing the cross: Martin Luther King and the Southern Christian Leadership Conference.* New York: Vintage.

Heller, S. (1989, November 8). Press for campus diversity leading to more closed minds, say critics. *The Chronicle of Higher Education*, pp. A13, ff A22.

Hirsch, E.D., Jr. (1987). *Cultural literacy: What every American needs to know.* Boston: Houghton Mifflin.

Jan, C. (1930). *The voyages of Christopher Columbus.* London: The Argonaut Press.

Lefcourt, H.M. (1976). *Locus of control: Current trends in theory and research.* New York: John Wiley.

Olsen, F. (1974). *On the trail of the Arawaks.* Norman, Okla.: University of Oklahoma Press.

Ravitch, D., and Finn, C.E., Jr. (1987). *What do our 17-year-olds know? A report on the first national assessment of history and literature.* New York: Harper and Row.

Ryan, W. (1971). *Blaming the victim.* New York: Vintage.

Starrs, J. (1988). *Cultural literacy and black education.* Paper submitted to James A.

Banks as a partial requirement for the course, EDC&I 469, University of Washington.

Chapter 6. Empowerment Through Media Literacy: A Multicultural Approach

References

Balon, R.E. (1978). The impact of "Roots" on a racially heterogeneous southern community: An exploratory study. *Journal of Broadcasting, 22*(3), 299-307.

Comstock, G. (1977). *The impact of television on American institutions and the American public.* Honolulu: East-West Communication Institute, East-West Center.

Cortés, C.E. (1981). The societal curriculum: Implications for multiethnic education. In Banks, J.A. (Ed.), *Education in the 80's: Multiethnic education* (pp. 24-32). Washington, D.C.: National Education Association.

Cummins, J. (1989). Empowering minority students. Sacramento: California Association for Bilingual Education.

Gans, H.J. (1967). The mass media as an educational institution. *Television Quarterly, 6,* 20-37.

Greenberg, B.S., and Reeves, B. (1976). Children and the perceived reality of television. *Journal of Social Issues, 32*(4), 86-97.

Howard, J., Rothbart, G., and Sloan, L. (1978). The response to "Roots": A national survey. *Journal of Broadcasting, 22*(3), 279-287.

Hur, K.K. (1978). Impact of "Roots" on black and white teenagers. *Journal of Broadcasting, 22*(3), 289-298.

Jowett, G. (1976). *Film: The democratic art.* Boston: Little, Brown.

Leckenby, J.D., and Surlin, S.H. (1976). Incidental social learning and viewer race: "All in the Family" and "Sanford and Son." *Journal of Broadcasting, 20*(4), 481-494.

Longstreet, W.S. (1989). Education for citizenship: New dimensions. *Social Education, 53*(1), 41-45.

Lopez-Johnson, P. (1989, May 29). "See No Evil"? Deaf film actors say they do. *Los Angeles Times,* p. VI-8.

Metabane, P.W. (1988). Television and the black audience: Cultivating moderate perspectives on racial integration. *Journal of Communication, 38*(4), 21-31.

O'Brien, S. (1989). How to produce a better Edsel—Writing U.S. history textbooks. *Social Education, 53*(2), 98-100.

O'Connor, J. E. (Ed.). (1989). *Image as artifact: The historical analysis of film and television.* Melbourne, Fla.: Krieger.

Peterson, R.C., and Thurstone, L.L. (1933). *Motion pictures and the social attitudes of children.* New York: Macmillan.

Pingree, S., and Hawkins, R.P. (1982). What children do with television: Implications for communication research. In Dervin, B., and Voigt, M.J. (Eds.), *Progress in communication sciences* (Vol. 3). Norwood, N.J.: ABLEX.

Raths, L.E., and Trager, F.N. (1948). Public opinion and "Crossfire." *Journal of Educational Sociology, 21*(6), 345-368.

Rosen, I.C. (1948). The effect of the motion picture "Gentleman's Agreement" on attitudes toward Jews. *Journal of Psychology, 26,* 525-536.

Schramm, W., Lyle, J., and Parker, E.B. (1961). *Television in the lives of our children.* Stanford, Calif.: Stanford University Press.

Shaheen, J.G. (1984). *The TV Arab.* Bowling Green, Ohio: Bowling Green State University Popular Press.

Singer, R., and Kazdon, R. (Eds.). (1976). Television and social behavior. *Journal of Social Issues, 32* (4).

Sklar, R. (1975). *Movie-made America: A cultural history of American movies.* New York: Random House.

Surlin, S.H. (1978). "Roots" research: A summary of findings. *Journal of Broadcasting, 22*(3), 309-320.

Vidmar, N., and Rokeach, M. (1974). Archie Bunker's bigotry: A study in selective perception and exposure. *Journal of Communication, 24*(1), 36-47.

Chapter 7.
Cooperative Learning as Empowering Pedagogy

Notes

1. For an excellent discussion of the many myths which influence our perspective and vision, see Arthur W. Combs, *Myths in education: Beliefs that hinder progress and their alternatives* (Boston: Allyn and Bacon, 1979).

2. See, for example, Barbara Kerr, *Smart girls: Gifted women* (Columbus, Ohio: Ohio Psychology Publishing Co., 1985), for an excellent documentation of the factors which limit girls' willingness and ability to achieve.

3. Intergroup competition is best exemplified in the work of Robert Slavin but is supported or used by a host of cooperative learning educators. See Robert Slavin, *Using student team teaching* (Baltimore, Md., Johns Hopkins University Press (1986).

4. Contrast this, for example, with the activity on advertising in Herb Perr's *Making art together* (San Jose, Calif.: Resource Publications, 1988).

References

Allport, G. (1954). *The nature of prejudice.* Cambridge, Mass.: Addison-Wesley.

Aronson, E. (1978). *The jigsaw classroom.* Beverly Hills, Calif.: Sage Publications.

Bell, L., and Schniedewind, N. (1987). Reflective minds, intentional hearts: Joining humanistic education and critical theory. *Journal of Education, 169*(2), 55-72.

Best, R. (1983). *We all got scars: What boys and girls learn in elementary schools.* Bloomington: Indiana University Press.

Cohen, E. (1986). *Designing groupwork.* New York: Teachers College Press.

Dishon, D., and O'Leary, P.W. (1984). *Guidebook for cooperative learning.* Holmes Beach, Fla.: Learning Publications.

Gallimore, R., and Howard, A. (1968). Studies in a Hawaiian community: Na Makanaka o Nanakuli. Hawaii: Bishop Museum, Pacific Anthropological Record 1, Department of Anthropology.

Johnson, D., and Johnson, R. (1975). *Learning together and alone.* Englewood Cliffs, N.J.: Prentice-Hall.

——— (1986). *Learning together and alone: Cooperation, competition and individualization.* Englewood Cliffs, N.J.: Prentice-Hall.

Johnson, D., Johnson, R., and Holubec, E.J. (1986). *Circles of learning.* Edina, Minn.: Interaction Books.

Johnson, D., Johnson, R., and Maruyama, G. (1983). Interdependence and interpersonal attraction among heterogeneous and homogeneous individuals: A theoretical formulation and a meta-analysis of the research. *Review of Educational Research, 53*(1), 5-54.

Kagan, S. (1980). Cooperation—Competition, culture and structural bias in classrooms. In S. Sharan, P. Hare, C. Webb, and R. Hertz-Lazarowitz (Eds.), *Cooperation in education* (p. 210). Provo, Utah: Brigham Young University Press.

———— (1988). Cooperative learning: *Resources for teachers.* University of California Press, Riverside, CA.

Kohn, A. (1986). *No contest: The case against competition.* Boston, Mass.: Houghton Mifflin.

Lickona, T. (1980). Beyond justice: A curriculum for cooperation. In D. Cochrane and M. Manley-Cosimir (Eds.), *Development of moral reasoning* (pp. 108-144). New York: Praeger Publishers.

Lockheed, M.R., and Harris, A.M. (1984). Cross-sex collaborative learning in elementary classrooms. *American Educational Research Journal, 21,* 275-294.

Miller, N., and Brewer, M. (Eds.). (1984). *Groups in contact: The psychology of desegregation.* New York: Academic Press.

Moorman, C., and Dishon, D. (1983). *Our classroom: We can learn together.* Englewood Cliffs, N.J.: Prentice-Hall.

Oakes, J. (1986). Keeping track, Part 2: Curriculum inequity and school reform. *Phi Delta Kappan, 36,* 148-154.

Owens, L. (1980). The development of a cooperative, competitive, and individualized learning preference scale for students. *British Journal of Educational Psychology, 50,* 147-161.

———— (1982). The relationship between cooperative, competitive, and individualized learning preferences and students' perception of classroom learning atmosphere. *American Educational Research Journal, 19,* 182-180.

Raviv, S. (1982). *The effects of three teaching methods on cross-sex cooperative and competitive behaviors of students in ethnically-mixed seventh grade classes.* Paper presented at the Second International Conference on Cooperation in Education, Provo, Utah.

Schniedewind, N., and Davidson, E. (1983). *Open minds to equality: Learning activities to promote race, sex, class and age equity.* Englewood Cliffs, N.J.: Prentice-Hall.

———— (1987). *Cooperative learning, cooperative lives: A sourcebook of learning activities for building a peaceful world.* Dubuque, Iowa: W.C. Brown. (Distributed by the Circle Books, 30 Walnut Street, Somerville, MA 02143.)

Sharan, S. (1984). *Cooperative learning in the classroom: Research in desegregated schools.* Hillsdale, N.J.: Lawrence Erlbaum Associates.

Slavin, R. (1982). *Cooperative learning: student teams.* Washington, D.C.: National Education Association.

———— (1983). *Student team learning*. Washington, D.C.: National Education Association.

———— (1986) *Using student team teaching*. Baltimore, Md.: Johns Hopkins University Press.

———— (1987, November). Cooperative learning and the cooperative school. *Educational Leadership, 45*, 7-13.

———— (1988, October). Cooperative learning and student achievement. *Educational Leadership, 45*, 31-33.

Solomon, D., Watson, M., Schaps, E., Battistich, V., and Solomon, J. (in press). Cooperative learning as part of a comprehensive classroom program designed to promote social development. In S. Sharan (Ed.), *Current research in cooperative learning*. New York: Praeger Publishers.

Webb, N. (1984). Sex Differences in interaction and achievement in cooperative small groups. *Journal of Educational Psychology, 76*, 33-44.

Yager, S., Johnson, R., Johnson, D., and Snider, B. (1986). The impact of group processing or achievement in cooperative learning groups. *Journal of Social Psychology, 125*, 389-397.

Chapter 8.
Teaching Children About Social Issues: Kidpower

Notes

1. Out of respect for religious diversity, including the right not to believe in God, some people would choose not to say this part of the pledge because of its reference to God.

References

Beyer, B. (1988). Developing a scope and sequence for thinking skills instruction. *Educational Leadership, 45*(7), 23-30.

Chavez, D. (1985). Perpetuation of gender inequality: A content analysis of comic strips. *Sex Roles, 13*(1-2), 93-102.

Comer, J. (1980). *School power*. New York: The Free Press.

Crooks, R.C. (1970). The effects of an interracial preschool program upon racial preference, knowledge of racial differences, and racial identity. *Journal of Social Issues, 26*, 137-143.

Derman-Sparks, L., Higa, C., and Sparks, B. (1980). Children, race, and racism: How race awareness develops. *Interracial Books for Children Bulletin, 11*(3-4), 3-9.

Durkin, D. (1978). *Teaching them to read* (3rd ed.). Boston: Allyn and Bacon.

Goodlad, J. (1984). *A place called school.* New York: McGraw-Hill.

Goodman, M.E. (1964). *Race awareness in young children.* New York: Collier Books.

Guidelines for selecting bias-free textbooks and storybooks. (1980). New York: Council on Interracial Books for Children.

Gutmann, A. (1987). *Democratic education.* Princeton, N.J.: Princeton University Press.

Hahn, C.L. (1984). Promise and paradox: Challenges to global citizenship. *Social Education, 48*(4), 240-243.

Harris, L., and associates. (1978). *A study of attitudes toward racial and religious minorities and toward women.* New York: author.

Herbers, J. (1978, February 26). Decade after Kerner report: Division of races persists. *New York Times,* p. 1ff.

Lenehan, A. (Ed.). (1989). *Soundings, 5*(6).

Lopach, J., and Luckowski, J. (1989). The rediscovery of memory in teaching democratic values. *Social education, 53*(3), 183-187.

Nakagawa, M., and Pang, V. (forthcoming). Cooperative pluralism: Moving from "me" to "we". *Social Studies and the Young Learner.*

Oakes, J. (1985). *Keeping track.* New Haven, Conn.: Yale University Press.

Porter, J.D.R. (1971). *Black child, white child: The development of racial attitudes.* Cambridge: Harvard University Press.

Sleeter, C., and Grant, C. (1987). An analysis of multicultural education in the United States. *Harvard Educational Review, 57*(4), 421-444.

State of Washington Office of the Superintendent of Public Instruction. (1977). *Guidelines for identifying and counteracting bias in instructional materials.* Olympia, Wash.: author.

Swadener, E.B. (1988). Implementation of education that is multicultural in early childhood settings: A case study of two day-care programs. *The Urban Review, 20*(1), 8-27.

Bibliography of Children's Books

Asian and Pacific Islander Americans

Clark, Ann Nolan. *To stand against the wind*. New York: Viking Press, 1978. (upper elementary)

Coutant, Helen. *First snow*. New York: Alfred A. Knopf, 1974. (primary)

Japanese American Curriculum Project. *The Japanese American Journey*. San Mateo, Calif.: Japanese American Curriculum Project, 1985. (intermediate and junior high)

Pinkwater, Manus. *Wingman*. New York: Dodd, Mead, 1975. (second grade and up)

Say, Allen. *A river dream*. New York: Houghton Mifflin, 1988. (primary)

Stock, Catherine. *Emma's dragon hunt*. New York: Lothrop, Lee and Shepard, 1984. (primary)

Takashima, Shizuye. *A child in prison camp*. Plattsburgh, N.Y.: Tundra Books of Northern New York, 1971. (intermediate and up, Japanese)

Uchida, Yoshiko.
    Best bad thing. New York: Atheneum, 1983.
    The happiest ending. New York: Atheneum, 1985. (trilogy, intermediate—about twelve years old and up)
    A jar of dreams. New York: Atheneum, 1981.
    Journey home. New York: Atheneum, 1978. (intermediate)
    Journey to Topaz. New York: Scribner's, 1971. (intermediate)
    Samurai of Gold Hill. New York: Scribner's, 1972. (intermediate)

Yep, Laurence.
    Child of the owl. New York: Harper and Row, 1977. (upper intermediate)
    Dragonwings. New York: Harper and Row, 1975. (junior high)
    Sea glass. New York: Harper and Row, 1979. (intermediate)
    Serpent children. New York: Harper and Row, 1984. (junior/senior high)

Black Americans

Adoff, Arnold. *All the colors of the race*. New York: Lothrop, Lee and Shepard, 1982. (primary)

Clifton, Lucille.
    Amifika. New York: Dutton, 1977. (primary)
    Everett Anderson's 1 2 3. New York: Holt, Rinehart and Winston, 1977. (primary)

Everett Anderson's goodbye. New York: Holt, Rinehart and Winston, 1983. (primary)
My friend Jacob. New York: Dutton, 1980. (primary)

Faulkner, William. *The days when the animals talked: Folktales of the Black American and how they came to be.* Chicago: Follett, 1977.

Feelings, Tom, and Greenfield, Eloise. *Day dreams.* New York: Dial Press, 1981. (elementary)

Greenfield, Eloise.
Honey I Love. New York: Thomas Y. Crowell, 1977. (primary)
Mary McLeod Bethune. New York: Thomas Y. Crowell, 1977. (primary)
Rosa Parks. New York: Thomas Y. Crowell, 1974. (primary)

Giovanni, Nikki. *Spin a soft Black song.* New York: Hill and Wang, 1971. (primary)

Hamilton, Virginia.
Junius over far. New York: Harper and Row, 1985. (junior high)
M.C. Higgins the Great. New York: Macmillan, 1974. (junior high)
The people could fly: American Black folktales. New York: Alfred A. Knopf, 1980. (intermediate and up)
Zeely. New York: Collier, 1971. (intermediate)

Mathis, Sharon Bell.
The hundred penny box. New York: Viking, 1975. (intermediate)
Sidewalk story. New York: Avon Books, 1971. (second grade and up)

Myers, Walter Dean. *The young landlords.* New York: Viking, 1979. (some profanity—junior high)

Steptoe, John. *Stevie.* New York: Harper and Row, 1969. (primary)

Taylor, Mildred.
The gold cadillac. New York: Dial Press, 1987. (intermediate)
Let the circle be unbroken. New York: Dial Press, 1981. (intermediate)
Roll of thunder, hear my cry. New York: Dial Press, 1976.

Walter, Mildred P.
Ty's one-man band. New York: Scholastic, 1980. (primary)
My mama needs me. New York: Lothrop, Lee and Shepard, 1983. (primary)

Winter, Jeanette. *Follow the drinking gourd.* New York: Alfred A. Knopf, 1988.

Yarbrough, Camille. *Cornrows.* New York: Coward-McCann, 1979. (elementary)

Hispanic Americans

Anaya, Rudolfo A. *Bless me Ultima.* Berkeley, Calif.: Tonatiuh International, 1972. (high school)

Gonzales, Rodolfo. *I am Joaquin.* New York: Bantam Books, 1967. (junior/senior high)

Native American

Baylor, Byrd. *Hawk, I'm your brother.* New York: Scribner's, 1976. (intermediate)

Blood, Charles, and Link, Martin. *The goat in the rug.* New York: Parents' Magazine Press, 1976. (primary)

George, Chief Dan, and Hirnschall, Helmut. *My heart soars.* Blaine, Wash.: Hancock House, 1982. (intermediate and up)

George, Jean Craighead.
Julie of the wolves. New York: Harper and Row, 1972.
The talking earth. New York: Harper and Row, 1983.

Highwater, Jamake
The ceremony of innocence. New York: Harper and Row, 1985. (junior high)
Moonsong lullaby. New York: Lothrop, Lee and Shepard, 1981. (primary)

Martin, Bill, Jr., and Archambault, John. *Knots on a counting rope.* New York: Henry Holt and Company, 1987. (primary)

Chapter 9.
Classroom Use of African American Language:
Educational Tool or Social Weapon?

References

Baugh, J. (1983). *Black street speech: Its history, structure, and survival.* Austin: University of Texas Press.

Davis, O., Gladney, M., and Leaverton, L. (1968). *The psycholinguistic reading series: A bi-dialectal approach.* Board of Education, City of Chicago.

Dillard, J.L. (1972). *Black English.* New York: Random House.

Labov, W. (1970). *The study of nonstandard English.* Champaign, Ill.: National Council of Teachers of English.

Shuy, R., et al. (1968). *Detroit dialect study.* Washington, D.C.: Center for Applied Linguistics.

Simpkins, G., Holt, G., and Simpkins, C. (1977). *Bridge: A cross-culture reading program.* Boston: Houghton Mifflin.

Simpkins, G., and Simpkins, C. (1981). The Cross-cultural approach to curriculum development. In G. Smitherman (Ed.), *Black English and the education of Black children and youth* (pp. 212-240). Detroit: Harlo Press.

Smitherman, G. (1977). *Talkin and testifyin*. Boston: Houghton Mifflin.

Wagner, S. (1981). The historical background of bilingualism and bi-culturalism in the U.S. In M. Ridge (Ed.), *The new bilingualism* (pp. 29-52). Los Angeles: University of Southern California Press.

West, E. (1972). *The Black American and education*. Columbus, Ohio: Charles E. Merrill.

Williams, S.W. (forthcoming). Substantive Africanisms at the end of the African linguistic diaspora. In S. Mufwene (Ed.), *Africanisms in Afro-American language varieties*. Athens: University of Georgia Press.

Chapter 10.
The Empowerment of Language-Minority Students

References

Cummins, J. (1979). Linguistic interdependence and educational development of bilingual children. *Review of Educational Research, 49*, 222-251.

———— (1986). Empowering minority students: A framework for intervention. *Harvard Educational Review, 56*, 18-36.

———— (1989). *Empowering minority students*. Sacramento: California State Department of Education.

Edwards, J. (1984). Language, diversity and identity. In J. Edwards (Ed.), *Linguistic minorities, policies and pluralism* (pp. 277-310). Orlando, Fla.: Academic Press.

Fanon, F. (1967). *Black skin, white masks*. Translated by C.L. Markmann. New York: Grove Press.

Freire, P. (1970). *Pedagogy of the oppressed*. Translated by M. B. Ramos. New York: Continuum.

Freire, P., and Macedo, D. (1987). *Literacy: Reading the word and the world*. South Hadley, Mass.: Bergin and Garvey.

Giroux, H.A. (1986, Spring). Radical pedagogy and the politics of student voice. *Interchange, 17*, 48-69.

Heath, S.B. (1985). Language policies: Patterns of retention and maintenance. In W. Connor (Ed.), *Mexican Americans in comparative perspective*. Washington, D.C.: The Urban Institute.

Hirsch, E.D. (1987). *Cultural literacy.* Boston: Houghton Mifflin.

Hornberger, N. (1988). *Bilingual education and language maintenance: A southern Peruvian Quechua case.* Providence, R.I.: Floris.

Kessler, C., and Quinn, M. (1980). Positive effects of bilingualism on science problem-solving abilities. In J. Atatis (Ed.), *Georgetown University round table on languages and linguistics 1980.* Washington, D.C.: Georgetown University Press.

Kjolseth, R. (1982). Bilingual education programs in the United States: For assimilation or pluralism? In P.R. Turner (Ed.), *Bilingualism in the southwest* (2nd. ed., rev., pp. 3-28). Tucson: University of Arizona Press.

Lambert, W. (1978). Some cognitive and sociocultural consequences of being bilingual. In J. Alatis (Ed.), *Georgetown University round table on languages and linguistics 1978.* Washington, D.C.: Georgetown University Press.

Macedo, D.P. (1983, Winter). The politics of emancipatory literacy in Cape Verde. *Journal of Education, 165,* 99-112.

McLeod, A. (1986, January). Critical literacy: Taking control of our own lives. *Language Arts, 63,* 37-50.

Moreau, N.B. (1984). Education, ideology, and class/sex identity. In C. Kamarae, M. Schulz, and W.M. O'Barr (Eds.), *Language and power* (pp. 43-61). Beverly Hills, Calif.: Sage Publications.

Nichols, P.C. (1984). Networks and hierarchies: Language and social stratification. In C. Kramarae, M. Schulz, and W.M. O'Barr (Eds.), *Language and power* (pp. 23-42). Beverly Hills, Calif.: Sage Publications.

Ruiz, R. (1988). Bilingualism and bilingual education in the United States. In C.B. Paulston (Ed.), *International handbook of bilingualism and bilingual education.* Westport, Conn.: Greenwood Press.

Smitherman, G. (1984). Black language as power. In C. Kramarae, M. Schulz, and W.M. O'Barr (Eds.), *Language and power.* Beverly Hills, Calif.: Sage Publications.

Valdes, G. (1981). Pedagogical implications of teaching Spanish to the Spanish-speaking in the United States. In G. Valdex, A.G. Lozano, and R. Garcia-Moya (Eds.), *Teaching Spanish to the hispanic bilingual: Issues, aims, and methods.* New York: Teachers College Press.

Wolfson, N., and Manes, J. (Eds.). (1985). *Language of inequality.* Berlin: Mouton.

Chapter 11. Changing Our Ideas About Ourselves:
Group Consciousness Raising with
Elementary School Girls as a Means to Empowerment

Notes

1. Project REACH was funded for 1987-88 by the Ford Foundation. Additional support during 1988-89 was provided by the New York African American Institute.

2. The names of the girls who participated in Project REACH have been changed. The names used in this chapter are pseudonyms. The names of the adults are actual.

3. See Campbell (1988) for an interesting discussion of the dilemmas that arise between school-university partnerships when the university has a research agenda and the school has an action agenda.

4. See Bell (1989) for further examples of the dilemmas that were developed into role plays for analysis.

References

Bell, L.A. (1989). Something's wrong here and it's not me: Challenging the dilemmas that block girls' success. *Journal for the Education of the Gifted, 12,* 118-130.

Campbell, D.R. (1988, Fall). Collaboration and contradictions in a research and staff development project. *Teachers College Record, 91,* 99-121.

Chodorow, N. (1974). Family structure and feminine personality. In M. Rosaldo and L. Lamphere (Eds.), *Women, culture and society* (pp. 43-66). Palo Alto, Calif.: Stanford University Press.

Dweck, C., Davidson, W., Nelson, S., and Enna, B. (1978). Sex differences in learned helplessness: II. The contingencies of evaluative feedback in the classroom and III. An experimental analysis. *Developmental Psychology, 14,* 268-276.

Freire, P. (1971). *Pedagogy of the oppressed.* New York: Herder and Herder.

Frieze, I.H. (1980). Beliefs about success and failure in the classroom. In J.H. McMillan (Ed.), *The social psychology of school learning.* New York: Academic Press.

Grant, L. (1984). Black females' "place" in desegregated classrooms. *Sociology of education, 57,* 98-111.

Horner, M. (1972). Toward an understanding of achievement-related conflicts in women. *Journal of Social Issues, 28,* 157-175.

Irvine, J.J. (1986). Teacher-student interactions: Effects of student race, sex and grade level. *Journal of Educational Psychology, 78,* 14-21.

Maehr, M.L. (1983). On doing well in science: Why Johnny no longer excels; why Sarah never did. In S.G. Paris, G.M. Olson, and H.W. Stevenson (Eds.), *Learning and motivation in the classroom.* Hillsdale, N.J.: Lawrence Erlbaum Associates.

Maehr, M.L., and Nicholls, J.G. (1980). Culture and achievement motivation: A second look. In N. Warren (Ed.), *Studies in cross-cultural psychology* (Vol. 3). New York: Academic Press.

Miller, J.B. (1976). Toward a new psychology of women. Boston: Beacon Press.

Sadker, M., and Sadker, D. (1982). *Sex equity handbook for schools.* New York: Longman.

Sassen, G. (1980). Success anxiety in women: A constructivist interpretation of its source and significance. *Harvard Educational Review, 50,* 13-25.

Scott-Jones, D., and Clark, M.L. (1986). The school experience of black girls: The interaction of gender, race and socioeconomic status. *Phi Delta Kappan,* Vol. 67, 520-526.

Stein, A., and Bailey, N. (1973). The socialization of achievement orientation in females. *Psychological Bulletin, 80,* 345-366.

Chapter 12. Who Is Empowering Whom?
The Social Construction of Empowerment

Notes

1. The two models with which the author is most familiar are the undergraduate sociological research projects at the University of Wisconsin, Parkside, and the undergraduate moot court program at the California State University, Dominguez Hills, both of which deal with issues of empowerment. Refer to Jeanne Curran (1989), *Interim Report on the Stanley Mosk Undergraduate Moot Court Competition* (Dominguez Hills: California State University); and James Benet (1977), "More than Techniques: A Research Center with Heart and Soul," *Change* 9:52-56.

2. Freire (1972) adds the following:

Narration (with teacher as narrator) leads the students to memorize mechanically the narrated content. Worse yet, it turns them into "containers," into "receptacles" to be "filled" by the teacher. The more completely he fills the receptacles, the better a teacher he is. The more meekly the receptacles permit themselves to be filled, the better students they are.

Education thus becomes an act of depositing, in which the students are the depositories and the teacher is the depositor. (p. 58)

Sometimes Freire refers to this as "banking education."

3. Phrase derived from discussions with Jeanne Curran.

4. The term and its definition and use are credited to Jeanne Curran.

5. The objectives of the Racine Gang Project were to develop a comprehensive understanding of the gang situation and to provide program and policy recommendations for community agencies to more effectively and efficiently address the problem of youth gangs. Refer to the following materials: S.R. Takata (1986), *The Racine Gang Project: Preliminary Report* (Racine: Task Force Commission on Gangs and Delinquency); and S.R. Takata and R.G. Zevitz (1987), "Youth Gangs in Racine: An Examination of Community Perceptions," *Wisconsin Sociologist* 24:142-151.

As a result of the Racine Gang Project, two follow-up projects were conducted. The Racine Community Collaboration Project was funded by the Wisconsin Council on Criminal Justice. This was a juvenile delinquency prevention project to improve community. Youth resources coordination, youth employment, and research and evaluation were the three major components of this project. For more information, refer to S.R. Takata (1988), *The Racine Community Collaboration Project: Final Report* (Kenosha: University of Wisconsin, Parkside). The third project, the Racine Youth Needs Assessment, was funded by the Johnson Wax Fund, Inc. The purpose of this project was to evaluate the effectiveness of youth programs and services in Racine. For more information, refer to S. Brudvig, S.R. Takata, and T. Nommensen (1988), *The Racine Youth Needs Assessment* (Kenosha: University of Wisconsin, Parkside).

In addition, one study of local gangs in the Kenosha area was conducted. The main objective of this project was to examine institutional records (police, school, and social services) of identified gang members. For more information, refer to S.R. Takata and S. Baskin (1987), *The Kenosha Gang Project: Preliminary Report* (Kenosha: Kenosha Task Force on Gangs).

6. Kenosha has a population of 77,685. There are 2,777 Blacks (3.6 percent of the city's population) and 3,110 Hispanics (4.0 percent). (1980 census).

7. In calculating the economic value of the labor of learning-by-doing students, it is conservatively estimated that personnel costs would have ranged between $8,500 to $10,400 (at ten to twelve hours a week for sixteen weeks with a pay rate of $4.50 an hour with twelve students). Despite some individuals who may consider this exploitation, students understand and realize that the kind of

learning that occurs has a lasting effect on their perceptions and expectations and an immeasurable value beyond the learning experience itself. Thus, labor value is easily ascertained, but calculating the value of the many short-term as well as long-term real-life lessons learned as a result of the course(s) is difficult. Students continue to tell me about how they have applied what they have learned in a variety of settings and situations.

8. Although there is an attempt to ensure success, this does not mean that students learn without experiencing failure, frustration, mistakes, and other obstacles. Real learning comes not without some struggle and effort.

9. "Earning your stripes" is another real-world lesson students must learn. Sometimes students naively believe that the diploma is the ticket to a high-paying job where they can immediately supervise others. Students frequently forget that stripes must first be earned.

10. Concept derived from discussions with Jeanne Curran.

11. Jeanne Curran is credited with this term, which describes what it is we attempt to do with our students.

12. From a discussion with Jeanne Curran.

References

Benet, J. (1977). More than techniques: A research center with heart and soul. *Change, 9,* 52-56.

Berger, P.L., and Luckmann, T. (1966). *The social construction of reality.* New York: Anchor Books.

Blauner, R. (1968). *Racial oppression in America.* New York: Harper and Row.

Bloch, A. (1977). *Murphy's law.* Los Angeles: Price/Stern/Sloan.

Bruner, J. (1966). *Toward a theory of instruction.* New York: W.W. Norton.

———— (1977). *The process of education.* Cambridge: Harvard University Press.

———— (1979). *On knowing: Essays for the left hand.* Cambridge: Harvard University Press.

Carnoy, M. (1974). *Education as cultural imperialism.* New York: David McKay.

Carroll, L. (1986). *Alice in Wonderland.* New York: Grossett and Dunlap.

Chickering, A.W., and Gamson, Z.F. (1987). Seven principles for good practice in undergraduate education. *The Wingspread Journal, 9,* special section.

Clark, K. (1965). *The dark ghetto*. New York: Harper and Row.

Cohen, E. (1986). *Designing groupwork*. New York: Teachers College Press.

Curran, J. (1977). *The social systems research center*. Unpublished manuscript.

—— (1989). *Interim report on the Stanley Mosk undergraduate moot court competition*. Dominguez Hills: California State University.

Curran, J., and Telesky, C. (1975). *A student-operated research center: A new climate of learning*. Unpublished manuscript.

Drucker, P. (1968). *The age of discontinuity*. New York: Harper and Row.

Freire, P. (1972). *Pedagogy of the oppressed*. New York: Herder and Herder.

Fromm, E. (1968). *The revolution of hope*. New York: Harper and Row.

Goffman, E. (1959). *The presentation of self in everyday life*. New York: Doubleday.

Guilford, J.P. (1967). *The nature of human intelligence*. New York: McGraw-Hill.

Holt, J. (1964). *How children fail*. New York: Dell.

National Institute of Education (1984). *Involvement in learning: Realizing the potential of American higher education*. Washington, D.C.: U.S. Government Printing Office.

Leonard, G. (1968). *Education and ecstasy*. New York: Dell.

MacKay, H. (1988). *Swim with the sharks*. New York: William Morrow.

Maslow, A.H. (1971). *The farther reaches of human nature*. New York: Viking.

McHugh, P. (1968). *Defining the Situation*. New York: Bobbs-Merrill.

Osborn, A.F. (1963). *Applied imagination*. New York: Scribner's.

Takata, S.R. (1988). *The importance of integrating 'divergent thinking' in today's criminal justice curriculum*. Unpublished manuscript.

Takata, S.R., and Leiting, W. (1987). Learning by doing: The teaching of sociological research methods. *Teaching Sociology, 15*, 144-150.

Wagner, J. (1985). *The search for signs of intelligent life in the universe*. New York: Harper and Row.

Weber, M. (1946). *From Max Weber: Essays in sociology*. New York: Oxford University Press.

Chapter 13.
The Rationale for Training Adults as Teachers

References

Carlozzi, A.F., Gaa, J.P., and Liberman, D.B. (1983). Empathy and ego development. *Journal of Counseling Psychology, 30*, 113-116.

Cummings, A.L., and Murray, H.G. (1989). Ego development and its relation to teacher education. *Teaching and Teacher Education, 5*(1), 21-32.

Erikson, E. (1963). *Childhood and society.* New York: W.W. Norton.

Heath, D. (1977). *Maturity and competence.* New York: Gardner.

Inhelder, B., and Piaget, J. (1958). *The growth of logical thinking from childhood to adolescence.* New York: Basic Books.

Keating, D.P. (1980). Thinking processes in adolescence. In J. Adelman (Ed.), *Handbook of adolescent psychology* (pp. 211-246). New York: John Wiley.

King, P.M. (1986). Formal reasoning in adults: A review and critique. In R.A. Mines and K.S. Kitchener (Eds.), *Adult cognitive development: Methods and models* (pp. 1-21). New York: Praeger Publishers.

Kitchener, K.S. (1986). The reflective judgment model: Characteristics, evidence and measurement. In R.A. Mines and K.S. Kitchener (Eds.), *Adult cognitive development: Methods and models* (pp. 76-91). New York: Praeger Publishers.

Kohlberg, L. (1976). Moral stages and moralization. In T.E. Lickona (Ed.), *Moral development and behavior: Theory, research and social issues* (pp. 2-15). New York: Holt, Rinehart and Winston.

Loevinger, J. (1976). *Ego development.* San Francisco: Jossey-Bass.

Marcia, J. (1976). Identity six years later: a follow-up study. *Journal of Youth and Adolescence, 5*, 145-160.

Markus, H., and Wurf, E. (1987). The dynamics of self concept: A social psychological perspective. *Annual Review of Psychology, 38*, 299-337.

Perry, W.G. (1981). Cognitive and ethical growth: The making of meaning. In A.W. Chickering (Ed.), *The modern American college* (pp. 76-116). San Francisco: Jossey-Bass.

Thies-Sprinthall, L. (1980). Supervision: An educative or miseducative process? *Journal of Teacher Education, 31*(4), 17-20.

———— (1984). Promoting the developmental growth of supervising teachers:

Theory, research programs and implications. *Journal of teacher education,* *35*(3), 53-60.

Thies-Sprinthall, L., and Sprinthall, N.A. (1987). Experienced teachers: Agents for revitalization and renewal as mentors and teacher educators. *Journal of Education, 169*(1), 65-77.

Waterman, A. (1985). *Identity in adolescence: New directions in child development* (pp. 59-164). San Francisco: Jossey-Bass.

Chapter 14. The Power to Empower: Multicultural Education for Student-Teachers

References

A.A.C.T.E. Commission on Multicultural Education. (1973). *No one model American.* A.A.C.T.E. Brochure. Washington, D.C.: A.A.C.T.E.

Andrzejewski, J. (1985). *Human relations and the study of oppression and human rights* (2nd ed.). Lexington, Mass.: Ginn Press.

Baker, G.C. (1983). *Planning and organizing for multicultural instruction.* Reading, Mass.: Addison-Wesley.

Banks, J.A. (1983). Multiethnic education and the quest for equality. *Phi Delta Kappan, 64,* 582-585.

——— (1984). *Teaching strategies for ethnic studies* (3rd ed.). Allyn and Bacon: Boston.

Banks, J.A., and Grambs, J.D. (1972). *Black self concept.* New York: McGraw-Hill.

Copeland, W.C. (1988). Student teachers and cooperating teachers: An ecological relationship. *Theory Into Practice, 33,* 3.

Dawson, M.E. (1981). A matter of linkage: Multicultural education and educational equity. In M.E. Dawson (Ed.) *Educational equity: The integration of equity into preservice teacher education programs.* ERIC Clearinghouse on Teacher Education, Washington, D.C., pp. 1-11.

Doyle, W., and Ponder, G.A. (1975). Classroom ecology: Some concerns about a neglected dimension of research on teaching. *Contemporary Education, 46,* 183-188.

Gay, G. (1977). Curriculum design for multicultural education. In C. Grant (Ed.). *Multicultural education: Commitments, issues and applications.* Washington, D.C.: Association for Supervision and Curriculum Development.

Gollnick, D.M., and Chinn, P.C. (1983). *Multicultural education in a pluralistic society* (2nd ed.). Columbus, Ohio: Merrill Publishing.

Grant, C.A. and Sleeter, C.E. (1985). The literature on multicultural education: Review and analysis. *Educational Review, 37,* 97-118.

——— (1989). *Turning on learning: Five approaches for multicultural teaching, plans for race, class, gender, and disability.* Columbus, Ohio: Merrill Publishing.

Howsam, R., Corrigan, B., Dean, C., Denemark, G., and Nash, R.J. (1976). *Educating a profession.* Washington, D.C.: American Association for Colleges of Teacher Education.

Martin, R.J. (1986). *A comparative analysis of the implementation of the human relations mandates in three selected teacher education institutions in the states of Iowa, Minnesota, and Wisconsin.* Unpublished doctoral dissertation, Iowa State University, Ames, Iowa.

National Council for the Accreditation of Teacher Education (N.C.A.T.E.). (1977). *Standards for accreditation of teacher education.* Washington, D.C.: N.C.A.T.E.

Nickolai-Mays, S., and Davis, J. (1986). In-service training of teachers in multicultural urban schools: A systematic model. *Urban Education, 21*(2): 169-179.

Terry, R. (1974). The white male club: Biology and power. *Civil Rights Digest, 6,* 66-77.

NOTES ON CONTRIBUTORS

JAMES A. BANKS is Professor of Education at the University of Washington, Seattle. He is a former Chair of Curriculum and Instruction and a Past President of the National Council for the Social Studies. Professor Banks specializes in social studies education and multicultural education and has published over 90 articles in these fields, in journals such as *Phi Delta Kappan, School Review, Educational Leadership,* and the *Elementary School Journal.* His books include *Teaching Strategies For Ethnic Studies, Multiethnic Education: Theory and Practice, Teaching Strategies for the Social Studies,* and (with Cherry A. McGee Banks), *Multicultural Education: Issues and Perspectives.* Professor Banks has held fellowships from the National Academy of Education, the Kellogg and the Rockefeller Foundations, and was named a Distinguished Scholar/Researcher on Minority Education by the American Educational Research Association in 1986. During spring of 1991, he will be a Hill Distinguished Professor of General Studies at the University of Minnesota.

LEE BELL is Assistant Professor in Educational Studies at SUNY-New Paltz where she codirects with Nancy Schniedewind the Masters of Professional Studies Program in Humanistic Education. Her research and writing focus on the areas of girls, women and achievement; humanistic education and critical theory; and feminist pedagogy. In 1989 she received The Distinguished Teaching Award from the New Paltz Alumni Association. Her most recent interests are challenging ethnocentrism and racism and developing fluency in Spanish.

KATHLEEN P. BENNETT is Assistant Professor of Social Foundations at the University of Tennessee-Knoxville. Her dissertation was a study of urban Appalachian first graders in an ability grouped reading program. Prior to moving to Tennessee, she served as a University of Alaska-Fairbanks regional coordinator for a field-based teacher education program for Native Alaskan students in villages surrounding Bethel, Alaska. While there she conducted research on Yup'ik Eskimo storyknifing, a play activity of young girls. She is currently involved in establishing a qualitative research program in the College of Education at the University of Tennessee. Her major interests are in the sociocultural foundations of education and the use of ethnography in the study of schooling. Her research and writing are concerned with equity issues in the structure and practice of schooling, particularly as related to women and minority students.

334   CONTRIBUTORS

CARLOS CORTES is Professor of History at the University of California, Riverside. He has edited three major book series on U.S. Hispanics, has written documentary films, and is writing a three-volume study of the history of the U.S. motion picture treatment of ethnic groups and foreign nations. Among his main publications are *Three Perspectives on Ethnicity* and *A Filmic Approach to the Study of Historical Dilemmas.* The recipient of the California Council for the Humanities' 1980 Distinguished California Humanist Award, he has lectured widely throughout the United States, Latin America, and Europe on such topics as media literacy, multicultural education, global education, and the implications of diversity for education, government, and private business. He has also appeared as guest host on the PBS national television series, "Why in the World?."

SIGNITHIA FORDHAM is Henry Rutgers Research Fellow and Assistant Professor in the Department of Anthropology at Rutgers University. Her research interests include contemporary adolescents, social stratification, race, ethnicity and inter- and intragroup relations. She has written several articles on the academic achievement of Black adolescents, including "Racelessness as a Factor in Black Students' School Success: Pragmatic Strategy or Phyrric Victory?" and (with John Ogbu) "Black Students' School Success: Coping with the 'Burden of Acting White.'" She is currently completing a book based on Black adolescents' school success at Capital High.

CARL A. GRANT is Professor in the Department of Curriculum and Instruction and Chair of the Department of Afro-American Studies at the University of Wisconsin-Madison. His major professional interests include multicultural education; race, social class and gender and school life; and preservice and inservice education. Among his books are *Turning on Learning,* with Christine Sleeter (1989), *Making Choices for Multicultural Education,* with Christine Sleeter (1988), *After the School Bell Rings,* with Christine Sleeter (1986), *Preparing for Reflective Teaching* (1984), *Bringing Teaching To Life* (1982), and *Community Participation in Education* (1979). His forthcoming book is *Research Directions for Multicultural Education.*

RICHARD RUIZ is Associate Professor at the University of Arizona. He received degrees in Romance Languages and Literature at Harvard College, and in Anthropology and Philosophy of Education at Stanford University. He was a member of the Department of Education Policy Studies at the University of Wisconsin-Madison for 9 years. His area of specialization is language planning and policy analysis.

VALERIE OOKA PANG is Assistant Professor at San Diego State University in the College of Education. Her major interests are multicultural education, incorporation of ethnic content into curriculum and instruction, equity education, and achievement of Asian and Pacific American students. She was a past

Spencer Foundation postdoctoral fellow and studied test anxiety in Asian American middle school children. She has published articles in a variety of journals such as *Harvard Educational Review, Social Education,* and *The Journal of Cross-Cultural Psychology.*

RENEE MARTIN is Assistant Professor at the University of Toledo in the Department of Educational Psychology, Research, and Social foundations. She is the former assistant director of the Office of Student Field Experiences and has had extensive experience as a student teaching supervisor.

MARTIN HABERMAN is Professor of Curriculum and Instruction, University of Wisconsin-Milwaukee. He develops programs for preparing urban teachers. The National Teacher Corps, university, union, and alternative certification programs have been based on his models.

MARA SAPON-SHEVIN is Associate Professor of Elementary and Special Education in the Center for Teaching and Learning at the University of North Dakota. Her major areas of interest include schooling for diversity, mainstreaming, cooperative learning, the politics of special education and school reform. She is a member of the Peace Studies Faculty at her institution as well as active in regional and national peace activist groups. She makes frequent presentations to school groups regarding integration/mainstreaming and cooperative learning. Her article "Giftedness as a Social Construct" appeared in *Teachers College Record.*

NANCY SCHNIEDEWIND is Professor of Educational Studies at State University College, New Paltz, where she teaches in a Masters Program in Humanistic Education. She is co-author of *Cooperative Learning, Cooperative Lives: Learning Activities For Building A Peaceful World* (W.C. Brown, 1987) and *Open Minds To Equality: Learning Activities To Promote Race, Sex, Class and Age Equity* (Prentice Hall, 1983). She is chair of the New York Cooperative Learning Association.

CHRISTINE E. SLEETER is Associate Professor of Education at the University of Wisconsin-Parkside. Her major research interests are multicultural education, school ethnography, teacher education, and sociology of special education. Her articles appear in journals such as *Teaching and Teacher Education, Harvard Educational Review, Teachers College Record,* and *Review of Educational Research.* Her books include *After the School Bell Rings, Making Choices for Multicultural Education,* and *Turning on Learning* (all three with Carl Grant); she is currently finishing a book, *Keepers of the American Dream.*

SUSAN R. TAKATA is Associate Professor of Sociology at the University of Wisconsin-Parkside. She received her Ph.D. in 1983 in Sociology from the University of California, Berkeley. Her areas of teaching interest are race and ethnic relations, criminology, and innovative approaches to undergraduate education. She recently published "Learning by Doing: The Teaching of Sociological Research Methods" in *Teaching Sociology*. In addition, she has co-authored a textbook titled *Controlling the Ascent Through Sociology*.

LOIS WEIS is Professor of Sociology of Education, and Associate Dean of the Graduate School of Education, at SUNY at Buffalo. She is the author or editor of numerous volumes, including *Working Class without Work: High School Students in a De-Industrialized Economy* (Routledge, 1990), and *Class, Race and Gender in American Education* (SUNY Press, 1988).

SELASE W. WILLIAMS has devoted his entire professional life to the study of the African World Experience and to the enhancement of educational opportunities for people of African descent and other peoples of color. He is currently Chair of the Pan African Studies Department at California State University-Northridge. He has studied German, French, Swahili, Mende, Bambara, and Hausa, in addition to Krio. He has published more than a half dozen scholarly articles and is nearing completion of two manuscripts (*A Guide to Krio Language* and *Oral Literature and Afro-Grammarian*). Concerned with the special educational challenges of African American public school students, Williams has conducted numerous in-service workshops for teachers in which he demonstrates how to use the language skills they bring to the classroom to teach them reading and writing skills.

INDEX

Ability, 44, 45, 51, 248
Ability groups, 29, 33, 35-38
Abrahams, R., 74
Academic achievement, 32, 38, 41,
45, 53, 70, 75, 77, 79, 81, 84, 87, 90,
92, 160, 163, 172, 223
Achievement, 51, 54, 69, 71, 87, 91,
229-32, 236-38, 240, 242, 248
AAL (African American Language),
13, 84, 129, 136-38, 140, 150, 200,
203-14, 224
American Indians, 18, 128, 130, 132,
144, 181-84, 191, 194
Appalachia, 5, 27, 28-32, 41, 44, 45,
47
A Raisin in the Sun, 138
Ashcroft, L., 3, 15, 50
Asian Americans, 2, 90, 144, 191, 194
Attitude, 33, 139, 144, 176, 180, 181,
188, 245

Bailey, F.G., 86
Baldwin, J., 132
Banks, J.A., 12, 13, 297
Bates, Daisy, 135, 136
Behavior, 34, 39, 42, 53, 88, 219
Benevolent helping models, 4-5
Bennett, C.I., 12
Bilingual education, 17, 202, 211,
217-20, 224-26
Black Americans, 54, 67, 73-76, 81,
84, 86, 92, 180
Black students, 5, 9, 16, 69-73, 75-78,
81, 83, 89-91, 167, 242
Black women, 18, 52

Bloom, A., 129
Brown vs. Board of Education,
167-68
Bruner, J., 252, 268

CAT (California Achievement
Tests), 32, 37, 38
Canon, 125, 127-30
Cartoons, 191, 193-96
Chan, A., 6
Chapter I, 37, 43
Charnofsky, S., 14
Checkoway, B., 7
'Civil Rights', 2, 292
Civil rights, 2, 70, 77, 85, 127, 129,
135, 137, 153
Clark, K., 252
Class, 95, 235
Classroom, 134, 169
Cohen, E., 176
Coleman, J.S., 129
Comer, J., 188
Competition, 71, 83, 87, 160, 162-
65, 174, 242
Conflict, 77, 79, 174, 224, 226, 234,
238, 242
Consciousness raising, 229-30,
232, 234, 235, 238, 241, 245, 248-
49
Co-operative learning, 13, 18, 86,
89, 90, 161, 165-75, 177, 178
Copeland, W.C., 293
Criteria, 38, 76
Critical thinking, 37, 50, 125, 126,
130, 131, 189, 221

Institution, 7, 62, 63, 65, 76, 141, 147
Instruction, 39, 41, 46, 92, 202
Integration, 213

Jordon Mott Junior High, 87, 88
Junior high, 5, 53, 81, 92, 132, 133, 213

Kagan, S., 169, 170
Kid power, 179, 196
Kinship, 53
Kipnis, D., 16
Kjolseth, R., 226
Knowledge, 3, 20, 36, 37, 49, 50-53, 55-57, 60, 63-66, 125-27, 186, 230
Kohn, Alfie, 160, 161

Language, 13, 41, 45, 195, 199, 200-03, 211, 215, 217-21, 223-26; minority communities, 13, 66, 74, 181, 220, 224; policies, 203, 204, 210-15
Lau vs. Nichols, 211
Learning, 147, 149, 166, 174
Learning by Doing, 252-61, 263, 265, 266, 269-71
Learning disabled, 34
Lewis, M., 7
Linguistic discrimination, 226

Maher, F.A., 20
Mainstream, 6
Male: dominance, 16, 91, 98; female, 8
Martin Luther King, Jr., 129, 196, 197
May, M., 96
McLaren, P., 3, 6, 45, 52
McRobbie, A., 99, 101
Media, 13, 136, 144, 145, 148, 149, 151, 153-56, 194, 245-47
Messages, 251, 252

Mexican American, 54, 140, 145, 150
Minority, 9, 147, 167, 169, 180, 217, 218, 220, 221, 227, 275-77
Mississippi Burning, 129, 153
Model, 3, 4, 19, 51, 180, 188, 191
Monroe, S., 72
Motive, 5, 83, 86, 153, 172
Multicultural Education: empowerment, 2, 13, 17, 22, 23; history, 291; people of color, 8, 9, 22, 147; political change, 1-3, 8, 10, 11, 17, 62, 139

Native American, 54; see American Indian
Neira, 79

O'Connor, J., 152
Ogbu, J., 72
Oppressed groups, 7, 16, 18, 164, 231
Oppression, 1, 2, 4-6, 10, 11, 22, 29, 230, 251, 269

Patriarchy, 103, 230
Pedagogy, 5, 20-22, 152, 159, 161, 166, 174, 217, 220, 222, 223, 225, 227
Peer influence, 69, 87, 168
People: of color, 130, 214, 238; peoplehood, 73-75
Perceptions, 36, 38, 39, 41, 72, 80, 163, 168, 175, 176, 183-85, 190, 229, 231, 264
Performance, 39, 41, 70, 71, 73, 77, 80, 85, 92
Policy, 43, 47
Power, 2, 3, 5, 15, 49, 63, 140, 217, 218, 222; see Empower/Empowerment
Powerless, 14, 49, 222
Professional Development Program, 90, 91